The Reform of FBI Intelligence Operations

PoliceFoundation

Written under the auspices
of the Police Foundation

The Reform of FBI Intelligence Operations

John T. Elliff

PRINCETON UNIVERSITY PRESS
PRINCETON, NEW JERSEY

Published by Princeton University Press, Princeton, New Jersey
In the United Kingdom: Princeton University Press, Guildford, Surrey

Library of Congress Cataloging in Publication Data will be found on the last printed page of this book

This book has been composed in VIP Primer

Clothbound editions of Princeton University Press books are printed on acid-free paper, and binding materials are chosen for strength and durability.

Printed in the United States of America by Princeton University Press, Princeton, New Jersey

The Police Foundation is a privately funded, independent, nonprofit organization established by the Ford Foundation in 1970 and dedicated to supporting research for innovation and improvement in policing and allied criminal justice agencies. The conclusions and recommendations of foundation-supported research projects are those of the authors and not necessarily those of the Police Foundation.

Contents

Preface

THIS book is the result of a three-year analysis and evaluation of FBI internal security intelligence operations conducted by the Police Foundation. Former FBI Director Clarence M. Kelley encouraged the Foundation to undertake an independent examination of FBI policies in this field, and the project began in 1974. The first year was devoted to interviews with FBI officials at headquarters and in selected field offices, with officials of the Department of Justice, with members of other law enforcement agencies, with congressional staff members and staff of the General Accounting Office, and others.

The project was interrupted for a year in 1975 while the author, who was principal consultant for the Foundation study, served as domestic intelligence task force leader for the United States Senate Select Committee to Study Governmental Operations with Respect to Intelligence Activities. The most significant effect of this one-year interruption was to cause a shift in focus from problems of the past to the proper role for FBI intelligence operations in the future. Extensive materials on the development of FBI internal security policies over the years were included in the final report of the Senate Select Committee. This body of information, coupled with the results of a General Accounting Office survey of field investigations, presented a detailed picture of how the FBI had discharged its intelligence responsibilities in the past. The result was that this study could build upon those findings without having the burden of retrospective inquiry.

The author is deeply grateful to Director Kelley, to Patrick V. Murphy, President of the Police Foundation, and to the Board of Directors of the Foundation for their support and encouragement.

Thanks are also due to the Brandeis University Department of Politics for granting the leave of absence necessary to complete the Foundation project.

Many people inside and outside the FBI have taken the time to answer questions, share their experiences, or read various preliminary drafts. Particular thanks go to Inspector John B. Hotis of the FBI; Bill Reed, executive assistant to Director Kelley; W. Raymond Wannall, former FBI Assistant Director; Mary Lawton, Deputy Assistant Attorney General; Jack Fuller, Attorney General Levi's special assistant; Michael E. Shaheen, Steve Blackhurst, and Ray Hornblower of the Justice Department's Office of Professional Responsibility; Tom Grady and Jeff Harris of the Attorney General's Investigation Review Unit; James Wilderotter, former Associate Deputy Attorney General; Richard Fogel of the General Accounting Office; Professor Christopher Pyle of Mount Holyoke College; Professor John Gardiner of the University of Illinois (Chicago Circle); Sanford J. Ungar; and Senate staff members Michael Epstein, Mark Gitenstein, and Tom Connaughton.

Although former Attorney General Edward H. Levi played no direct role in the development and conduct of the study, his contribution to the understanding of the problems was immense. His landmark efforts to establish guidelines for FBI intelligence investigations are a principal subject of this book.

Members of the Police Foundation staff contributed to a productive and enjoyable year of full-time association. John Heaphy, Tom Brady, and Mara Adams deserve special thanks for their assistance in developing the project, carrying it forward to completion, and preparing the manuscript for publication. The research assistance of Craig Charney was especially helpful in the project's early stages.

As with all studies of current public policy issues, events sometimes make observations outdated or cast new light on continuing problems that have been addressed from the perspective of a given moment. An attempt has been made to take account of developments that took place after this study was completed in 1977. However, the specific issues raised by proposed charter legislation for FBI intelligence operations are not discussed. The question whether policies and procedures of the FBI and the Justice Department should be embodied in legislation was outside the scope of the Police Foundation-supported inquiry. However, the reforms that were developed and implemented during the mid-1970s supplied at least partial models for legislation; and the analysis of those reforms presented here suggests further alternatives. Whatever the outcome of efforts to enact a legislative charter for the FBI, the maintenance of a free society will continue to require that public officials and citizens weigh carefully the need for FBI domestic security and foreign counterintelligence operations.

The Reform of FBI Intelligence Operations

CHAPTER I

Introduction: The Reform of FBI Intelligence

THE Federal Bureau of Investigation underwent significant change during the 1970s. After Director J. Edgar Hoover's death in 1972 and the constitutional crisis of Watergate, revelations of abuses of power tarnished its public image. For the first time in fifty years there were credible allegations of illegality in the FBI. While these painful disclosures took place, Director Clarence M. Kelley began reconsidering the Bureau's traditional investigative priorities and administrative practices. Congressional committees and the Attorney General looked into the FBI's secret past and sought ways to hold it accountable in the future. These efforts focused, to a great extent, on the Bureau's role as an intelligence agency. Some of the most highly publicized abuses and alleged violations of the law had occurred as part of FBI operations to protect the nation's security. In response, there were major reforms to ensure that privacy and freedom would be protected and legitimate public interests served by FBI intelligence programs.

This study of FBI intelligence operations describes how these reforms emerged, and what their impact was. The general aim is to contribute to a more systematic understanding of the FBI's domestic security and foreign counterintelligence functions, and how they may be carried out in a manner consistent with constitutional requirements.

The Problems

FBI intelligence operations pose difficult problems for a nation committed to constitutional government and the rule of law. We live in a world where acts of terrorist violence and foreign espionage are considered serious present dangers to the security of the United States. Yet post-Watergate disclosures demonstrated the great risks in giving an agency such as the FBI unlimited authority to conduct intelligence activities against terrorists and spies.

Charges that the White House misused the FBI and other U.S. intelligence agencies played a central part in the events leading to President Nixon's resignation in 1974. The House Judiciary Committee's second article of impeachment cited as abuses of presidential power certain FBI wiretaps and other investigations authorized by the President and his aides, the concealment of wiretap records, the attempt to have the CIA curtail the FBI's investigation of the Watergate break-in, and the use of intelligence resources against the President's partisan opponents. After serving as special prosecutor, Archibald Cox attributed many of the events leading to the Watergate scandal to "a neurotic passion for spying as a means of ensuring loyalty and coping with supposed threats to domestic security." A prime example was the so-called "Huston plan" developed in 1970 for the use of illegal surveillance techniques against Americans.

Similar activities had occurred under previous administrations. Army intelligence surveillance of civilian political activity grew dramatically in the last years of the Johnson Administration, although it was cut back after public exposure in the early 1970s. Later, as a byproduct of the Watergate investigations, reports surfaced that the FBI had committed burglaries before 1966, that journalists were wiretapped during the Kennedy Administration, and that President Johnson ordered an FBI check of vice-presidential candidate Spiro Agnew's phone records during the 1968 campaign. Following President Nixon's resignation, Attorney General William Saxbe issued a report on a 15-year FBI domestic counterintelligence program labeled COINTELPRO, carried out at least until 1971, to disrupt dissident groups and discredit Americans using tactics

Saxbe described as "abhorrent in a free society." Shortly thereafter, major newspapers reported that the CIA had conducted surveillance of Americans in the United States, in violation of its charter, and that the FBI had spied upon political activities at the 1964 Democratic National Convention for the Johnson White House.

Watergate unleashed a torrent of revelations about questionable FBI intelligence activities, going far beyond abuses tied to the Nixon Administration. In his first appearance before a congressional committee after taking office in 1975, Attorney General Edward H. Levi confirmed the existence of previously undisclosed files maintained by former Director J. Edgar Hoover and containing derogatory information on public figures. Levi also presented the results of an inquiry by outgoing Deputy Attorney General Laurence Silberman and the FBI Inspection Division into misuse of the Bureau to gather political intelligence for administrations of both parties and to discredit the FBI's critics.

In reaction to these disclosures, Congress and the legal profession began looking more closely at the FBI, particularly at its internal security operations. Select Committees of the House and Senate included FBI abuses in their investigations of intelligence activities, and the House Judiciary Committee asked the General Accounting Office (GAO) to review FBI domestic intelligence policies and procedures. The American Bar Association set up a Special Committee to Study Federal Law Enforcement Agencies. Within the Justice Department, Attorney General Levi established a committee to draw up guidelines for FBI investigations.

The FBI, under Director Clarence M. Kelley, worked with the Attorney General and with congressional investigators to assess what had gone wrong in the past and what should be done in the future. The new revelations were sometimes shocking, especially the details of FBI efforts to "neutralize" Dr. Martin Luther King, Jr., as an effective civil rights leader during the 1960s. Former top officials of the FBI and CIA had acted on the assumption that they could disregard the normal legal rights of domestic groups because their work was so important to the national security that they were not governed by legal and constitutional standards applying to the rest of the law enforcement community. They made this claim in defense of opening mail, breaking into homes and offices without a warrant, and using what the Senate Select Committee to Study Governmental Operations with respect to Intelligence Activities (the Church committee) found to be "dangerous and degrading tactics" to disrupt and discredit lawful domestic political activities of Americans.

Even after the congressional committees issued their reports and Attorney General Levi adopted his first FBI guidelines in 1976, Director Kelley discovered that some of his subordinates had "deceived" him by not revealing FBI break-ins that had taken place in 1972-1973. This information triggered still another inquiry—a criminal investigation by the Justice Department leading to indictments of former FBI officials in 1977-1978. Director Kelley summed up the problems in a landmark address at Westminster College in May 1976. Admitting that some FBI activities had been "clearly wrong and quite indefensible," he declared that the Bureau should never again occupy the "unique position that permitted improper activity without accountability."

The Reforms

Accountability was the key to the efforts to bring FBI intelligence activities within the rule of law. Briefly, what happened was that FBI internal security operations were subjected to formal guidelines, procedures were established for regular oversight by the Attorney General, the foreign and domestic sides of the Bureau's intelligence work were sharply divided, and FBI agents discovered that their use of illegal methods risked criminal prosecution.

Before the Attorney General's guidelines were issued, the

source of the Bureau's legal authority was obscure, and the legal restrictions applying to intelligence operations were unclear. J. Edgar Hoover assumed he had broad authority from the President, going back to directives from Franklin D. Roosevelt in the 1930s, for conducting intelligence operations against "subversive activities" in the United States. The scope of that authority was never adequately defined, the practical meaning of "subversion" varied according to the political climate of the times, and the Attorney General's role in supervising the FBI was uncertain because the FBI director's mandate came directly from the President. As for legal restraints on intelligence techniques, neither Congress nor the courts had fully addressed the issues; the interpretations by successive Attorneys General were incomplete and often contradictory.

Attorney General Levi did not have to start from scratch in clarifying the legal standards for FBI intelligence. The Supreme Court already had laid down some basic principles in the pioneering *Keith* case in 1972, which ruled unconstitutional the use of electronic surveillance without a judicial warrant in a "domestic security" investigation of persons suspected of sabotaging a CIA office in Ann Arbor, Michigan, to protest the Vietnam War.[2]

The first principle was that the Constitution and the law applied to intelligence activities. FBI officials had believed for many years that legal standards did not govern collecting intelligence if the information was not used in a criminal prosecution. The operating premise was that, so long as the government was not gathering evidence for prosecution, its intelligence techniques need not adhere to constitutional requirements. The Supreme Court clearly rejected this distinction: "Official surveillance whether its purpose be criminal investigation or ongoing intelligence gathering, risks infringement of constitutionally protected privacy and speech."[3] There was no exception to basic constitutional standards for intelligence activities.

The second principle set forth in the *Keith* opinion was that domestic security investigations might differ in some significant respects from investigations of "ordinary crime." The Court said that, because intelligence gathering about domestic violence emphasizes "the prevention of unlawful activity," its focus "may be less precise than that directed against more conventional types of crime." The Court went so far as to suggest that Congress could adopt more flexible standards for judicial warrants in domestic security cases than for regular criminal investigations, and that Fourth Amendment standards could vary, so long as they were "reasonable both in relation to the legitimate need of Government for intelligence information and the protected rights of our citizens."[4]

The third principle suggested in *Keith* was that, while domestic security investigations must satisfy such requirements as a prior judicial warrant for electronic surveillance, the Constitution might allow other procedures where foreign powers or their agents are involved. The Court specifically refused to express an opinion on whether a warrant was required in cases "where there is collaboration in varying degrees between domestic groups or organizations and agents or agencies of foreign powers." It noted, however, that lower federal courts and the American Bar Association held the view that such warrantless surveillance "may be constitutional."[5] Thus, in the area of foreign counterintelligence, the Supreme Court clarified very little. It did not resolve the question of whether the President had the constitutional power, as several lower courts have held, to authorize warrantless electronic surveillance of foreign agents. Nor did it say where to draw the line between foreign and domestic intelligence. These became the most troublesome issues for Attorney General Levi and his successor, Attorney General Griffin B. Bell.

The fourth and final principle was a warning expressed throughout the Court's opinion that intelligence operations conducted in the name of national security need careful control because of their proven danger to the rights of Americans:

> National security cases, moreover, often reflect a convergence of First and Fourth Amendment values not present in cases of "ordinary" crime. Though the investigative duty of the executive may be stronger in such cases, so also is there greater jeopardy to constitutionally protected speech. . . . History abundantly documents the tendency of Government—however benevolent and benign its motives—to view with suspicion those who most fervently dispute its policies. Fourth Amendment protections become the more necessary when the targets of official surveillance may be those suspected of unorthodoxy in their political beliefs. The danger to political dissent is acute where the Government attempts to act under so vague a concept as the power to protect "domestic security." Given the difficulty of defining the domestic security interest, the danger of abuse in acting to protect that interest becomes apparent. . . . The price of lawful public dissent must not be a dread of subjection to an unchecked surveillance power.[6]

The Supreme Court's interpretation of the legal principles applying to intelligence activities supported FBI reforms. It supplied not only constitutional standards for the development of FBI domestic security guidelines, but also a legal basis for the criminal investigation of possible civil rights violations by FBI officials in connection with warrantless searches for domestic security purposes. The investigation of FBI break-ins made clear that FBI officials could no longer disregard legality, except at the risk of prosecution under the federal civil rights statutes.

As for the Attorney General's guidelines, in accordance with the *Keith* principles they treated FBI domestic security investigations separately from FBI foreign intelligence collection and foreign counterintelligence investigations. Domestic security investigations (not involving foreign powers or their agents) were linked closely to law enforcement standards. Subsequently, this separation took a tangible form when Director Kelley shifted supervision of domestic security cases from the FBI Intelligence Division to the Criminal Investigative Division in mid-1976.

Clarifying the sources of the FBI's intelligence authority was more difficult because the best solution, a new legislative charter, could not be enacted overnight. By basing domestic security investigations on the likelihood of federal law violations, the Attorney General could invoke his broad statutory authority to appoint officials "to detect and prosecute crimes against the United States."[7] However, Director Kelley told the Senate Intelligence Committee that the guidelines did not "in any manner diminish the need for legislation" defining FBI jurisdiction in the domestic security and intelligence fields.[8]

FBI foreign counterintelligence investigations posed a different problem, because they were not as closely tied to criminal activity. In theory, such investigations could rely on a statutory provision authorizing "such other investigations regarding official matters under the control of the Department of Justice and the Department of State as may be directed by the Attorney General." But Congress nowhere defined these official matters, and the legislative history of the provision was obscure, if not completely unintelligible.[9]

To resolve this problem, legal authority for FBI foreign counterintelligence was specifically included in Executive Orders on U.S. foreign intelligence activities. President Ford's Executive Order 11905 issued in 1976 asserted an inherent presidential authority under the Constitution; it directed the FBI to prevent as well as detect certain activities of foreign powers; and it retained the traditional catch-all term "subversion" as one of those activities. The greatest advantage of the new Executive Order over the old presidential directives going back to Roosevelt was that it required the FBI to operate "under the supervision of the Attorney General and pursuant to such regulations as the Attorney General may establish." The Attorney General was specifically ordered to "issue guidelines relating to the activities of the Federal Bureau of Investigation in the areas of foreign intelligence and counterintelligence."[10] President Carter's superseding order in 1978 gave the Attorney General "sole authority to issue and revise procedures" for FBI foreign intelligence and counterintelligence activities. The Carter order dropped the term "subversion," substituting instead a counterintelligence mandate "to protect against espionage and other clandestine intelligence activities . . . conducted for or on behalf of foreign powers, organizations or persons."[11]

The Attorney General's guidelines included a procedure for warrantless electronic surveillance of foreign agents with the specific approval of the Attorney General in each case. However, as a practical matter, Attorney General Levi did not approve any request for warrantless surveillance of an American citizen under this procedure during his last eighteen months in office, and he proposed legislation to require a special form of judicial warrant for electronic surveillance of foreign agents in the future. Attorney General Bell received presidential approval for warrantless television surveillance of one citizen in 1977, while continuing to press for similar legislation. The Foreign Intelligence Surveillance Act of 1978 superseded the guidelines and required a court order for any FBI electronic surveillance that might overhear an American citizen or resident alien in the United States.

Thus, reform of FBI intelligence meant splitting foreign intelligence and counterintelligence operations from domestic security investigations, bringing both sides of the FBI's intelligence work under the rule of law as embodied in formal guidelines and the 1978 surveillance act, and establishing that the FBI's legal authority flows through and must be supervised by the Attorney General. The balance of this study examines in greater depth how these reforms came about and what they could accomplish. Rather than exploring various models for legislation, this analysis concentrates on the structure, policies, and programs of the FBI and the Justice Department.

The first three chapters examine the changes made in the structure and policy framework for FBI intelligence operations during the mid-1970s: What were the issues in the debate over FBI intelligence policy? How did the Attorney General's guidelines develop, and what was the FBI's initial response? What were some of the reasons for the reorganization that transferred domestic security investigations from the Intelligence Division to the Criminal Investigative Division? What objectives did Attorney General Levi, Attorney General Bell, and Director Kelley seek to achieve by these reforms? The next two chapters address some of the issues that were not fully resolved by the reorganization and the guidelines: What policies for FBI domestic security investigations of terrorists can best serve law enforcement needs and minimize unnecessary risks to individual privacy? How should the FBI handle investigations of foreign spying and foreign-directed covert political activities sometimes labeled "foreign subversion"?

A final chapter covers the standards and procedures for dealing with possible misconduct by FBI personnel, including departures from professional norms and abuses of authority: What should be the procedures within the FBI for conducting and reviewing internal inquiries? How should the Justice Department oversee the handling of possible misconduct in the FBI? Confidence in the FBI's adherence to professional and legal standards depends in large measure upon the effectiveness of these auxiliary safeguards as a means of holding Bureau officials accountable for their conduct.

The tension between security and liberty has existed throughout American history; and the pendulum may again swing in the direction of sacrificing freedom for the sake of order. In a climate of relative tranquility, and with the memory still vivid of the excesses committed in the name of national security or "law and order," important new safeguards were established. However, striking the right balance between the nation's security and the principles of liberty under law requires anticipating different circumstances. The aim must be to institutionalize the concerns for freedom and legality, so that they are not easily cast aside or forgotten under the pressure of some future crisis or emergency. This means enacting certain standards into law and organizing the conduct of security operations in such a manner as to provide lasting internal and external checks.

CHAPTER II

The Policy Debate

REFORM of FBI intelligence represented more than just policies of the Attorney General and the FBI Director. They were part of a wider reconsideration of the FBI's role by the Congress, the organized legal profession, and the American public. Attorney General Levi's guidelines and Director Kelley's reorganization paralleled recommendations of the Church committee, the General Accounting Office study requested by the House Judiciary Committee, and the Special American Bar Association Committee to Study Federal Law Enforcement Agencies. All of them cast aside old assumptions about FBI intelligence, and tried to find a new, more justifiable basis for FBI domestic security and foreign counterintelligence programs.

Some participants in the policy debate found no justification at all for FBI activities going beyond criminal investigations. The American Civil Liberties Union (ACLU), for example, represented the view that FBI intelligence operations were inconsistent with civil liberty. An older generation of critics identified J. Edgar Hoover's FBI with the excesses of McCarthyism in the 1950s. Their fears, expressed in books on the Bureau by Max Lowenthal in 1950 and Fred J. Cook in 1964, seemed exaggerated at the time, but by the mid-1970s they appeared tame in comparison with the documented abuses.[1] A younger generation's perceptions of the FBI were shaped by the civil rights and anti-Vietnam War movements, which brought hundreds of thousands of Americans into active opposition to their government's policies and, often, within the scope of FBI intelligence-gathering. For them the FBI symbolized repression of lawful dissent and protest, the antithesis of political liberty and individual rights. Thus, unlike the years when the FBI was sacrosanct, the mid-1970s saw civil liberties groups subject the Bureau to a steady flow of lawsuits and public criticism.

The policy debate centered on whether the FBI should maintain a modified security intelligence role or terminate such functions entirely.

There were sharp differences over the practical benefits of intelligence investigations and the extent to which they should depart from conventional criminal law enforcement standards. It was almost impossible to measure objectively some of the claimed advantages of intelligence surveillance; it was equally difficult to estimate accurately the harm done by such surveillance to a free and open society. Where foreign powers were involved, weighing the competing interests was even harder because most of the crucial information about the nature of the foreign threats and the FBI's response was secret.

All sides urged FBI adherence to the rule of law. This most often meant linking FBI investigations to criminal law violations with such legal requirements as "reasonable suspicion" or "probable cause." However, neither side in the debate fully realized that effective reform of FBI intelligence required more than such simple remedies. The criminal law is extraordinarily broad, especially in respect to the law of conspiracy and certain registration statutes. Law enforcement officials have enormous discretionary power over the use of these and other instruments of criminal investigation. The criminal law alone does not supply effective standards to guide the exercise of this discretionary authority, to ensure that decisions on priorities are not made for arbitrary or politically motivated reasons, and to maintain accountability to the public. Consequently, the development of standards for FBI intelligence operations was part of the larger enterprise of regulating law enforcement discretion generally.

Historical and Comparative Perspectives

To understand the traditional assumptions behind FBI intelligence, some historical and comparative background is needed. These observations may help explain where the FBI has been, if not where it may be headed.

In 1924, while he was Attorney General, Harlan Fiske Stone appointed J. Edgar Hoover as Director of the FBI, instructed him to clean house in the wake of the Harding scandals, abolished the Bureau's first domestic intelligence program, and limited it "strictly to investigations of violations of law." In the 1930s, Supreme Court Justice Stone looked back over the first decade of Hoover's administration of the FBI, thought the Director had done an outstanding job, and urged that President Roosevelt retain him in office. Stone's one concern was his wish that Hoover follow the example of Scotland Yard in Great Britain and avoid wide publicity. Instead, with strong encouragement from President Roosevelt, Hoover had become the nation's most famous crime fighter, and the "G-men" were popular heroes.[2]

Justice Stone's comparison between the FBI and Scotland Yard is a useful place to start. Despite their contrasting approaches to publicity, as well as their structural differences, the FBI and its British and Canadian counterparts have had one thing in common—their ability to maintain popular support for secret intelligence operations. The contrast with the political police of totalitarian societies was striking. One student of intelligence has commented that "secret police . . . are everywhere hated and feared," but the circumstances in free societies are different: "The FBI as a crime buster, the 'Mounty' as symbol of the Canadian nation, the cool secret agent of the British Secret Service as leading man in the spy thriller—all evoke considerable enthusiasm."[3]

The uncritical public adulation of J. Edgar Hoover enhanced his power and prestige, but the British services had a compensating advantage for their lack of such popular leadership. Under the Official Secrets Act, the public could learn little about the counterespionage security service (long known as MI-5), or about Scotland Yard's Special Branch, which makes arrests and conducts domestic investigations. Hoover's capacity to escape outside inquiry because of his overwhelming prestige was matched in Britain by what a perceptive observer has called "a wall constructed by craftsmen with a mania for secrecy."[4]

Like the pre-1976 FBI Intelligence Division, the British Special Branch has had both domestic security and foreign counterintelligence responsibilities. It was created in the late nineteenth century to cope with Irish Fenian and anarchist terrorism; its investigations extended by the 1920s to cover the Communist party and other seditious activities. With respect to foreign espionage, the Special Branch became the overt investigative arm of MI-5, and thus engaged in "the observation, procuring of evidence and general enquiries into the activities of persons suspected of espionage and kindred offenses."[5] MI-5 and the Special Branch are accountable to the Home Secretary, and MI-5 also has direct access to the Prime Minister. The confidentiality of MI-5 operations is seldom breached, the identity of its chief was kept secret until the 1960s, and its formal existence is not recognized by statute or common law.[6]

Secrecy and effective public relations were not the only sources of public support for Anglo-American internal security agencies. Until Watergate, domestic intelligence operations did not seem to endanger the mainstream of political life. British journalist Edward Crankshaw made this point by comparison with the Gestapo, saying that British and American security police exercised "a purely defensive function, designed to uphold the status quo as sanctioned by the people as a whole," while the Gestapo was "an instrument not of defense but of attack," created "to impose the will of Hitler upon his political opponents."[7] For the most part, the use of intelligence techniques within the United States was thought to involve surveillance of only those few dissenting groups that used violence or served the interests of a hostile foreign power.

There were even civil libertarian impulses behind the FBI's expansion of domestic intelligence work under President Roosevelt in the late 1930s. The threat was perceived as coming not from purely domestic dissent, but from Nazi and Communist movements whose "fifth column" activities served hostile foreign interests. The lesson of Hitler's rise to power seemed to be that those who would destroy freedom should not be able to pursue that goal by taking advantage of the rights established to advance the cause of liberty. At the same time, Roosevelt Administration officials realized that innocent people could be harmed by national hysteria over the danger of Nazis and Communists. Soon after taking office in 1940, Attorney General Robert Jackson warned against labeling as "subversive" those whose activities seem "helpful to wage earners" or "those who would bring about a change of administration."[8]

To Robert Jackson and his predecessor, Frank Murphy, FBI internal security investigations were a way of discouraging the widespread local vigilantism that had occurred during World War I. When war broke out in Europe in 1939, Attorney General Murphy declared, "Twenty years ago inhuman and cruel things were done in the name of justice; sometimes vigilantes and others took over the work. We do not want such things done today, for the work has now been localized in the FBI."[9] President Roosevelt issued a statement stressing the need "to avoid confusion and irresponsibility," and calling on all local law enforcement officials to turn over to the FBI any information relating to "subversive activities."[10] After Nazi troops occupied France and threatened to invade Britain in 1940, Attorney General Jackson convened a conference of state law enforcement officials and asked them to defer to the FBI, because it was conducting "steady surveillance over individuals and groups within the United States who are so sympathetic with the systems or designs of foreign dictators as to make them a likely source of federal law violation."[11]

This stress on political sympathies as the basis for investigations gave the FBI an extraordinarily broad intelligence mandate. However, there was confidence in the FBI's ability to exercise responsible discretion because it stressed scientific crime detection without resort to the third-degree methods of interrogation still prevalent among local police. J. Edgar Hoover also won lasting respect for his opposition to the mass arrest and detention of Japanese-Americans on the West Coast in 1942.

Public and even civil libertarian acceptance of the FBI's security role from World War II through the Cold War era was rooted in these factors—Hoover's ability to portray the FBI as heroic defenders of "the American way of life," the general belief that the FBI's targets were on the political fringes rather than in the mainstream, and the hope that the centralization of security responsibilities in the FBI would reduce hysterical reactions and discourage local vigilantism. During the Korean War in 1950, for example, congressional liberals supported as the alternative to prosecution and forced registration of Communists an Emergency Detention Act, which contemplated FBI investigations of potentially dangerous persons who would not be arrested unless there was a war with the Soviet Union.[12]

Finally, the constitutional legitimacy of FBI security operations in this period depended primarily upon the link with foreign threats. The Supreme Court in 1956 viewed FBI intelligence as part of an "all-embracing program for resistance to the various forms of totalitarian aggression."[13] As late as 1961, Justice William O. Douglas concurred with the decision that the law compelling registration of Communists did not violate the First Amendment. "The Bill of Rights was designed to give fullest play to exchange and dissemination of ideas that touch the politics, culture, and other aspects of our life," Justice Douglas wrote. "When an organization is used by a foreign power to make advances here, questions of security are raised beyond the ken of disputation and debate between the people resident here."[14]

So long as the FBI's security program focused mainly on "the ever-increasing and continual threat from international communism and Soviet-bloc espionage and subversion," as J. Edgar Hoover advised the incoming Kennedy Administration in 1961, it remained substantially immune from constitutional or political challenge.[15] The Cold War consensus was not seriously challenged until the Vietnam War.

The Watergate "Revolution"

In his definitive study of modern political repression, Professor Otto Kirchheimer of Columbia University was "tempted to define a revolution by the willingness of a regime to open the archives of its predecessor's political police." Even under constitutional governments, internal security agencies seemed "foolproof against any investigation" of their operations. "Measured by this yardstick," he concluded, "few revolutions have taken place in modern history."[16]

Viewed in this light, the impact of Watergate in the mid-1970s approached revolutionary dimensions. Information from the FBI's intelligence files was spread out upon the public record in the House Judiciary Committee's impeachment investigation, by the Church committee, and in a continuing stream of disclosures by way of skeptical courts and a Freedom of Information Act expanded by Congress, largely in reaction to Watergate abuses. The revelations were unprecedented, even though concerns for privacy, for the sensitivity of counterespionage cases, and for the protection of informants from reprisal placed some limits on the flow of data. President Nixon's unsuccessful attempt to hide his administration's misuse of power not only produced his own fall, but also opened the way for an evaluation of how the FBI had strengthened presidential power and ignored the restraints of legality for decades.

The breach of secrecy greatly weakened support for the FBI. J. Edgar Hoover's image was transformed posthumously from that of a heroic crime fighter to that of a bureaucratic politician who did favors for his President (regardless of party), waged vendettas against his critics (including the most prominent civil rights leader of the 1960s), and used the FBI's resources to buttress his own power within the government.[17] It became clear that FBI intelligence operations were not aimed just at the extremes, but also at lawful domestic dissent. In the search for potentially violent or foreign-directed protest activities, law-abiding citizens had been targeted for surveillance, for investigations of their private lives and personal beliefs, and even for covert action (COINTELPRO) to disrupt or discredit their political activities.[18]

The investigations also established that succeeding Presidents and Attorneys General bore major responsibility for reorienting FBI intelligence in the 1960s toward domestic rather than mainly foreign threats. They had placed sweeping demands on the FBI for information about domestic unrest, and had given the Bureau virtual carte blanche to conduct its intelligence operations as it saw fit.[19] In the 1940s and 1950s, intrusive surveillance techniques had been adopted without regard for the law for use against foreign-dominated Nazi and Communist activities. But in the 1960s, the FBI had been encouraged, along with other U.S. foreign and military intelligence agencies, to use these methods against purely domestic groups, without regard for the consequences.[20] Broad segments of the American public, including many participants in civil rights and antiwar activities, had reason to fear that they had become the targets of FBI investigations.

Finally, the public learned that FBI intelligence had sometimes served the partisan political interests of the White House. The investigations confirmed what one FBI intelligence official had described in a confidential position paper written shortly after J. Edgar Hoover's death: "Over the years it became common practice for White House staff members to telephone requests for information or investigations to Mr. Hoover's office or the office of one of his officials. Such requests were usually considered as being within the constitutional Executive power. . . . Occasionally, however, requests were made—and complied with—which in retrospect appear to have been beyond any recognized Executive authority."[21] As Attorney General Levi stressed, in testimony on some of the most dramatic abuses, they "were not unique to any particular Administration or to any political party"; and "many of the improper requests for information or activity were cast in terms of 'national security' or other legitimate law enforcement purposes."[22]

In the aftermath of the Watergate "revolution," the American people were forced to recognize that this nation, like every other modern state, whether totalitarian or constitutional, had a "security police." All three branches of government had to face up to the question of how, if at all, FBI internal security functions could be reconciled with constitutional principles that had been disregarded for decades. This meant taking into account some of the persistent realities of security police operations, as described by Professor Kirchheimer:

> First, the area of opinions and actions kept under watch by the police of any modern state includes far more than what constitutional governments could and would want to take up with the courts. Second, control through police channels covers a wide range of means, including infiltration, intimidation, and corruption. They might be infinitely more effective as instruments of control than resort to criminal prosecution; and they narrow down the necessity or desirability and, to a much smaller extent, the chances of successful criminal prosecution. Third, to the extent that prosecution presupposes unveiling some part, however small, of the knowledge of the police in regard to the plans and organization of its foes, it might, at least temporarily, counteract their successful control. . . .

> The head of the political police, whether under civil service or considered a political officeholder, whether restricted to political supervision jobs or, as in the United States, master of the whole federal police establishment, may outlast many a government. His could be an independent and strategic position in the government because of his intimate knowledge of the personal background of the political personnel, as well as by the prestige which his organization might have built up with the public at large as the chosen custodian of national security. While he officially only advises the government on a certain course of action, disregard of his advice is liable to cast aspersion on the good judgment of the government and may easily be used to impeach the government's patriotic loyalty should its decision in an individual instance become a matter of public controversy. . . .
>
> Neither the spotless image of self-effacing patriotism nor the traditional watchdog concern over the main threat against civil liberties fits the very complicated reality of present-day political police organizations.[23]

Thus, the Attorney General and the Congress had to decide whether the FBI should investigate only criminal cases for prosecution, whether it should use "means of control" other than criminal prosecution, and whether its independent power could be reduced without increasing the risk of partisan misuse. The question, in short, was whether the United States should continue to have a "security police."

Domestic Security Investigations

Upon issuing his guidelines in early 1976, Attorney General Levi described them as intended to "tie domestic security investigations closely to the violation of federal law." He added that their purpose "must be the detection of unlawful conduct and not merely the monitoring of disfavored or troublesome activities and surely not of unpopular views."[24] This did not mean the FBI had to wait until a federal crime was committed before it could begin an investigation. Nor did it restrict the purpose of FBI investigations to the development of evidence for use in criminal prosecutions. Instead, the Attorney General, along with the Church committee and the General Accounting Office, adopted the twin premises that FBI investigations were needed to *anticipate* certain violent crimes, and that their purpose should be *prevention* as well as prosecution.

As Levi put it, "the detection of crime in some areas requires preparation and at least some knowledge of what is likely to be going on. What is at issue, I think, is the proper scope, the means and methods used, the attention paid to conduct and not views, and the closeness of the relationship of the conduct and that which is forbidden by laws of the United States."[25]

Along the same lines, the Church committee recommended that the FBI be authorized to conduct "preventive intelligence investigations" of terrorist and hostile foreign intelligence activities, although it "sought substantially to narrow, and to impose special restrictions on the conduct of, those investigations which involved the most flagrant abuses in the past."[26] The report of the Comptroller General on the GAO review of FBI domestic intelligence operations stated that they had produced "few tangible results." Nevertheless, the GAO concluded that there should be FBI domestic intelligence investigations of "groups involved in activities that have resulted, or are likely to result, in use of violence," and that the FBI should "continually assess the extent to which individuals in the groups might be involved in criminal conspiracies or acts involving use of violence."[27]

The ABA Committee to Study Federal Law Enforcement Agencies did not confront the issue directly, but its proposals accepted the idea that the FBI would continue to conduct investigations "in anticipation or prevention of a crime," and engage in "intelligence gathering and the investigation of alleged subversives or extremists." Although the ABA Committee criticized FBI surveillance of "legitimate activities of American citizens," it attributed past abuses to "vague guidelines, the growth of Presidential power accompanied by Presidential requests and directives, international tensions and subsequent internal security problems, and the lack of any control over the FBI."[28]

The most thoughtful dissent was expressed by the late Senator Philip A. Hart in the separate views he appended to the report of the Church committee. Authorizing "preventive intelligence" investigations beyond the investigation of committed crimes would be, in Senator Hart's view, "a dramatic and dangerous step." The crucial question was whether such investigations "might prevent a significant amount of terrorist activity without posing unacceptable risks for a free society." In comparison with "the shocking record of widespread abuse," Senator Hart believed that there had not been a "rigorous presentation of the case" for preventive intelligence. The FBI had provided "a handful of substantiated cases" that produced warnings of terrorist activity, but most of those investigations "could not have been opened under the Committee's proposed restrictions." Hart said the American people were being asked "to accept the risks of preventive intelligence on the hypothetical possibility that the worst imaginable terrorist acts might be averted." He concluded that there was "no substantial record before the committee that preventive intelligence, under the restrictions we propose, would enable the Government to thwart terrorism." Yet those restraints, if not more rigorous ones, were essential for preserving civil liberties and preventing the United States from becoming a police state.[29]

In defense of its recommendation, the Church committee contended that its limits on preventive intelligence "should increase the efficiency of Bureau investigations." The aim was to "avoid the wasteful dispersion of resources which has characterized the sweeping (and fruitless) domestic intelligence investigations of the past." The committee cited the GAO finding that when the FBI "initiated its investigations on harder evidence, its ability to detect imminent violence improved significantly."[30] The GAO's own final report concluded that the FBI had not obtained "positive results" because it had "diffused its domestic intelligence coverage" rather than concentrating "on those groups and individuals who really represent the greatest threats to national security," and that more sharply focused investigations were likely to be "more productive."[31]

This debate over the probable benefits of carefully restricted domestic intelligence investigations could not be fully resolved because the FBI had never determined the sort of investigations that best supplied advance warning of serious violence. The GAO was candid about the problem when it observed that "no one can say with assurance what might happen were the scope of the FBI's domestic intelligence operations changed."[32]

Another difficulty was that some of the most important risks and advantages of domestic intelligence investigations were impossible to measure objectively. There was no way to assess adequately the impact of such investigations on the sense of privacy and the willingness of Americans to assert their beliefs openly. Nor could anyone be sure of the effects on the nation as a whole. "Persons most intimidated may well not be those at the extremes of the political spectrum, but rather those nearer the middle," the Church committee concluded. "Yet voices of moderation are vital to balance public debate and avoid polarization of our society."[33]

On the other hand, the GAO gave weight to the idea that the FBI's domestic intelligence program might accomplish the purpose of preventing violence "by its mere existence," even if it seldom provides advance warning of specific acts of violence.[34] The argument, in effect, was that FBI investigations deter those who might otherwise turn to violence. Former Attorney General Nicholas Katzenbach made this point by citing with approval the FBI's investigations of the Ku Klux Klan in the mid-1960s. He believed the FBI had deterred murders, bombings, and beatings by its use of such techniques as repeated interviews and open surveillance of Klan members, as well as by making Klan members aware of the Bureau's "extensive informant system." Katzenbach said he authorized such operations and "would do so again today" in the same circumstances.[35]

One other aspect of the debate on how to handle domestic intelligence was not directly addressed in the various reports. Many of the nation's largest cities confronted the same issues that were being raised at the federal level by the FBI. In the 1960s presidential commissions on crime and civil disorders encouraged them to develop their own police intelligence operations to cope with urban riots. Some of these cities later encountered allegations of abuse comparable to the disclosures about the FBI, and some abolished their police intelligence units with the decline in civil disturbances. But in the largest and most volatile urban areas, such as New York and Los Angeles, police intelligence became a permanent part of law enforcement. Police administrators sought to reassure their communities that these activities would be carefully controlled; and with outside legal advice they formulated and published standards for investigations that in some cases predated the Attorney General's FBI guidelines. The institutionalization of police intelligence had important consequences for the FBI. It suggested that the FBI could not lay claim to exclusive authority or expertise in the field. Given the essentially local character of many of the activities that trigger violence in different communities, there was less need for the FBI to duplicate these police functions—if they were needed at all.

Foreign Counterintelligence Investigations

FBI intelligence operations are not limited to problems of domestic violence. As Director Kelley told the House Appropriations Subcommittee in 1976, "the FBI's responsibilities in the internal security field involve detecting and combating hostile activities by foreign intelligence services and terrorism by persons acting in behalf of foreign powers, groups, or movements."[36] After the 1976 reorganization of intelligence operations, these became the sole functions of the FBI Intelligence Division.

Although FBI foreign counterintelligence activities may affect the rights of Americans, they receive less public attention, because the problems are complex and sometimes classified for national security reasons. Most of the discussion has focused on electronic surveillance, in the context of proposed legislation requiring court orders for FBI foreign intelligence surveillance in the United States.

On the surface, there is overwhelming agreement that counterintelligence operations are needed to uncover potential acts of espionage and terrorism by foreign agents, even if the foreign agents happen to be Americans. But the debate over the electronic surveillance bill revealed differences of opinion over the proper scope and basis for these investigations. Should counterintelligence investigations of Americans be as closely linked to violations of federal law as investigations of domestic violence? Or do such general threats as "foreign subversion," or "clandestine intelligence activities," require wider counterintelligence investigations of Americans?

FBI surveillance of political groups had significant foreign counterintelligence dimensions during the 1960s and early 1970s. Any participation by a Communist party member in a group (openly or secretly) would trigger an FBI investigation to determine the degree of Communist influence over the group's activities. Moreover, when a protest group's leaders traveled abroad to attend international meetings involving Communist representatives, the FBI suspected possible foreign influence over their plans. FBI reports reinforced the belief that domestic dissent, particularly against the Vietnam War, was inspired by foreign governments. Presidents Johnson and Nixon demanded from the FBI and CIA increasingly broad surveillance to discover proof of such foreign controls, even though substantial positive evidence never turned up. The White House, the State Department, the CIA, military intelligence, and the Secret Service received a constant flow of information from the FBI about domestic political activities having some possible connection (via Communist participation or otherwise) with foreign powers considered hostile to the United States. The purpose was never law enforcement; instead, the ostensible function was to supply "pure intelligence" for top officials, who could then assess the impact of any foreign effort in this country. Every President since FDR had received such reports on foreign "subversion."

The breadth of FBI surveillance to uncover foreign influence on domestic politics led the Church committee to conclude that "the concern for 'foreign subversion' was distorted so far beyond reasonable definition the term 'subversion' should be abandoned completely."[37] But defining the permissible objective of FBI foreign counterintelligence investigations was more difficult. Americans are recruited by foreign intelligence services, and current federal law does not specify which activities of foreign agents justify investigation.

Attorney General Levi vigorously opposed rewriting the espionage laws for this purpose, and defended the use of other standards for FBI counterintelligence surveillance. On constitutional grounds, he argued that the Fourth Amendment permitted "searches for purposes other than criminal law enforcement if reasonable in light of the circumstances and the governmental interests involved." As a matter of policy, he stressed the difference between counterintelligence and law enforcement investigations. The purpose of criminal investigations is prosecution "to deter certain activities deemed contrary to the public interest." By contrast, the purpose of counterintelligence is "to gain information about the hostile actions and intentions and capabilities of foreign powers." Such information is sometimes "more vital to the nation's safety than preventing or deterring the activities through criminal prosecution." Moreover, Levi said, changing the espionage laws to encompass all the clandestine intelligence activities undertaken on behalf of a foreign power "would be difficult and could make the espionage laws too broad."[38]

This issue remained unresolved when Attorney General Levi left office. His successor, Attorney General Griffin Bell, agreed to a modified criminal standard in the Foreign Intelligence Surveillance Act of 1978, but what standard would apply to FBI counterintelligence investigations involving less intrusive techniques was far from clear. Nonetheless, the area of dispute moved significantly away from the sweeping intelligence operations of the past aimed at political subversion and Communist influence in the United States.

Finally, there was agreement that proposals to divest the FBI of its foreign counterintelligence duties were misconceived. Such proposals arose, in part, out of a concern that intelligence activities that might be justified against foreign spies would be improper for domestic law enforcement and that, as Attorney General Levi put it, "the combination can work a contamination." Levi concluded that the dangers were greater if a separate agency were to be created. He stressed that "the fact that the FBI has criminal investigative responsibilities, which must be conducted within the confines of constitutional protections strictly enforced by the courts, gives the organization an awareness of the interests of individual liberties that might be missing in an agency devoted solely to intelligence work."[39] The Church committee agreed that keeping these functions in the FBI would make it easier for the Attorney General to control them, inasmuch as he appeared to be "the most appropriate official to be charged with ensuring that the intelligence agencies of the United States conduct their activities in accordance with the rule of law."[40]

Beyond the Criminal Law Standard

The touchstone of virtually every aspect of FBI intelligence reform has been Attorney General Harlan Fiske Stone's statement in 1924 that the FBI should not be "concerned with political or other opinions of individuals." It should be "concerned only with their conduct and then only with such conduct as is forbidden by the laws of the United States." Stone believed that a police system that passed beyond these limits was "dangerous to the proper administration of justice and to human liberty, which it should be our first concern to cherish."[41] However, this principle was the beginning—not the end—of the reform enterprise. Even if the FBI is viewed just as a criminal investigative agency, its powers are tremendous and require careful control when they approach the borderline between criminal conduct and lawful political dissent.

Once again, it was Attorney General Robert Jackson who diagnosed the dangers. Even in 1940 the law books were "filled with a great assortment of crimes," and the government stood "a fair chance of finding at least a technical violation of some act on the part of almost anyone."[42] There are many more federal criminal laws today, especially in such areas as organized crime, civil rights, bombings and riots, assaults on American and foreign officials, and white-collar crime. In combination with the law of conspiracy and the federal fugitive laws, which allow investigations to locate persons who cross state lines to avoid prosecution, the scope of federal jurisdiction is immense. As a result, the FBI and the Justice Department have enormous discretionary power to decide how they will allocate their limited resources. This means, in turn, that adherence to the rule of law demands much more than simply requiring that investigations be linked to violations of federal law. There must also be principled standards for the exercise of discretion and the establishment of priorities.[43]

Two examples may help explain the problem. One involves the law of conspiracy and domestic political activities. The other deals with laws concerning registration of foreign agents and "clandestine intelligence activity."

In 1968 Dr. Benjamin Spock and others were convicted of conspiracy to aid and abet violation of the Selective Service laws. The evidence introduced at the trial included political statements opposing the war in Vietnam, and participation in antidraft protest activities. Harvard Law Professor Alan Dershowitz later observed that the government had charged "the kind of crime—a loosely knit, widespread and uncircumscribed conspiracy—that would have the greatest impact on discouraging organized opposition to the Vietnam War."[44] The convictions were reversed on appeal, but the Court of Appeals' opinion on the law of conspiracy, as applied to the First Amendment context, still supplied a legal basis for wide-ranging conspiracy investigations.

In one respect, the court tried to narrow conventional conspiracy doctrines. Ordinarily, so long as there is some circumstantial evidence of agreement among the alleged conspirators, each defendant is held responsible for the acts and statements of his co-conspirators. An individual need not have committed an illegal act himself; the question is whether he is a "partner" in an illegal enterprise. In the *Spock* case, the court ruled that "partnership" was not enough. Where the enterprise has both legal and illegal objectives, and is "political within the shadow of the First Amendment," an individual's participation cannot be made criminal by the conduct or statements of others in the movement.

Nevertheless, the court held firm to the basic conspiracy doctrine that persons may be convicted for what they *intend* to do. It ruled that "an individual's specific intent to adhere to the illegal portions" of the undertaking may be shown not only by the commission of the illegal act that is contemplated, but also by the individual's "unambiguous statements" or by the commission of a legal act "for the specific purpose of rendering effective the later illegal activity."[45]

Thus, under the law of conspiracy as interpreted by the courts, there is a wide exception to the First Amendment principles forbidding the prosecution of speech falling short of "incitement to imminent lawless action."[46] If persons make "unambiguous statements" that they intend to violate the law, or if they commit a lawful act specifically intended to "render effective" their eventual crimes, they may be investigated and, if it suits the Justice Department's priorities at the time, prosecuted for conspiracy. This is, in effect, a sweeping legal charter for criminal investigations that would produce, as a side benefit of the search for further evidence of the conspiracy, "preventive intelligence" information. Even the most rigorous probable cause standard is not much of a restraint if all that is needed is probable cause of a conspiracy.

The laws requiring registration of foreign agents offer a comparable example. There is more than one law for this purpose, although the Foreign Agents Registration Act of 1938, as amended, is the only statute regularly enforced.[47] Another law dating from 1917 makes it a blanket crime for anyone other than a diplomatic officer to act in the United States "as an agent of a foreign government without prior notification to the Secretary of State."[48] In addition, a law enacted in 1956 requires the registration of all persons who have received assignments, instructions, or training in the espionage, counterespionage, or sabotage tactics of a foreign government. This statute extends beyond persons who have a "principal-agent" relationship with a foreign power; and willful failure to register is punishable by up to five years in prison and a $10,000 fine.[49]

Registration laws widen the scope of criminal law enforcement to reach activities that, in the absence of the disclosure requirement, would be entirely lawful. Indeed, this may be the only constitutionally permissible function of registration laws, because the Supreme Court has ruled that laws compelling the disclosure of criminal activity violate the Fifth Amendment privilege against self-incrimination.[50]

Thus, the foreign agents registration laws—particularly the 1956 "spy registration" statute—may encompass most of the otherwise noncriminal "clandestine intelligence activities" that were the subject of the debate over FBI foreign counterintelligence surveillance. The congressional committee reports on the 1978 electronic surveillance bill recognized the danger that the foreign agents registration laws might cover not only spying, but also activities normally protected by the First Amendment. Publishing literature favoring the cause of a foreign government, or organizing a meeting to promote the views of a foreign political party might technically violate the registration law if the publisher or organizer took confidential directions from the foreign power. Therefore, the committee reports stressed that Americans who fail to comply fully with the foreign agents registration acts should not be placed under surveillance if all they are doing on behalf of a foreign power is to lobby Congress or influence public opinion on matters relating to the national defense or foreign affairs.[51] However, the committees did not address the question of when the registration laws might allow the FBI to investigate such activities, using less intrusive techniques than electronic surveillance.

These examples show why Attorney General Stone's principle that the FBI should investigate only conduct forbidden by federal law does not go far enough. The law of conspiracy and the foreign agents registration laws circumvent the First Amendment in ways that are not always obvious to anyone but the experienced investigator or prosecutor; there are other statutes and legal doctrines designed to provide flexible instruments for federal law enforcement. Therefore, what may count as the critical protection for civil liberties in the future are the standards governing the exercise of investigative and prosecutorial discretion within the broad framework of the criminal law.

That FBI intelligence investigations should be linked to possible violations of the law was the first principle in the effort to strike the right balance between security and liberty, yet it was not the only one. Some federal laws, such as the Smith Act and the Voorhis Act, which on their face punish political advocacy, obviously needed revision or repeal. The espionage and foreign agents laws probably required modernization. Perhaps the FBI should be given authority to investigate certain terrorist activities that may violate state laws, without making them federal crimes, so there would be no artificial gaps in its "preventive intelligence" coverage. All these changes were recommended by the Church committee.[52]

The spirit behind them, as Attorney General Levi observed regarding the proposal to modernize the espionage laws, derived "from a perceived need for complete symmetry between this area and the traditional law enforcement area." But Levi believed this symmetry might "not be possible in the working out of the details of policy, no matter how inviting it may be in its spirit."[53] Levi's skepticism about the value of perfect symmetry makes sense in another way. Law enforcement agencies never have enforced with equal vigor all the criminal laws, nor should they. Instead, they set priorities, sometimes openly and sometimes behind the screen of what Kenneth Culp Davis calls "the pervasive false pretense of full enforcement."[54]

It is not enough to say that the FBI shall investigate only where it has credible information or reasonable suspicion that a crime has been or may be committed. Nor is it adequate to say that the FBI shall use certain intrusive techniques only where it or the Attorney General or a court finds reasonable suspicion or probable cause that a criminal enterprise is underway. These may be the outer limits, but they provide little guidance for those discretionary decisions at the heart of the power of a law enforcement agency. If we are to apply the rule of law effectively to the exercise of investigative powers, our thinking must go beyond the criminal laws and beyond procedures linked to the criminal law by such shorthand terms as reasonable suspicion or probable cause. The FBI has been told what it should not do—that is, investigate without reasonable suspicion of criminal activity—but it has not been told what it should concentrate on doing. There must be a more systematic and principled analysis of where and why domestic security and foreign counterintelligence investigations are necessary.

Traditionally, there has been a wide gap between law enforcement officers, who know the practical problems of discretionary choice, but often cling to the myth that they act as neutral instruments of the law, and those who frame criminal laws and procedures from a distance. Bridging this gap is vital to any long-term improvements in the system of criminal justice. We have forced the FBI to bare its secrets. Now there is an obligation on those who set the standards. As Professor Davis observed, "perhaps all of us who work on legal problems should be wondering whether judicial opinions, lawyers' thinking, and legal education are too much focused on the formality of law (words in statutes and in case law) and give insufficient emphasis to the reality of law (what enforcement officers do in fact)."[55] Failure to confront these realities can render the most idealistic legal safeguards for individual rights ineffective because they turn out, in practice, to be irrelevant.

CHAPTER III

Development of the Attorney General's Guidelines

THE impression that the Bureau was completely on its own for forty years is false: Attorneys General have always given some degree of guidance to the FBI for its intelligence operations. There were instructions governing the compilation of emergency detention lists, guidelines for designating and prosecuting subversive organizations, and orders dealing with domestic violence and civil disorder. The FBI kept the Justice Department generally informed of its domestic intelligence investigations through a continuing stream of reports to the department's Internal Security Division (abolished in 1973), Criminal Division, Civil Rights Division, and special units such as the Interdivisional Intelligence Unit (1967-1974) and Intelligence Evaluation Committee (1971-1973), which the department created specifically to receive FBI civil disturbance intelligence reports.

Attorneys General may not have known much about the Bureau's most questionable activities, including its surreptitious entries and its harassment of civil rights and antiwar groups, but part of the reason for their not knowing was that they did not ask. Nor did any Attorney General ever promulgate a set of legal or administrative principles to govern FBI intelligence activities. Even without going into all the details of Bureau operations, an Attorney General could have interpreted the constitutional requirements. None chose to do so. The courts did not compel such an interpretation because cases that threatened to disclose intelligence techniques were never brought. Congress was not interested in anything but electronic surveillance, and it became the one intelligence technique specifically regulated by the Attorney General.

In place of sporadic and incomplete instructions and legal intepretations, Attorney General Levi in 1975-1976 substituted a coherent framework of law and policy for the FBI and other U.S. intelligence agencies. Whether or not one agrees with all aspects of Attorney General Levi's guidelines and his constitutional interpretations, one must respect his contributions to clarifying the issues and encouraging public debate. His successor, Attorney General Bell, carried forward Levi's policies in most respects, and the guidelines became the focus for consideration of legislative charters for FBI foreign counterintelligence and domestic security investigations.

Development of the guidelines must be viewed against a background of FBI efforts to shore up the legal basis for domestic intelligence investigations in 1972-1974. Even before J. Edgar Hoover's death, Bureau executives realized they might be in a vulnerable position, and Hoover himself was not always willing in his later years to act without support from the Attorney General. For these and other reasons, FBI intelligence officials attempted to rationalize their existing operations in terms of the criminal law, and to secure new Justice Department authorization. In 1974, under Attorney General William Saxbe, they succeeded in getting broad departmental endorsements. But the disclosures spawned by Watergate, including the FBI's domestic counterintelligence program (COINTELPRO) and political misuse of the Bureau by various Presidents, made reconsideration of FBI guidelines imperative for Attorney General Levi when he arrived in 1975.

Levi confronted two parallel sets of issues. The first involved the standards and procedures for FBI intelligence operations using conventional investigative methods. The second dealt with the use of the most intrusive techniques, such as warrantless electronic surveillance and surreptitious entry. The formulation of guidelines for FBI investigation was assigned to a Justice Department committee, and in many areas the preliminary drafts were submitted to Congress for public debate.

The process of arriving at standards for using intrusive techniques in the foreign intelligence area could not be fully publicized. Instead, Attorney General Levi used as his stalking horses a bill to require court orders for foreign intelligence electronic surveillance within the United States, and a Justice Department report on CIA mail opening. Attorney General Bell pursued these initiatives further in a revised wiretapping bill and more detailed internal regulations.

The task of developing intelligence guidelines inevitably went beyond the FBI. Levi and Bell articulated constitutional criteria governing the full range of intelligence surveillance and search techniques, including by implication both the CIA and the ultrasecret activities of the National Security Agency (NSA). The problem of regulating the FBI at home was in many ways the same as the problem of restricting the activities of other U.S. intelligence agencies that affect Americans. Although the Attorney General did not have direct authority over agencies outside the Justice Department, Levi used his position as chief legal officer of the United States to extend the rule of law to the entire intelligence community and to bring the issues to public attention. Taking up where Levi left off, Attorney General Bell obtained formal authorization from the President to review and approve procedures for all intelligence activities, at home and abroad, affecting the rights of Americans.[1]

The FBI and Guidelines

FBI executives approached the guidelines with, to say the least, ambivalence. They strongly believed that FBI intelligence programs served necessary and popular interests, and they feared that outside guidelines would curb or publicly disclose these operations, harming the Bureau's effectiveness and reputation. On the other hand, if the Attorney General took on more responsibility for authorizing intelligence activities, he and not the Bureau would take the legal or political heat. Passing the buck to the Attorney General could protect the FBI from embarrassment or criticism. These contradictory impulses existed within the Bureau under J. Edgar Hoover, years before Clarence Kelley and Edward Levi arrived on the scene.

Director Hoover's Restrictions

During the mid-1960s, J. Edgar Hoover decided to withdraw his approval for some of the FBI's most intrusive intelligence operations, including warrantless surreptitious entries and mail openings. According to some of his associates, Hoover feared exposure by a Senate subcommittee, even though Attorney General Nicholas Katzenbach had persuaded the committee to bypass the FBI. Others believed that he came to feel insecure after passing the mandatory retirement age in 1964. However, it is just as plausible that Hoover, with a keen sense for changing public attitudes, realized that the Bureau could no longer count on a popular consensus favoring unrestricted surveillance operations. A particularly acrimonious exchange with Attorney General Katzenbach over disclosure of FBI electronic bugging in organized crime investigations also may have convinced Hoover that he could no longer count on Justice Department support. The political tides clearly had turned by 1967, when Attorney General Ramsey Clark began rejecting FBI requests for electronic surveillance in all domestic security and even some foreign intelligence cases, reversing a long-standing policy of permissiveness.

Hoover's reluctance to act without authorization continued into the Nixon Administration. It was one of the main reasons why the head of the FBI Intelligence Division, William C. Sullivan, worked through White House aide Tom Huston in 1970 to secure formal presidential permission for resuming surreptitious entry and mail-opening operations, and for more extensive electronic surveillance. The CIA and military intelligence endorsed Sullivan's proposal, because the restrictions by Hoover prevented the FBI from undertaking foreign intelligence operations on their behalf. Even then, Hoover rejected the sweeping mandate offered by the Huston plan. The risk of exposure, with copies of the plan in the files of other agencies, was far too great. Hoover told Attorney General Mitchell that the FBI would implement the plan only if Mitchell directed it to do so on a case-by-case basis.[2] Mitchell recoiled at the prospect of his signature on every questionable surveillance authorization, and persuaded President Nixon to withdraw his formal approval of the plan.

Hoover's position was probably best summed up by his comments in the margin of a 1965 memorandum regarding the Senate subcommittee investigation: "I don't see what all the excitement is about. I would have no hesitance in discontinuing all techniques—technical coverage (i.e., wiretapping), microphones, trash covers, mail covers, etc. While it might handicap us I doubt they are as valuable as some believe and none warrant FBI being used to justify them."[3]

Nonetheless, Hoover was willing to approve other questionable intelligence operations, including the COINTELPRO operations to harass and disrupt activities of the Ku Klux Klan, the New Left, and black nationalists. COINTELPRO, which consisted largely of poison pen letters, was infinitely more secure than surreptitious entries or mail openings. Where the Bureau did use outsiders for harassment, most were trusted informants.[4] Hoover rescinded his authorization for COINTELPRO only after the theft of documents from an FBI office in Media, Pennsylvania, in 1971 breached the Bureau's tight security.

The Media break-in and the subsequent publication of internal documents on FBI intelligence operations coincided with renewed congressional concern about government surveillance. Senator Sam J. Ervin's Subcommittee on Constitutional Rights held highly publicized hearings in 1971 on the Army's surveillance of civilians, and later turned its spotlight on the Justice Department's Interdivisional Intelligence Unit, which collated civil disturbance data. Although the Ervin subcommittee treated the FBI with great caution, Hoover ordered the preparation of a summary of relevant FBI manual provisions, in case the subcommittee forced the Bureau to produce its "guidelines."[5]

The Security Index and Administrative Index

Concern inside the Bureau increased later in 1971, when Congress repealed the Emergency Detention Act of 1950. That act, passed at the height of the Cold War, authorized the detention of suspected subversives without a criminal trial in times of unspecified crisis, providing a degree of legislative authority for the FBI's Security Index of "dangerous individuals." In 1968 the FBI Intelligence Division and Justice Department attorneys made a joint study of the detention program, and concluded that the criteria for placing persons on the Security Index should be broader than the standards for detention under the law, on the grounds that "flexibility and discretion at the operating level" were needed for "an effective surveillance program." Thus, under Attorney General Ramsey Clark, the Justice Department encouraged the FBI to mark for detention anyone who belonged to or participated in "a basic revolutionary organization" or entertained "anarchistic or revolutionary beliefs" indicating that they might seize upon an emergency to interfere with the effective operation of government. The FBI interpreted this authorization to permit listing racial militants, black nationalists, and persons involved in the New Left.[6]

After the repeal of the Emergency Detention Act, the FBI saw a need to ask the Justice Department whether "the essence of the Security Index and emergency detention of dangerous individuals could be utilized under Presidential powers." The Bureau's legal counsel also recommended asking the Attorney General to reaffirm the FBI's entire "investigative and record-keeping authority concerning subversive matters," so as to protect the Bureau in case "some spokesman of the extreme left" claimed that repeal of the Detention Act revoked this authority. FBI intelligence officials shared these concerns about possible "charges that we are evading the will of Congress."[7] Director Hoover asked Attorney General Mitchell to authorize the FBI "to continue investigations of those who pose a threat to the internal security of the country and to maintain an administrative index of such individuals." Mitchell endorsed the proposed Administrative Index, and advised Hoover that the FBI retained full power to investigate "subversive activities" under "both statutory and Presidential authority."[8]

This blanket authorization permitted the FBI to place names on the Administrative Index without first clearing them with the department's Internal Security Division attorneys. Thereafter, the Bureau widened the criteria to incorporate individuals "who are in a position to influence others to engage in acts inimical to the national defense or are likely to furnish financial aid or other assistance to revolutionary elements because of their sympathy, associates, or ideology." The FBI reported the revised standard to Attorney General Kleindienst and received no reply.[9] The Security and Administrative Indexes showed how easy it was for the FBI to secure an Attorney General's approval for its own sweeping "guidelines," even if particularly sensitive techniques still caused problems. It made little difference whether the Attorney General was a liberal like Ramsey Clark or a conservative like John Mitchell or Richard Kleindienst. Whatever their ideological bent, Attorneys General usually preferred to let the FBI set its own guidelines or, where it sought direction, to grant whatever investigative authority the Bureau desired.

"Subversion" Guidelines and Revision of the FBI Manual

When Richard Kleindienst testified at his nomination hearings in 1972, he said he was not sure what the FBI's guidelines were, but he believed its investigations were "restricted to criminal conduct or the likelihood of criminal conduct." Director Hoover promptly sent him a summary of the Bureau's "guidelines," stressing that, although investigations were based partly on criminal statutes, subversive activity "often does not clearly involve a specific section of a specific statute." In those instances, Hoover noted, the FBI derived its authority from presidential directives dating back to 1939. Investigations of subversion, he added, were not just to "obtain evidence for prosecution," but to "obtain intelligence data" for the purpose of making "a day-to-day appraisal of the strength, dangerousness, and activities" of subversive groups.

According to the summary prepared for Attorney General Kleindienst, the FBI's standards for subversion investigations covered: (1) any organization "which has as an objective" the violent overthrow of the government or "other criminal activity detrimental to the National defense"; (2) any individual who is "affiliated with or adheres to the principles of" such an organization; and (3) "other individuals with anarchistic, revolutionary or extremist beliefs."[10] Kleindienst did not question these standards.

When Hoover died several months later, Deputy Attorney General L. Patrick Gray was appointed Acting FBI Director. Gray immediately asked for a review of the Bureau's authority to investigate "where there is no direct violation of laws," and his request triggered a sharp debate within the FBI Intelligence Division.

Assistant Director Edward S. Miller had been placed in charge of the Intelligence Division in 1971, when Hoover demoted his predecessor in an effort to keep intelligence operations under his control.[11] Miller and his principal deputy, Thomas J. Smith, concluded that the FBI should try to base its domestic intelligence investigations on federal criminal statutes rather than rely on the more vulnerable presidential directives. Others in the division disagreed. While Acting Director Gray was preoccupied with the Watergate scandal, Miller and Smith proceeded to revise the pertinent FBI manual sections. They had support from the FBI's Legal Counsel Division, whose staff anticipated further congressional intervention, and recommended developing "tight internal controls and carefully developed guidelines."[12]

Miller and Smith began their revision with the Administrative Index. They decided that some of the people on the list did "not realistically pose a threat to the national security," and that leaving their names on it would place the FBI "in a vulnerable position if our guidelines were to be scrutinized by interested Congressional committees." By trimming the list to those who were an actual danger, they could reduce its number by two-thirds. The new standard covered individuals "who have shown a willingness and capability" to commit acts that would interfere with the effective operation of government.[13]

The first change in the FBI manual was to define "subversive activities" solely by reference to the broad federal criminal statutes dealing with rebellion or insurrection, seditious conspiracy, and advocating violent overthrow of the government (the Smith Act).[14] Under the new standards, the FBI would investigate: (1) any "group or movement which is known to engage in *or advocate* activities which *are aimed* at overthrowing, destroying or undermining the Government of the United States or any of its political subdivisions by the illegal means prohibited by [these] statutes"; (2) any individual who is "reported to be engaged in activities which *may result* in a violation of [these] statutes"; (3) any individual who is a "current active member" of an organization or movement under investigation; (4) any individual who is "actively supporting the goals" of such a movement, "where formal membership in [the] movement does not exist."[15] The standards were essentially the same for investigations of "racial extremist activities," except that reference was also made to the equally broad federal civil rights conspiracy statute.[16]

The second revision involved making a distinction between

full investigations, which had to meet the enumerated standards, and 90-day preliminary investigations, relying upon established sources, which could be opened on the basis of fragmentary information that a person had contact with groups or individuals already under investigation, but where the purpose of the contact was not known.[17]

From the point of view of agents in the field, the changes made little difference. They now had to secure headquarters approval for each full investigation and attach a brief "statutory predication" to their requests, but once they satisfied these formalities, they were free to continue the same kinds of investigations as before.[18] The FBI still could conduct sweeping preliminary investigations, such as those of all black student leaders and all members of campus groups such as Students for a Democratic Society, which had been ordered in 1970. Those preliminary inquiries using established sources had been based on the theory that, even if there was no specific information linking the students to violent activity, their active participation in movements that had some violent members was enough to suggest that they, too, might turn to violence.[19]

According to a former FBI official who worked on the revision of the manual, the statutory approach advocated by Miller and Smith did not prevail within the Bureau until June 1973, when Senator Edward M. Kennedy asked for a copy of the manual sections on subversive investigations. By then the Watergate investigations had driven Acting Director Gray from office, and the management of day-to-day Bureau affairs was in the hands of career Associate Director W. Mark Felt. Although Felt had been afraid that Miller's statutory approach cast doubt on the validity of past intelligence investigations not linked to specific statutes, Senator Kennedy's request and the prospect of attendant publicity changed his mind.[20] Another factor may have been Attorney General Kleindienst's decision in early 1973 to abolish the Justice Department's Internal Security Division and transfer its attorneys to the Criminal Division.

Marking Time

In retrospect, it is clear that Watergate and the impeachment process made the task of reconsidering legal and policy standards for FBI intelligence operations impossible in 1973-1974. Four different Attorneys General held office in a period of less than two years, and members of Congress who might otherwise have called for FBI reforms were preoccupied with removing President Nixon from office.

There was some movement toward congressional action. A new Senate Judiciary Subcommittee on FBI Oversight drafted a bill setting a ten-year limit to the FBI director's term, and expressing the sense of the Congress that a director should not be removed for political reasons. Subcommittees headed by Senators Ervin and Kennedy held hearings to pave the way for legislation regulating national security wiretaps and bugs. In the midst of its impeachment investigation, the House Judiciary Committee asked the General Accounting Office to survey FBI domestic security investigations. On the other hand, Watergate investigators in both the Senate and the House chose not to pursue reports that misuse of the FBI had precedents in recent Democratic administrations, and Senators aware of COINTELPRO did not demand an immediate public accounting. In this area, as in virtually every other field of national policy, the government was marking time.

What changes took place occurred on the margins of existing policy. In mid-1973, when Clarence Kelley testified at his confirmation hearings, he was questioned closely about the FBI's reliance on presidential rather than legislative authority for intelligence investigations. Kelley, in turn, asked Attorney General Elliott L. Richardson for "authoritative *and* definitive guidelines" spelling out "the nature and type of intelligence data" required from the FBI by the President, defining the Bureau's "national security objectives," and "conforming to the principles of the Constitution and the Bill of Rights."[21] William Ruckelshaus, upon becoming Deputy Attorney

General-designate after a brief tour as Acting FBI Director, questioned FBI intelligence standards and proposed "an in-depth examination of some of the problems facing the Bureau in the future."

COINTELPRO

The "Saturday night massacre" aborted this enterprise in the Fall of 1973. Richardson and Ruckelshaus were swept from office, and the Acting Attorney General, Solicitor General Robert Bork, faced a more pressing problem. Newsman Carl Stern had obtained a copy of an FBI document stolen from the Media resident office in 1971, bearing the caption "COINTELPRO—New Left" and recommending the anonymous mailing of an article criticizing student demonstrators to university officials. When Stern's request for documents describing COINTELPRO was denied, he filed suit in federal court under the Freedom of Information Act. The judge ordered the Attorney General to produce the documents. The FBI urged then-Solicitor General Bork to appeal; but as one close observer has put it, Bork believed "that a strong dose of openness and candor, rather than the usual tilt against disclosure, was in order."[22]

Disclosure of COINTELPRO put Director Kelley in a difficult position. He faced a choice between denouncing the disruptive practices authorized by J. Edgar Hoover, and defending them so as not to jeopardize the legal position of many agents who had implemented Hoover's program, and who now faced the prospect of civil suits and possible criminal prosecution. Even if he stood up for the agents, Kelley could not oppose restrictions on the use of disruptive operations in the future. When Solicitor General Bork and Attorney General-designate William Saxbe formed a joint Justice Department-FBI committee to find out what COINTELPRO had been all about, Kelley saw a threat to foreign counterintelligence operations, as well. FBI officials had spent most of their time worrying about domestic intelligence problems; now the

COINTELPRO controversy endangered the foreign side of the Intelligence Division, which also engaged in harassment tactics against foreign agents.

To protect the Bureau's continuing activities, Director Kelley asked the new committee, headed by the Assistant Attorney General for the Criminal Division, Henry Petersen, to exclude from its review the FBI's "extremely sensitive foreign intelligence collection techniques," on the grounds that they were too sensitive to be included in a report that might eventually be made public. One Bureau representative on the Petersen committee even suggested that the Attorney General did not have authority over foreign counterintelligence operations, because the FBI was accountable in that area directly to the United States Intelligence Board (chaired by the Director of Central Intelligence) and the National Security Council. The Petersen committee rejected this theory out of hand, but quietly agreed not to seek the details of harassment activities outside the domestic realm.[23]

In its report to Attorney General Saxbe, the Petersen committee made three basic recommendations. The first proposed that "a sharp distinction . . . be made between FBI activities in the area of foreign counterintelligence and those in the domestic field." The second was that the FBI take "no disruptive action . . . in connection with its investigative responsibilities involving domestic based organizations, except those which are sanctioned by rule of law, procedure, or judicially recognized and accepted police practices, and which are not in violation of state or federal law." The third urged that "where a proposed action may be perceived, with reason, to unfairly affect the rights of citizens," it should be "the responsibility of the FBI as an institution and of FBI agents as individuals to seek legal advice from the Attorney General or his authorized representative."[24]

Attorney General Saxbe neither accepted nor rejected these recommendations. Instead, he simply expressed approval of an order by Director Kelley that declared that "FBI employees must not engage in any investigative activity which could abridge in any way the rights guaranteed to a citizen of the United States by the Constitution and under no circumstances shall employees of the FBI engage in any conduct which may result in defaming the character, reputation, integrity, or dignity of any citizen or organization of citizens of the United States."[25] Even these standards, however, lost much of their force when Kelley subsequently defended COINTELPRO as necessary in the circumstances of the 1960s, and declared that all he would do differently in the future would be to obtain the Attorney General's advance approval.[26]

Director Kelley's stand on COINTELPRO was a critical misjudgment of the FBI's needs. Relying for knowledge of its past operations upon what his subordinates told him, he did not realize the full dimensions of what had been done; nor did he insist upon a complete internal accounting, as had CIA Director James Schlesinger in 1973. Consequently, when congressional and Justice Department investigations later uncovered more damaging information about an ill-conceived program that far exceeded reasonable preventive measures, Kelley was left in the embarrassing position of learning more about the Bureau from outside sources than from his own inquiries. Kelley's attempt to justify, in retrospect, the FBI's use of disruptive tactics was equally mistaken. He personally sympathized with Bureau officials who had acted under pressure to cope with widespread violence, and he allowed those feelings to stand in the way of exercising firm leadership. He placed himself in the position of defending actions that involved not only the prevention of imminent violence, but also secret suppression of unpopular political dissent.

1974 Justice Department Authorizations

Under Attorney General Saxbe in 1974, the Justice Department handled FBI requests for guidance piecemeal, essentially approving existing Bureau policies on the basis of long-standing departmental positions. There was one visible change when Saxbe abolished the twenty-five-year-old "Attorney General's List" of subversive organizations. This list had not been updated since the mid-1950s, but it still provided a source of authority for FBI intelligence investigations to obtain information for the federal employee security program; abolishing the list redefined this intelligence-gathering authority. (The Administrative Index continued to serve as the FBI's own internal list of priority investigative targets until its termination in 1976.)

Under Executive Order 10450, which governed the employee security program, the FBI originally was required to gather information about any person who belonged to or associated with an organization that: (1) was "totalitarian, fascist, communist, or subversive"; (2) had "adopted a policy of advocating or approving the commission of acts of force or violence to deny others their rights under the Constitution of the United States"; (3) was "seeking to alter the form of government of the United States by unconstitutional means."[27] In 1971 President Nixon had modified this order on the recommendation of Assistant Attorney General Robert Mardian of the Internal Security Division, who hoped to reach "the new brand of radical in this country." The revised standards spoke only of unlawful advocacy, but extended beyond federal crimes to include violations of the "laws . . . of any State."[28] Thus, they required no connection whatsoever with federal criminal offenses.

Along with the Emergency Detention Program, the employee security program with its Attorney General's list was a basic element of the federal government's Cold War approach to internal security. Just as FBI intelligence investigations served to identify persons whose potential dangerousness might justify detention without trial in an emergency, they also spotted individuals whose "subversive" associations might disqualify them from federal employment. During the 1950s, association with the Communist party or Communist-front groups could put someone on the Security Index and deprive him of a federal job. Twenty years later, association with the New Left and black nationalist activities involving violence resulted in listing a person on the Administrative Index. Mardian's aim had been to revive the employee security program as a way of using FBI intelligence to deny federal jobs to individuals associated with such groups as the Black Panther party, Progressive Labor party, Young Socialist Alliance, and Ku Klux Klan.[29]

When Attorney General Saxbe abolished the Attorney General's list in 1974, the FBI asked the Justice Department to furnish guidelines for the conduct of any intelligence-type investigations still required by Executive Order 10450, as amended.[30] The department replied, through the Assistant Attorney General for Administration, that the FBI should undertake to uncover organizations that "potentially" fell within the terms of the order, and to investigate "individuals who are active either as members of or as affiliates of" such organizations. The FBI was told that it was "not possible to set definite parameters covering the initiation of" these investigations, but that a crime need not have occurred, and the FBI should make "a reasonable evaluation of the available information." Investigations could continue so long as an organization or individual "is engaged in . . . potentially illegal activities."

These instructions constituted virtually complete Justice Department authorization of the FBI manual standards for investigations of subversion and extremism. Indeed, they went beyond the recently revised FBI manual, because they required no federal statutory predicate for investigations conducted on the basis of Executive Order 10450. The department declared that investigations could be based "on a possible violation of a federal (such as the Smith Act) *or state* statute prohibiting unlawful advocacy or the commission of any unlawful act of force or violence."[31]

The FBI also asked in 1974 for guidelines with regard to gathering and reporting information concerning civil disturbance. In this area, the Bureau's authority had support from a 1967 directive by Attorney General Ramsey Clark ordering the FBI to "use the maximum available resources, investigative or intelligence, to collect and report all facts bearing upon the question as to whether there has been or is a scheme or conspiracy by any group of whatever size, effectiveness or affiliation, to plan, promote or aggravate riot activity." For this purpose, Clark had instructed the Bureau to develop and expand its "sources or informants in black nationalist organizations . . . to determine the size and purpose of these groups and their relationship to other groups, and also to determine the whereabouts of persons who might be involved in instigating riot activity in violation of federal law." Clark had stressed the President's desire for "extensive and comprehensive investigations of these matters."[32]

In 1971 Assistant Attorney General William Rehnquist told Senator Ervin's subcommittee that the laws authorizing the President to use troops to put down domestic violence, combined with inherent constitutional powers of the Executive Branch going beyond federal statutes, justified "investigative activities . . . directed to determine the possibility of domestic violence occurring at a particular place or at a particular time."[33] The Justice Department reiterated Rehnquist's position in 1974. Although the FBI suggested that its "reporting be limited to those particular situations which are of such a serious nature that Federal military personnel may be called upon for assistance," Assistant Attorney General Petersen advised that this was not practical, but that the Bureau need not report "each and every relatively insignificant incident of a strictly local nature coming to its attention."

Petersen's criteria were unclear, but they appeared to authorize: (1) full investigations of "extremist organizations such as the Communist Party, the Ku Klux Klan, or Black Panther Party . . . so that the Attorney General may be apprised of potential civil disturbances" that such groups would "instigate or exploit"; (2) investigations to "gather and report (information) on significant civil disorders . . . which may develop into major incidents of violence"; and (3) obtaining information about other "disturbances and patterns of disorder" and "potential disorders" through the Bureau's "liaison with local and state police departments and other law enforcement agencies."[34] The FBI Intelligence Division considered these instructions to be "consistent with what we have already been doing for the past several years," and it was pleased to have "an official, written mandate from the Department."[35]

In late 1974 the FBI could say with confidence that its domestic intelligence investigations were fully authorized by the Department of Justice. By asking for guidance, the Bureau had won more discretion than it sought. Although the Petersen committee privately characterized COINTELPRO as "an unwarranted interference with First Amendment rights of free speech and associations of the target individuals and organizations," it recommended against any criminal investigation of past or present FBI personnel.[36] Not until November 1974, nearly six months after it was submitted, did Attorney General Saxbe release a public version of the Petersen committee report. By that time, the Watergate investigations were ending, President Ford wanted a nonpolitical Attorney General to restore confidence in the Justice Department, and Congress was ready to turn from impeachment to the underlying problems of the FBI and the CIA.

The chairman of the House Judiciary Subcommittee charged with FBI oversight was Representative Don Edwards, a former FBI agent and liberal Democrat from California. Edwards made clear his subcommittee's intentions at the first public hearings on COINTELPRO in November 1974. He was disturbed by Director Kelley's defense of the program's "frightening litany of Government violations of constitutional rights," and he denounced the philosophy "that any public official, the President or a policeman, possesses a kind of inherent power to set aside the Constitution whenever he thinks the public interest, or national security warrants it." The subcommittee intended, particularly through its request for a General Accounting Office review, to make sure "that serious efforts are begun for exercising responsible congressional oversight in this area."[37]

The Attorney General's FBI Guidelines

During the hearings on his confirmation in early 1975, Attorney General Levi made a commitment to preparing new guidelines for the FBI, but he did not fully realize the importance of this task until he took office and immediately confronted the record of abuses.

The first thing Levi discovered was that, since J. Edgar Hoover's death in 1972, the FBI had been hiding the existence of certain of Hoover's files marked "Official and Confidential" (OC). In addition to materials on policy, administrative, and personnel matters, the OC files contained what Levi later described as "derogatory information concerning public figures or prominent persons." These files had been removed from Hoover's office suite after his death and lodged in the office of the Associate Director. Levi also learned that there had been other personal files in Hoover's office that had been destroyed.

The OC files had come to light only when Deputy Attorney General Laurence Silberman, at the request of the Edwards subcommittee, asked the FBI for a full review of its practices for maintaining files on public officials, members of Congress, and private citizens. The review of FBI files on individual Congressmen disclosed that fifteen folders relating to Congressmen were in the OC files, and that in one instance derogatory information about a Congressman who had attacked Hoover "was improperly disseminated." The OC files also revealed that executive officials in other agencies of government requested the FBI to take certain actions, directing that it maintain no records of those actions. Therefore, as Levi explained, one could not "always know what action, if any, was taken with respect to these files."[38]

But Silberman's inquiry went beyond the OC files. During the early stages of the Watergate investigations in 1973, White House Counsel John Dean had turned over several memoranda, prepared for him by former FBI executive William C. Sullivan, recounting political misuse of the FBI by Presidents before the Nixon Administration. The Senate Watergate Committee later obtained copies of these memoranda, and minority staff members interviewed Sullivan and other former FBI officials about the allegations. The committee decided not to include these findings in its public report.[39] Silberman asked the FBI to have its Inspection Division investigate the charges made in the Sullivan memoranda; Attorney General Levi received the reports when he arrived at the Justice Department.

They revealed that the FBI had been used by Presidents and their White House aides to gather "political intelligence information during the course of election campaigns and a political convention, as well as to report on activities of critics of administration policies, including members of Congress." The FBI also had disseminated derogatory information to others in the Executive Branch "to enable them to discredit their critics." This, at least, was the understated way Levi described his findings to the Edwards subcommittee after only three weeks in office.[40] The details of these political abuses did not become public until eight months later, when the Church committee held hearings to disclose the results of its investigation into FBI misconduct.[41]

The Agenda for FBI Guidelines

From the outset, Attorney General Levi gave priority to FBI problems and, as he put it, "to the development of standards or rules which may minimize the possibilities for abuse." His testimony before the Edwards subcommittee claimed only to report "the beginning steps in this endeavor." Even at that early stage, however, the outline of the FBI guidelines began to emerge.

There was an obvious need to limit requests from White House personnel, and to emphasize what Levi described as "the availability of the Attorney General as a 'lightening rod' to deflect improper requests." Accordingly, Levi instructed Kelley "to report to me immediately any requests or practices which in his judgment are improper, or which, considering the context of the request, he believes present the appearance of impropriety."[42]

As for guidelines generally, Levi declared that they would sort out the relationships between the FBI's "investigatory practices" and its "jurisdiction and authority." They also would take up "the question of retention and disclosure of information." Finally, because the FBI was supposed to operate under the supervision of the Department of Justice, of which it is a part, the guidelines would address "the effectiveness of this supervision."

Levi did more than present an agenda for FBI guidelines; he made significant initial policy decisions as well. First, he stated that under its statutory authority to detect federal crimes, the FBI could investigate "persons or incidents when there is reason to believe that a Federal crime has been *or is likely to be* committed so that the violators can be prosecuted *or the crime prevented*" (emphasis added). Second, presidential directives authorizing the FBI to conduct national security surveillance were, in Levi's view, "conditioned by the developing constitutional law on the powers of the President, and . . . [by] legislative enactments and court decisions on the appropriate procedures for investigation." Third, Levi rejected the federal employee security program as a basis for FBI intelligence investigations. As Levi saw it, the Executive Order authorized the Bureau only to investigate Executive Branch employees and applicants. It could not supply a basis for the FBI's authority to conduct domestic intelligence investigations in general.

These policy statements repudiated the standing Justice Department instructions for FBI intelligence investigations.

They undercut the 1974 departmental memos instructing the FBI to investigate subversives and extremists so as to have data for checking out applicants for federal jobs and for anticipating civil disorders. Nevertheless, Levi did retain the idea of presidential authorization for FBI surveillance, even if it might be qualified by statutes or court decisions.

When Levi finished explaining his plans to the Edwards subcommittee, Director Kelley declared that he "wholeheartedly endorsed" Levi's objectives and his "constructive approach." Kelley said the FBI would "work with him each step of the way in carefully laying out the facts and in analyzing them judiciously so that definitive guidelines and safeguards can be developed wherever the need exists." Kelley added that he was "very much aware . . . of the potential for misuse" of the FBI, although he did not know of any effort since he took office "to use the FBI for partisan political purposes."[43]

The Work of the Guidelines Committee

Soon thereafter, Levi set up a committee to draft FBI guidelines, chaired by Deputy Assistant Attorney General Mary C. Lawton of the Office of Legal Counsel, who was the department's expert on the law of privacy. Director Kelley's representative on the committee was the head of the FBI's Office of Congressional Affairs, John B. Hotis, and Levi's personal staff representative was Jack Fuller, a former Chicago journalist with a Yale law degree. Other members came from the department's Criminal and Civil Rights Divisions and the Office of Policy and Planning. The committee's mandate was "to reconsider the whole range of Bureau investigative practices from the use of organized crime informants to the use of warrantless electronic surveillance to collect foreign intelligence information."

In August 1975, after the committee had been meeting several times a week for five months, Attorney General Levi announced that it had completed draft guidelines in four areas: investigations requested by the White House, investigations for congressional and judicial staff appointments, the handling of unsolicited allegations received by mail, and investigations to obtain domestic intelligence. Speaking to the American Bar Association, Levi promised that the committee would go on to "areas such as organized crime intelligence, criminal investigations, the federal employee security program, counterintelligence and foreign intelligence investigations, and background investigations for federal judicial appointments."[44]

The new standards for White House requests were designed expressly to prevent presidential assistants from using the FBI for partisan political purposes through requests "couched in terms of law enforcement or national security." The guidelines required that all requests be made in writing, that only specified officials could make requests, that the official initiating the request be identified, and that the purpose of the investigation be stated from among four "routine areas." These included: (1) suitability for presidential appointment; (2) suitability for position on the staff of the Executive Office; (3) clearance for access to classified information; and (4) clearance for access to "places under the protection of the U.S. Secret Service in connection with its duties to protect the President and the Vice President." Requests for a field investigation, as opposed to a mere review of existing files, had to be "accompanied by a signed statement by the subject of the investigation acknowledging that he has consented to the investigation with knowledge that facts or information gathered shall be retained" by the Bureau. Special controls were placed on access to and dissemination of information in White House investigative files.[45]

These guidelines and the ones governing requests for staff employee background investigations from congressional committees and judges, lacking an Executive Order or legislation, were not formally imposed on the Bureau, but Levi gave his assurance that the Bureau followed them "substantially."[46] All contact between the White House and the FBI, except that specifically authorized by the guidelines, was regulated by the Attorney General's office. Direct contact from any member of the White House staff or the Cabinet about a criminal case received a reply from the Attorney General's office. Nevertheless, Levi's failure to secure an Executive Order was unfortunate: although President Ford was willing to abide by the guidelines in practice, a successor possibly could be unwilling to do so, especially if the rules could be changed without a formal order. (See Appendix III for the draft guidelines for "White House Personnel Security and Background Investigations.")

The domestic intelligence guidelines raised more problems and went through several drafts before they were finally adopted in March 1976. By then, Attorney General Levi had dropped a proposal for FBI preventive action to avert violence in certain circumstances, and had changed the label from "domestic intelligence" to "domestic security investigations." A separate set of guidelines was developed for reporting on civil disorders and demonstrations involving a federal interest. Later, recognizing that there were special problems with the FBI's use of informants, the committee drafted additional guidelines for informants in domestic security, organized crime, and other criminal investigations. The committee devoted the first half of 1976 primarily to the guidelines for FBI foreign intelligence and counterintelligence investigations, which were required by President Ford's Executive Crder on U.S. foreign intelligence activities.[47] These guidelines were issued by June 1, 1976, but could not be made public because they included classified information.

Before Attorney General Levi left office, he said the committee was still "working on guidelines concerning cooperation with foreign police and other overseas aspects of the Bureau's work, organized crime . . . and the government loyalty-security or, as it is sometimes called, employment suitability program." Levi admitted that the process had "taken a great deal of time" because of its "unprecedented nature." The committee had tried "to be realistic about the exercise of discretion and to impose special controls to guide sensitive decisions."[48]

The Domestic Security Guidelines

The guidelines for domestic security investigations authorized the FBI to collect "information on the activities of individuals, or the activities of groups, which involve or will involve the use of force or violence and which involve or will involve the violation of federal law." Specific federal criminal statutes were not listed. Instead, the guidelines covered any federal crime committed for the purpose of overthrowing the federal government or a state government; substantially interfering in the United States with the activities of a foreign government or its authorized representatives; substantially impairing the functioning of federal or state government or interstate commerce for the purpose of influencing U.S. government policies or decisions; or depriving persons of their civil rights under the Constitution, laws, or treaties of the United States.

Investigations could be conducted at three levels—preliminary investigations, limited investigations, and full investigations—differing in scope and in investigative techniques to be used. All investigations had to be "designed and conducted so as not to limit the full exercise of rights protected by the Constitution and laws of the United States."

Preliminary investigations could be undertaken on the basis of "allegations or other information," and were confined to determining whether there was "a factual basis for opening a full investigation." FBI field offices were authorized to open preliminary investigations on their own initiative, but the techniques they could use were limited to the examination of FBI files, public records, and records of government agencies; inquiry of existing sources of information and use of previously established informants; and physical surveillance and interviews of other persons for the purpose of identifying the subject of an investigation. If these techniques were inadequate, the Special Agent in Charge of the field office (or FBI headquarters) could authorize a limited investigation involving physical surveillance for purposes other than identification, and more extensive interviews.

Preliminary and limited investigations had to be closed within ninety days of their initiation, unless FBI headquarters authorized an extension based upon a written statement of the information and circumstances justifying the extension. The FBI was required to report periodically to the Justice Department on all limited investigations and all preliminary investigations that were extended beyond ninety days.

Full investigations required authorization by FBI headquarters on the basis of "specific and articulable facts giving reason to believe that an individual or group is or may be engaged in activities which involve or will involve the use of force or violence and which involve or will involve the violation of federal law." In addition, consideration had to be given to the magnitude of the threatened harm, the likelihood it would occur, the immediacy of the threat, and the danger to privacy and free expression posed by a full investigation. FBI headquarters was directed to review the results of full investigations periodically, and to terminate them when the standards could no longer be satisfied and all logical leads had been exhausted or were "not likely to be productive."

The FBI was to advise the Attorney General or his designee within one week of the opening of each full domestic security investigation, setting forth the basis for the investigation. A progress report was to be made to the Justice Department within ninety days, and the results of the investigation were to be reported at the end of each year an investigation continued. No full investigation could continue beyond one year unless the Department determined in writing that continued investigation was warranted.

The guidelines placed certain limitations on the techniques

used in full investigations. The use of informants to gather information required approval of FBI headquarters, subject to review at intervals not longer than 180 days. When persons were arrested or charged with a crime, and criminal proceedings were still pending, informants could not be used to gather information from the person charged with the crime. Informants could not be used to obtain privileged information; and where an informant obtained such information on his own initiative, the Bureau could make no record or use of that information. "Mail covers" (recording the names and addresses from the outside of envelopes or packages) had to be conducted pursuant to postal regulations, and only with the approval of the Attorney General or his designee. Electronic surveillance could be conducted only in accordance with the criminal law enforcement procedures requiring a judicial warrant, based on probable cause that a crime had been or was about to be committed. The guidelines committee was not satisfied, however, that all sensitive techniques had been covered, citing inquiries made under "pretext," "trash cover," and photographic or other surveillance techniques.

Regarding dissemination of information, the guidelines allowed the FBI to disseminate to other federal authorities any information that fell within their investigative jurisdiction, that might assist in preventing the use of force or violence, or that might be required by statute, interagency agreement approved by the Attorney General, or presidential directive. All such agreements and directives were to be published in the Federal Register. The FBI could disseminate information relating to possible violent activities to state and local law enforcement authorities under similar standards. Information about other criminal activities could be referred to state or local authorities only if it related to "serious crimes." The guidelines placed no limit on the FBI's authority "to inform any individual(s) whose safety or property is directly threatened by planned force or violence, so that they may take appropriate protective safeguards." (The full text of the Attorney General's guidelines for domestic security investigations appears in Appendix I.)

The policies of the guidelines provided the impetus for major changes in the scope of FBI domestic intelligence operations. The implementation of the guidelines, and their impact on the FBI's activities, are described in the next chapter.

Foreign Intelligence Surveillance

Shortly before his departure, Levi recounted an episode that showed how he began his process of rethinking the standards and procedures for the use of controversial techniques such as warrantless electronic surveillance for foreign intelligence purposes:

> I vividly recall that quite late in the afternoon on my first day as Attorney General this issue arose immediately. Just as I was settling into my chair and observing the handsome wood paneling of the office, an FBI agent appeared at my door without announcement. He put before me a piece of paper asking my authorization for the installation of a wiretap without court order and he waited for my approval. For close to forty years the Department of Justice had been called upon to undertake electronic surveillance in certain cases without prior judicial approval. But I thought it was a bit unusual that I was expected to sign it automatically, if that really was the expectation. I asked the agent to leave the request with me—I think, perhaps, to his surprise—so that I could consult other officials in the Department.[49]

Attorney General Levi played his most active personal role in this area, and called upon the advice of academic consultants, including such distinguished legal scholars as Herbert Wechsler of the Columbia Law School and Philip B. Kurland of the University of Chicago Law School. Among other responsibilities, Wechsler and Kurland were specially appointed consultants to evaluate the Justice Department's report on CIA mail-opening activities.

Warrantless Electronic Surveillance

The first problem involved warrantless electronic surveillance standards. Following the *Keith* decision in 1972, the Justice Department took the position that warrantless surveillance could not be used against domestic organizations unless there was "substantial financing, control by, or active collaboration with a foreign government and agencies thereof in unlawful activities directed against the Government of the United States." In an analysis prepared for Attorney General Richardson in 1973, the Office of Legal Counsel assumed that this meant "that before electronic surveillance power is used against groups composed of citizens a rather clear showing of possible law violation must be shown."[50]

Richardson explained publicly that such surveillance "was carried out to meet the obligations of the President as both Commander-in-Chief and as the Nation's instrument for foreign affairs." Although Congress had never authorized warrantless surveillance, it had suggested the contours of the President's power in Title III of the Omnibus Crime Control Act of 1968, which provided for electronic surveillance with judicial warrants in certain criminal investigations. Citing the language of Title III, Richardson stated, "in general, before I approve any new application for surveillance without a warrant, I must be convinced that it is necessary (1) to protect the nation against actual or potential attack or other hostile acts of a foreign power; (2) to obtain foreign intelligence information deemed essential to the security of the United States; or (3) to protect national security information against foreign intelligence activities."[51] However, Richardson did not make clear whether his standards modified the earlier requirement of possible violation of the law for surveillance of American citizens; and he did not specify the necessary "relationships . . . between domestic groups or organizations and foreign powers, or their agents."[52]

Attorney General Saxbe announced in 1974 that, under his criteria, "there was no domestic activity subject to warrantless wiretapping unless it was demonstrated in the application that it was financed by, organized by and directed by a foreign power outside our borders." But confusion remained because he claimed at one point to be following the unlawful activities standard for citizens, and later asserted that "in intelligence work you can't always allege a crime." Saxbe's most significant modifications of the Richardson standards came in two areas, the definition of "foreign power," and the application of constitutional protections to American citizens abroad. The term "foreign power" was to include foreign terrorist groups, and Saxbe was attempting "to insure that no American citizen can be wiretapped any place in the world without the approval of the Attorney General,"[53] under the same limitations applying within the United States.

Richardson and Saxbe had sharply contrasting views on the proposal that court orders be required for national security electronic surveillance. Although he did not have an opportunity to consider all the practical problems, Richardson stated after leaving office that warrants should be required "at least for any electronic surveillance of an American citizen," and said that he and Deputy Attorney General Ruckelshaus had hoped to find a way to construct that kind of warrant without having to formulate new legislation. Warrantless surveillance would be confined "to the facilities and personnel of certain foreign powers."[54]

After some initial hesitation, Saxbe came down strongly against judicial warrants. "The sensitivity of the intelligence in these cases cannot possibly be evaluated by persons who do not regularly deal with foreign affairs and intelligence matters," he said. "The judgment requires consideration of information that cannot be available to the judiciary." Saxbe was particularly concerned that proposed warrant legislation would seriously impair the FBI's ability to protect the nation from foreign powers that both send agents to the United States, and recruit American citizens to obtain intelligence about our military affairs and for purposes of "terrorism and subversion." FBI Director Kelley agreed, and stressed that the distinction between foreigners and American citizens had "no practical, logical basis" because it ignored the fact that Americans "have been, are, and always will be influenced and in some cases directed by foreign powers."[55]

Thus, in 1975 Attorney General Levi faced constitutional and policy issues encompassing the powers of the presidency, the principles of the Bill of Rights, the need to combat hostile intelligence operations, the desires of the CIA and the State and Defense Departments for foreign intelligence information, and the insistence of Congress that it play a much greater role in regulating surveillance practices. Attorney General Saxbe's commitment to supervising the electronic surveillance of Americans abroad forced Levi to deal not only with the FBI, but with the CIA and the highly secret programs of the National Security Agency, as well.

Other Warrantless Search Techniques

Other techniques than conventional electronic surveillance were involved. Levi decided to oppose the Watergate Special Prosecutor's position, expressed in the prosecution of John Ehrlichman for approving the Nixon White House "plumbers" burglary, that the President has no constitutional power to authorize warrantless searches other than electronic surveillance. Similar issues arose when the Justice Department completed its criminal investigation of CIA mail-opening activities.

The magnitude of this enterprise was vividly demonstrated in late 1975, when the Church committee held the first public hearings on NSA since its establishment in 1952. General Lew Allen, NSA Director, described its mission as obtaining "foreign intelligence . . . from foreign electrical communications," which are "intercepted by many techniques and processed, sorted, and analyzed by procedures which reject inappropriate or unnecessary signals." Under these procedures, NSA used "lists of words, including individual names, subjects, locations, et cetera . . . to sort out information of foreign intelligence value from that which is not of interest." General Allen testified that during the period 1967-1973, the names of "about 1,200" U.S. citizens or organizations had been placed on these lists at the request of the FBI, the CIA, the Secret Service, the Bureau of Narcotics (now DEA), and the Defense Intelligence Agency (DIA). Of these, the FBI had submitted "about 1,000" names for "watch lists" to obtain information "on foreign ties and support to . . . 'so-called' extremist persons and groups, individuals and groups active in civil disturbances, and terrorists."[56]

General Allen also provided the committee a copy of a 1971 memorandum from his predecessor to the Attorney General and the Secretary of Defense, which purported to reflect their authorization for NSA to contribute "intelligence bearing on domestic problems" obtained from "telecommunications with at least one foreign terminal." It made no reference to "watch list" practices, but described the scope of NSA reporting as including "intelligence bearing on: (1) criminal activity, including drugs; (2) foreign support or foreign basing of subversive activity; (3) Presidential and related protection."[57]

In 1973, Attorney General Richardson learned of these NSA practices, and advised General Allen that, in view of the *Keith* decision, they raised "serious legal questions which have yet to be resolved." He ordered NSA to stop "disseminating to the FBI and Secret Service information acquired by you through the use of electronic devices pursuant to requests from FBI and Secret Service." Although NSA could continue furnishing to appropriate agencies "relevant information acquired by you in the routine pursuit of the collection for foreign intelligence," it was to avoid "responding to a request from another agency to monitor in connection with a matter that can only be considered one of domestic intelligence."[58] General Allen replied that he had "directed that no further information be disseminated to the FBI and Secret Service, pending advice on legal issues."[59]

Attorney General Levi tried to clarify these legal issues in 1975-1976. He considered a wide range of intelligence techniques that fell within the meaning of "search and seizure" under the Fourth Amendment, including conventional electronic surveillance, surreptitious entry and other forms of search, mail opening, and NSA's techniques for intercepting foreign electrical communications. He concluded that the Constitution did not require a judicial warrant or a showing of unlawful activities for the use of these techniques against Americans who are foreign agents, but he approved no warrantless surveillances of Americans during his last eighteen months in office. In one case he authorized surveillance with a court order, using special procedures departing from the statute governing surveillance in criminal cases. However, the legality of this experiment was uncertain, because it relied on a theory of inherent judicial authority. Thus, Levi urged that Congress legislate standards and procedures, and he persuaded President Ford to endorse legislation requiring a court order for electronic surveillance within the United States, including surveillance of foreigners.

Constitutional Standards and Executive Policy

In the absence of legislation or definitive judicial rulings, Attorney General Levi set forth standards for the use of these techniques on the basis of presidential authority. Within these minimum constitutional standards, he considered the decision to use a particular technique in specific circumstances to be a matter of executive policy. Levi told the Church committee, after presenting a comprehensive analysis of Fourth Amendment principles, that "the legality of the activity does not remove from the Executive or from the Congress the responsibility to take steps, within their powers, to seek an accomodation between the vital public and private interests involved."[60]

As expressed in the Justice Department report on CIA mail opening, Levi's minimum constitutional standards were these:

> The Executive Branch may exercise its constitutional authority to engage in certain forms of surveillance without the prior approval of the Judicial Branch only if it determines whether the facts justify the surveillance, renders a formal, written authorization, and places a time limitation upon the surveillance. The authorizing officer must act pursuant to an express, written delegation of presidential authority. . . . There must in each case be a sufficient basis, measured in light of the private interests the surveillance invades, for believing that the surveillance is necessary to serve the important end that purportedly justifies it. It must, in other words, be reasonable in scope and duration, as "reasonable" has come to be defined by the courts in cases involving wiretapping. No open-end authorization . . . would be sufficient. The Department does not suggest that this means that there must be probable cause to believe that every letter sought to be opened under such an authority would contain foreign intelligence information, any more than there must be probable cause to believe that every telephone call that might be overheard during a wire interception for criminal investigative purposes will include a discussion of crime. But there must, at a minimum, be a determination that the facts justify the surveillance and that it is no more intrusive than is necessary to that end. The standards that guide presidential conduct and the conduct of the Department of Justice draw their sub-

> stance from the evolving principles of Fourth Amendment jurisprudence.[61]

This summary of the standards did not deal with the question of when particular Americans may be targeted for surveillance. However, in the body of the report, the department indicated that where there is "a close analogy" to conventional electronic surveillance, the *Keith* case and subsequent lower court decisions allowed warrantless electronic surveillance only "of foreign powers or their agents."[62] The report also implied that there may be somewhat more leeway where the search or surveillance is not purely "domestic" in the geographical sense. For example, the "expectation of privacy" for international communications, such as mail, could not "easily be equated" with the expectation of privacy in domestic communications.[63]

These constitutional standards did not dispose of the policy issues regarding the authorization for using particular search or surveillance techniques affecting Fourth Amendment interests. Under Attorney General Levi, conventional electronic surveillance by the FBI within the United States was authorized, subject to the Attorney General's personal approval in each case. It was Levi's policy that such surveillance would under no circumstances be "directed against any individual without probable cause to believe he is a conscious agent or collaborator of a foreign power."[64] Similarly, NSA's General Allen stated in 1975, "as to the future, the Attorney General's direction is that we may not accept any requirement based on the names of U.S. citizens unless he has personally approved such a requirement; and no such approval has been given."[65] With respect to surreptitious entries by the FBI within the United States, the Church committee reported in 1976 that such entries were "not presently being conducted," except for electronic surveillance purposes.[66] The Justice Department report on mail opening indicated that there was no authorization for opening first-class mail in United States postal channels without a warrant, although it implied this could be done upon "express, properly limited Presidential authority."[67]

There was no publicly stated executive policy for other search or surveillance techniques that might affect Fourth Amendment interests, such as CIA electronic surveillance directed against Americans abroad, or other forms of unconsented search in the United States or directed against Americans abroad. President Ford's Executive Order on intelligence activities required that such techniques could be used only under "lawful . . . procedures approved by the Attorney General."[68] But neither the Executive Order nor any other public directive had expressly authorized their use. Although Justice Department lawyers debated the point, the restrictions section of Ford's order did not constitute a grant of authority sufficiently explicit to meet the standards set out in the mail-opening report.

Thus, Attorney General Levi's minimum standards for the use of sensitive foreign intelligence-gathering techniques retained substantial flexibility. Despite the historical and conceptual differences among the various search techniques, there now existed coherent measures for deciding when an Attorney General should seek explicit presidential authorization for resuming such practices as surreptitious entry or mail opening. He could do so if the technique were directed against "foreign powers or their agents," if its use were "reasonable in scope and duration," and if the invasion of private interests were "no more intrusive than is necessary" to serve an "important end" relating to "the President's foreign affairs powers."

These standards were embodied in President Carter's 1978 order, and further procedures were adopted by Attorney General Griffin Bell. Executive Order 12036 authorized electronic surveillance, the use of television cameras and other electronic or mechanical devices for continuous monitoring, physical searches, and the opening of mail of United States persons abroad. Whenever such techniques would require a judicial warrant if undertaken for law enforcement rather than intelligence purposes, the order required that the President must authorize "the type of activity involved" and that the Attorney General must approve "the particular activity" and determine that there is "probable cause to believe" that any United States person against whom the technique is directed is "an agent of a foreign power." The Carter order prohibited the CIA from engaging in any electronic surveillance within the United States. No intelligence agency except the FBI could conduct unconsented physical searches within the United States. Further detailed procedures approved by the Attorney General were required to "protect constitutional rights and privacy, ensure that information is gathered by the least intrusive means possible, and limit use of such information to lawful governmental purposes." These procedures could "be classified because of the sensitivity of the information and its relation to national security," but all procedures had to "be made available to the Congressional intelligence committees."[69]

Inherent Presidential Power

What Attorney General Levi and Attorney General Bell failed to do was to set forth a strong argument for the constitutional basis of this presidential power. Neither their formal statements nor their public speeches addressed this issue in depth. To do so would have detracted from their efforts to persuade Congress that legislation was necessary. Nevertheless, the President's authority did have a foundation in Article II of the Constitution.

From the very first years of the nation, Presidents have authorized intelligence activities on the basis of their powers as commander-in-chief of the armed forces and as the nation's representative for the conduct of foreign affairs. The Chief Executive also has the duty faithfully to execute the full body of laws of the United States, including the statutes enacted by Congress, the treaties ratified by the Senate, and the provisions of the Constitution itself. These three grants of power in Article II—the commander-in-chief power, the foreign affairs power, and the responsibility to execute the laws—are independent constitutional sources of presidential authority. Each can support measures taken by the President to secure intelligence for protecting the nation's security and enhancing its ability to deal with foreign powers and international events. Even domestically, the President's duty to execute the laws is a source of authority to protect the rights guaranteed by the Constitution.

None of these "inherent" presidential powers is immune from constitutional restraint. They cannot be exercised in ways that violate the Bill of Rights or other prohibitions in the Constitution. Nor are they immune from regulation by Congress, which has paramount authority under Article I to make "all laws which are necessary and proper . . . for carrying into execution . . . all other powers" granted to any department of government. But if Congress has not enacted legislation, the President may be free to act on his own authority so long as he does not infringe rights protected by the Constitution. As Justice Robert Jackson wrote in the *Steel Seizure* case of 1952,

> When the President acts in absence of either a congressional grant or denial of authority, he can only rely upon his own independent powers, but there is a zone of twilight in which he and Congress may have concurrent authority, or in which its distribution is uncertain. Therefore, congressional inertia, indifference or quiescence may sometimes, at least as a practical matter, enable, if not invite, measures on independent presidential responsibility. In this area, any actual test of power is likely to depend on the imperatives of events and contemporary imponderables rather than on abstract theories of law.
>
> When the President takes measures incompatible with the expressed or implied will of Congress, his power is at its lowest ebb, for then he can rely only upon his own constitutional powers minus any con-

> stitutional power of Congress over the matter. Courts can sustain exclusive Presidential control in such a case only by disabling the Congress from acting upon the subject. Presidential claim to a power at once so conclusive and preclusive must be scrutinized with caution, for what is at stake is the equilibrium established by our constitutional system.[70]

In each area of presidential authorization for intelligence activities, there must be a clear relationship between the measures adopted and the constitutional source of presidential power. Hence, the collection of military intelligence on the capabilities and disposition of foreign forces, including strategic warning of possible hostilities, directly relates to the commander-in-chief power. So do counterintelligence operations to protect vital information and facilities from foreign spies and saboteurs. Similarly, gathering intelligence about the intentions of foreign governments and international political or economic developments clearly supports the President's conduct of American foreign policy. And counterintelligence information about foreign intelligence operations against this country enables the Chief Executive to gauge foreign objectives or, if necessary, take diplomatic action against nations seeking to interfere in our internal affairs.

Finally, both counterintelligence and domestic security measures fulfill the President's duty to protect constitutional rights. Foreign intelligence agents who spy on Americans, intimidate émigrés seeking refuge in the United States, or secretly attempt to manipulate domestic political or economic activities, endanger individual rights and the integrity of the processes of free government. Likewise, those who use violence to achieve their political ends infringe not only the rights of the victims of terrorism, but also the freedom of others to participate in public life without fear for their personal safety. Where these threats to individual liberties reach national proportions—either because a foreign intelligence service or an international terrorist group is involved or because domestic violence exceeds local law enforcement capabilities—an exercise of presidential authority is justifiable.

In none of these areas may the President disregard laws passed by Congress to regulate such actions or conceal his decisions from congressional inquiry. Indeed, his best course ordinarily should be to seek legislative backing, so that necessary measures have the legitimacy that comes from participation by both branches in the policy-making process. But if Congress fails to legislate and leaves a policy vacuum, or if new problems arise that federal statutes do not reach, the Executive Branch is not powerless to deal with the matter. The Attorney General's explanation of the legal framework for U.S. intelligence operations was incomplete because it avoided this question. But the answer given here was implicit in the policy decisions of Levi and Bell.

By enacting the Foreign Intelligence Surveillance Act of 1978, Congress provided the "exclusive means" by which the President could authorize electronic surveillance within the United States. However, the President retained his ability under the Constitution to authorize other FBI intelligence activities.

CHAPTER IV

Reorganization of FBI Domestic Security Operations

THE most dramatic reform of FBI intelligence operations was Director Kelley's reorganization in August 1976, transferring domestic security investigations from the Intelligence Division to the Criminal Investigative Division. The reorganization was accompanied by a sharp reduction in the number of domestic security cases, from nearly five thousand to fewer than three hundred, during the first nine months after Attorney General Levi imposed his domestic security guidelines. By 1978 the number had fallen well below one hundred. Director Kelley said the reorganization was intended "to better facilitate our efforts" in complying with the guidelines. He said his "express purpose" was to have domestic security cases managed as much as possible "like all other criminal cases." The Intelligence Division would handle only the Bureau's foreign intelligence and counterintelligence operations, and Kelley announced that he had already "directed a revitalization" of those efforts. He stressed that domestic intelligence cases raised "entirely different and complex considerations," because the Bureau was "involved with threats from within," and the Attorney General's guidelines directed that such investigations be pursued "in accordance with . . . criminal statutes."[1]

The Attorney General's guidelines were not the only reason for the reorganization. The sharp drop in the number of cases was the result of policy and personnel changes within the FBI, as well as of the requirements of the guidelines. The guidelines established procedures for the review of domestic security investigations by the Attorney General's office, but the cutback within the FBI occurred partly in anticipation of these outside review procedures.

This is not to say that every case was closed by the FBI on its own, rather than through review by the Attorney General's office. Terminating the thirty-five-year investigation of the Socialist Workers party (SWP) required thorough study by the Attorney General's review unit and a final decision by Levi himself. The same process led to a decision to treat the Communist party as a foreign counterintelligence, rather than a domestic security, problem and to transfer cases relating to the Communist party back from the Criminal Investigative Division to the Intelligence Division.

The reorganization itself came about less because the new Domestic Security Section fit in the Criminal Investigative Division than because the Internal Security Branch of the Intelligence Division had become a political embarrassment. In fact, the work of the new section was not fully comparable to the regular criminal cases that were supervised in the Criminal Investigative Division. If anything, it was more like the Bureau's organized crime intelligence activities. But where to place supervision of the domestic security investigations at FBI headquarters was less important than to take them out of the Intelligence Division, reassign personnel, and break down long-established norms and incentives at both the headquarters and field-office levels.

Why was this kind of reorganization necessary? How might it "facilitate" the FBI's efforts to conform to the Attorney General's guidelines and to Director Kelley's policies? What led to the drastic reduction in caseload? What were the implications of closing the Socialist Workers party investigation and treating the Communist party as a foreign counterintelligence problem? We can find some answers by looking at past decisions within the FBI concerning structural changes in intelligence work, by examining the crucial provisions of the Attorney General's guidelines, and by tracing personnel and policy changes within the Bureau during 1976.

The Organization of Intelligence Operations

The FBI Intelligence Division had undergone reorganization before. From its formation shortly before World War II until the early 1960s, the division focused primarily (although not exclusively) on foreign counterintelligence, the Communist party, and Communist-front activities. In 1964, however, the division moved substantially into the field of domestic violence by taking on responsibility for investigating resurgent Ku Klux Klan activities. Thereafter, its domestic operations expanded to deal with black militants and New Left movements. In 1971, criminal bombing investigations were shifted to the Intelligence Division. The arguments made within the FBI at the time of these reorganizations shed considerable light on the 1976 decision to reverse these trends.

The reasons advanced in 1964 for moving Klan investigations to the Intelligence Division were that Klan groups were "essentially subversive," that the Intelligence Division had more experience in using aggressive techniques to penetrate such groups, and that it could use "counterintelligence and disruption tactics" developed to deal with the Communist party and Soviet intelligence operations.[2] Opinion within the Intelligence Division was sharply divided on the merits of the 1964 decision. Some saw it as an attempt to bring the division's expertise in penetrating secret organizations to bear on a problem—Klan involvement in the murder of civil rights workers—that the Bureau was under tremendous pressure to solve. Traditional law enforcement measures were insufficient because of the inàdequacy of federal statutes and the lack of cooperation from local law enforcement. Others thought that the Klan's activities were essentially a law enforcement problem, and that the transfer would dilute the Intelligence Division's major responsibility for dealing with foreign threats.

Those who opposed the transfer lost, and they traced many of the division's subsequent difficulties to this "substantial enlargement" of its responsibilities.[3]

Using the Intelligence Division to cope with domestic problems was not entirely the FBI's own idea. In 1964, Attorney General Robert F. Kennedy, on the recommendation of Civil Rights Division executives Burke Marshall and John Doar, urged that President Johnson instruct the FBI to adopt against the Klan "the techniques followed in the use of specially trained, special assignment agents in the infiltration of Communist groups." The President called on retired CIA Director Allen Dulles to evaluate the situation, and accepted Dulles' advice that the FBI be used to "control the terrorist activities." Similarly, after the ghetto riots in Detroit and Newark in 1967, Attorney General Ramsey Clark asked the FBI to "use the maximum resources, investigative and intelligence," to collect information about plans "by any group of whatever size, effectiveness or affiliation" to aggravate riot activity.[4]

In 1971 the main reason for placing bombing investigation in the Intelligence Division was that the Justice Department had shifted such cases to its Internal Security Division under Assistant Attorney General Robert Mardian. The change was also a logical result of the 1964 decision and of subsequent events that had given the Intelligence Division responsibility for infiltrating domestic extremist groups. As stated in an FBI Inspection Division memorandum, the basic principle was

> that individual violations of applicable statutes arising from the activities of subversive organizations of groups should be supervised within the same division [Intelligence] that has the basic and continuing responsibility for supervision of the overall investigations of these organizations and groups as well as the members thereof and the development of informants within the groups. . . . Informants who may be utilized in specific violations or who are developed in

> the course of investigation of such violations must of necessity be closely correlated with the supervision of these informant programs which now rest with [the Intelligence Division].[5]

This principle could be turned around, of course, as indeed it was in 1964 by those who opposed giving the Intelligence Division jurisdiction over domestic groups engaged in violence. One official argued that the Criminal Investigative Division should retain "hate group informants and intelligence functions" because a transfer would

> create an undesirable division of authority and responsibility . . . our best chance to break major civil rights cases such as bombings, murders, etc., is through information developed from the inside as a result of coverage established in the community where the crime occurred; i.e., informants and sources in the Klan, hate groups, subversive organizations, but also sources not connected with any group, who will report potential violence and individuals prone to violence.[6]

It made as much sense to put Klan intelligence work in the hands of criminal investigators as it did to place investigation of Klan crimes in the hands of intelligence agents.

By 1976, the other reasons for the shifts to the Intelligence Division were no longer valid. The Justice Department had abolished its Internal Security Division and returned bombing cases to the Criminal Division. Most important, the FBI had renounced the use of "counterintelligence and disruption tactics" against domestic groups.

The remaining argument for keeping domestic security investigations in the Intelligence Division was that foreign and domestic terrorist and revolutionary activities were closely related. One FBI Intelligence Division official, whose duties encompassed the supervision of bombing investigations and the collection of intelligence about foreign-based terrorists, contended that the domestic and foreign aspects of extremist violence could not be separated without hampering the effective coordination of terrorism investigations. For example, there were allegations that Cuban agents had been associated with both Puerto Rican terrorists and the Weather Underground, and that Americans had given assistance to Arab terrorists.

Thus, some FBI officials saw advantages to having domestic security investigations supervised by the division that was also responsible for handling foreign threats. How else, they asked, could there be an adequate estimate of the relative weight of foreign influence on domestic violence? Although the FBI and CIA did not find substantial evidence of foreign financing or control of domestic protest activity in the late 1960s and early 1970s, FBI officials insisted the *potential* was there because Soviet and bloc intelligence services were committed, ideologically at least, to exploiting domestic dissent wherever possible.[7] In operational terms, the informants and sources used in domestic security investigations were in a position not only to detect potential violent crimes, but also to look for any indications of foreign direction or control. As William R. Harris of the RAND Corporation argued, in opposing a split between FBI foreign counterespionage and domestic intelligence duties, "Discreet inquiries and analytical finesse are required to cope both with those inclined to violence and those associated with foreign intelligence organizations. Indeed, many of the key foreign intelligence organizations have sabotage or paramilitary directorates, and many seek to penetrate and support, as opportune, indigenous groups which are prone to violence."[8]

In short, proponents of the arrangements thought that transfer of domestic security investigations to the Criminal Investigative Division could deprive those cases of the knowledge and expertise of intelligence personnel. In the larger field offices, it might overburden the regular criminal investigative supervisors with responsibilities for which they lacked the special skills; shifts in agent assignments would risk losing valuable contacts with sources and informants.[9]

On the other hand, as long as the Intelligence Division was expending a major part of its resources on domestic intelligence work, its foreign counterintelligence investigations suffered. Despite some connections between foreign and domestic matters, there were increasingly wide differences in policy and organizational practice between counterintelligence and domestic security. Director Kelley sought to give higher priority to foreign counterintelligence, and efforts had begun to enhance such operations through specialized career development and training programs. Besides these internal developments, the outside policy framework of court decisions, Executive Orders, guidelines, and possible legislation had more sharply distinguished foreign from domestic FBI intelligence activities. President Ford's Executive Order granted authority only for FBI foreign intelligence and counterintelligence operations, unlike previous presidential directives, which encompassed both foreign and domestic "subversion." The Attorney General's guidelines for FBI domestic security investigations differed from those for foreign intelligence collection and counterintelligence investigations. Proposed legislation on electronic surveillance for intelligence purposes covered only the surveillance of foreign agents.

Structural change also could be an effective way to bring about the circulation of personnel between regular criminal investigations and domestic security investigations, substantially changing both attitudes and organizational incentives. The Intelligence Division at headquarters and its counterparts in the field did not have the close, regular contact with the United States Attorneys' offices that routinely provided guidance to agents conducting criminal investigations, because few security investigations led to prosecutions. Some security squads had engaged in domestic intelligence work for many years, without exposure to regular interchange with prosecutors and courts. Moreover, supervisory personnel and agents working in this area could remember when they had been formally directed to use techniques generally considered illegal. "The end justifies the means" had been explicit headquarters policy until the risk of possible exposure persuaded Hoover to stop approving "black bag jobs" (illegal entries) and disruptive COINTELPRO operations. The use of a "do not file" procedure requiring the destruction of records of the authorizations for "black bag jobs" had also been a formal headquarters policy.[10]

By contrast, the norms of the Criminal Investigative Division were more conducive to internal and external controls. For example, until the establishment of the FBI's Legal Counsel Division in 1971, the Intelligence Division seldom sought legal advice on its operations, either from the FBI's own legal staff or from the Justice Department, sharply differing from the practice of the Criminal Investigative Division. At least one former high-level career Justice Department attorney with lengthy experience in internal security matters contended that the shift would strengthen the department's ability to oversee domestic security investigations, because of the good relationship and patterns of interchange between the Criminal Investigative Division and the department's Criminal Division.

Operationally, the Criminal Investigative Division had substantial experience in managing "major cases" requiring the temporary assignment of extensive resources and sometimes nationwide coordination. If dramatic and highly publicized acts of terrorism, such as the Patty Hearst kidnaping case, should occur, this division could combine this expertise with its ability to use sources and informants already developed in its domestic security investigations.

In terms of attitudes and perspectives, agents who handled regular criminal investigations were not only more accustomed to working with the U.S. Attorneys' offices and appearing in court, but also more clearly oriented toward finding hard evidence of crime rather than amorphous intelligence about "potential" law violation. They knew and understood the discipline of due process. Many agents experienced with criminal cases disliked the traditional type of domestic intelligence investigation because it lacked a tangible focus and produced few concrete results. Thus, a reorganization could encourage new attitudes more in line with the Attorney General's guidelines, and reinforce them in the future.

The Response to the Guidelines

The story of how this reorganization took place involves a combination of events and people. Director Kelley's philosophy of leadership was one of participatory management, rather than the Hoover mode of autocratic domination or L. Patrick Gray's brief attempt to impose his own ideas. Thus, Kelley relied heavily on the collective judgment of his top subordinates, who composed the FBI Executive Conference. Until mid-1976, his principal advisors were mainly career Bureau headquarters administrators, most of whom believed strongly in the importance of the FBI's traditional domestic intelligence programs. Associate Director Nicholas P. Callahan and the two Deputy Associate Directors—James B. Adams for investigations and intelligence, and Thomas J. Jenkins for administration—had worked together for many years in the FBI's Administrative Division under one of J. Edgar Hoover's closest and most powerful aides, John P. Mohr.

Nevertheless, some officials were willing to reconsider past policies. Assistant Director Edward S. Miller, who had attempted to protect domestic intelligence investigation by cosmetic manual revisions, retired in 1974. His successor in charge of the Intelligence Division, W. Raymond Wannall, had been a counterintelligence section chief for more than a decade, and brought to the office a different perspective on intelligence problems. He realized that Miller's statutory approach did not begin to resolve the more complex questions of FBI domestic security and foreign counterintelligence authority. Shortly after taking over the division, Wannall testified publicly before the House Internal Security Committee, defending Miller's domestic intelligence manual standards.[11] By 1975, however, he had developed a new divisional position paper that candidly acknowledged that part of the basis for FBI intelligence-gathering activities had to be "the intention of the President to delegate his constitutional authority."[12] In general, Wannall sought to restore foreign counterintelligence to its proper place as the division's highest priority, after years of preoccupation with domestic concerns; he was receptive to outside ideas and new approaches to domestic security investigations, but he concentrated his efforts on strengthening the foreign side of the division's work.

Early in 1976, Wannall retired, and Thomas J. Leavitt, whose experience was mainly in the field rather than at headquarters, became Assistant Director. He, too, believed that foreign counterintelligence was the division's primary job, although both he and Wannall allowed their subordinates to press their case for domestic intelligence at highest levels of the Bureau and with the Attorney General. Thus, the main burden of defending domestic intelligence operations fell upon the division's Internal Security Branch and its two principal sections: the Internal Security Section and the Extremist Activities Section. The first supervised investigations of Communist and "revolutionary" activities, ranging from the Weather Underground to the Socialist Workers party and the Communist party, USA. The second handled black and white racist groups (such as the Black Panther party, the Black Liberation Army, and the Klan), American Indian violence, and the collection of civil disturbance and demonstration intelligence.

Until mid-1976, the weight of opinion within the FBI Executive Conference fell on the side of existing domestic intelligence policies. But Director Kelley ensured that different viewpoints would be considered, especially where Congress or the Attorney General appeared to move in new directions. One important voice was that of his executive assistant, William

Reed, who had worked with Kelley in the Kansas City Police Department before heading a new state law enforcement department in Florida. Kelley also relied heavily on the FBI Legal Counsel Division, headed by career Bureau lawyer John Mintz. One of Kelley's crucial early decisions in 1974 had been to shift the FBI's congressional liaison office from the External Affairs Division, which handled press and public relations, to the Legal Counsel Division. The head of the new office, John B. Hotis, also served as Director Kelley's representative on the Attorney General's guidelines committee.

The guidelines were the first step toward reorganization. The first public draft of Levi's domestic security guidelines did not vary much from the revised FBI manual. It listed several factors to be considered in opening an investigation, including information that individuals (a) "are now, or have been, advocating or engaging in" activities which may involve violence; (b) "are members of, or have expressed public support for, an organization which has as its objective" such activities; or (c) "have engaged in prior acts of violence."

These initial standards would have allowed the FBI to begin investigating an individual solely on the basis of membership or "expression of public support," without any direct indication that he or she might go beyond lawful speech and association protected by the First Amendment. As a practical matter, they would have given the FBI authority to conduct sweeping surveys of politically active individuals, similar to the preliminary inquiries about all black student leaders and all members of campus groups like SDS that occurred in 1970-1971. All the Bureau needed was a general finding that such leadership or membership constituted an "expression of public support" for political movements that engaged in violence. Thus, the draft did not significantly change the revised manual provisions for opening investigations. As the General Accounting Office observed, "no substantive difference existed between the draft guidelines and current FBI policy."[13]

The final version of the guidelines adopted a more restrictive approach for opening investigations. This approach emphasized information about "activities," not mere advocacy or association, and the information had to be serious enough to justify a full investigation if corroborated. Preliminary and limited investigations were designed to verify the initial allegations or information.

Full investigations required "specific and articulate facts giving reason to believe" that an individual or group was engaged in "activities which involve or will involve the use of force or violence." FBI headquarters was required periodically to review full investigations and terminate those unlikely to be productive. Finally, four factors had to be considered before a full investigation could begin or continue: "(1) the magnitude of the threatened harm; (2) the likelihood it will occur; (3) the immediacy of the threat; and (4) the danger to privacy and free expression posed by a full investigation." The guidelines did not define further such crucial terms as "activities which will involve violence" or a "productive" investigation; nor did they give more or less weight to any of the four "balancing factors." Nonetheless, the stress on activities instead of advocacy or association, and the requirement for specific facts rather than conclusory statements, were very different from previous Bureau standards.

Whether these differences in theory would have a substantial impact on FBI investigations depended on their practical application. The work of the Attorney General's review unit and Levi's own decisions were critical in the early stages. The review unit was formed in April 1976, and initially included three attorneys: one with four years experience as an Assistant U.S. Attorney in the Southern District of New York, another who had served for three years as a trial attorney in the Civil Rights Division, and a third who had been a staff counsel to the Church committee. The first cases reviewed were full investigations of groups, because the unit believed resolution of such cases would dispose of the largest number of individual investigations linked to the groups. In several of these initial cases, which the FBI considered representative of many others, the review unit found the factual justifications weak. Assumptions were presented as facts, and in one major instance Bureau officials had overlooked the only persuasive data in their files that might have justified the case. It appeared as if the officials supervising the investigations either did not know what they were doing, or could not effectively marshal the facts to justify their actions.

These events signaled to Director Kelley that, if the FBI continued to submit similar cases to the Attorney General, it would find itself constantly overruled. Rather than allow the Bureau to remain in this uncomfortable position, Kelley halted the submission of cases and began his own internal review.

At the same time, other forces precipitated change in FBI executive ranks. Director Kelley learned that records of possibly illegal break-ins during 1972-1973 had been found in the New York field office. He passed the information to Attorney General Levi, who ordered a criminal investigation, and Kelley admitted publicly that some of his subordinates had "deceived" him into believing that such operations had stopped in the 1960s. If that were not enough, another Justice Department investigation of alleged administrative improprieties in the Bureau had reached the highest levels, including Kelley himself.

Partly because of these inquiries, several top executives either chose or were forced to retire in the summer of 1976. Among them were Associate Director Callahan and several Assistant Directors. Their departures gave Kelley an opportunity to bring freshness to the Bureau hierarchy. One such new executive was Associate Director Richard Held, whose long career as Special Agent in Charge of field offices in Minneapolis and Chicago had made him sympathetic to the problems of street agents, and not a headquarters type. One of the new Assistant Directors, Vincent DeBruler, headed a reorganized Planning and Inspection Division with a mandate from Kelley to reexamine traditional internal inspection procedures. Finally, the Legal Counsel Division under John Mintz was given increased authority and direct access to Kelley and Held.

The domestic security reorganization was part of those administrative reforms. The purposes were to strengthen accountability and to change supervisory personnel. In another respect, the domestic security shift was part of longer-term plans for the Bureau. Director Kelley considered consolidating all FBI criminal investigative activities into the Criminal Investigative Division, bringing white-collar crimes, organized crime, and domestic security together with more conventional cases. An alternative was to use the Special Investigative Division, where organized crime cases were supervised, as the new home for domestic security. Even after he placed it in the Criminal Investigative Division, Kelley studied a third option: merging organized crime with the Criminal Investigative Division and shifting domestic security matters and civil rights cases to the Special Investigative Division, where they would join federal employee background investigations and fugitive cases—a potpourri of separate investigative functions requiring special procedures.

All this structural tinkering might have amounted to very little without other steps taken in response to the signals from Attorney General Levi. Initially, all the cases handled by the Internal Security Branch were transferred to the new Domestic Security Section, along with criminal bombing investigations and cases involving violent nationality groups, which had been handled by a section in the Counterintelligence Branch. The personnel of the Domestic Security Section were drawn from the Internal Security Branch, although about half of the supervisors and the Internal Security Section chief were transferred elsewhere. The Extremist Activities Section chief became the first head of the new section, and he reported to a new Deputy Assistant Director who had supervised bombing cases and related security investigations in the New York field office. It was not until the end of 1976 that outside supervisors began to replace the holdovers from the Internal Security Branch. In some instances, the holdovers were retained because their knowledge of discontinued investigations was needed to compile materials for pending lawsuits.

Director Kelley did not rely only on the new Domestic Security Section, with its close ties to past domestic intelligence policies, for a reassessment of ongoing investigations. He formed a special team of seasoned criminal investigators to conduct a thorough review of all the Bureau's domestic security cases. To head the team, Kelley chose Neil Welch, Special Agent in Charge of the Philadelphia field office, who had strong doubts about the usefulness of domestic intelligence investigations. In the Philadelphia office, Welch had had the experience of weighing both the usefulness of intelligence information and the seriousness of current terrorist threats, because of the possibility of violence during bicentennial celebrations. The absence of violent demonstrations reinforced Kelley's judgment that, with the end of the Vietnam War, domestic violence was on the wane. In Kelley's view, people the Bureau had investigated since the peak of antiwar protest "no longer were engaged in activities that were likely to involve violations of Federal law." Finally, Kelley had decided, on the basis of an experiment with criminal cases in four field offices, "that a quality, rather than a caseload quantity, approach in the assignment of our manpower and other resources would produce better results."[14]

Welch's team consulted the FBI representative on the Attorney General's guidelines committee and adopted rigorous "productivity" standards. Field offices were told they had the burden of showing why each domestic security case was likely to uncover serious violence. There were some differences among the reviewing agents over whether to insist upon evidence of current criminal activity, and the FBI's member of the guidelines committee had to point out that Attorney General Levi approved investigating activities "which involve *or will involve* the violation of federal law" (emphasis added). But by giving the task to agents without a personal stake in the outcome, Kelley did much to ensure an objective and credible review.

The caseload reduction also resulted from one across-the-board policy change. The Domestic Security Section decided, with approval from the director, to discontinue investigations of rank-and-file members of organizations, and to confine its attention to organizations and individuals "in a policy-making position in those organizations or who have engaged in activities which indicate they are likely to use force or violence in violation of Federal law."[15] FBI officials believed they could collect sufficient information about rank-and-file members (and, presumably, about other persons who support or associate with groups) in the course of the investigations of the groups themselves, of their leaders, and of members likely to commit violence.

It is debatable whether the Attorney General's guidelines would have automatically required closing all rank-and-file membership cases. On the one hand, simple membership in or active association with a group committed, at the leadership level, to the use of violence might not meet the guideline standards of "specific and articulable facts giving reason to believe that an individual . . . may be engaged in activities which . . . will involve the use of force or violence." The fact of membership might be clear, but the likelihood that mere association would indicate a serious or immediate threat of violent activity might be remote. On the other hand, membership or active association could arguably serve as a basis for a ninety-day preliminary investigation to determine whether there was a factual basis for opening a full investigation.

These policy changes and the dramatic caseload reduction—from more than twenty-one thousand domestic security investigations in mid-1973 to fewer than three hundred by the end of 1976—did not fully represent a comparable decline in investigative activities affecting individual privacy. For example, closing rank-and-file cases did not necessarily affect the extent of FBI informant coverage, because informants were used primarily to investigate groups. The main impact was upon the large volume of preliminary inquiries and relatively low-level investigative measures, such as locating alleged members through existing informants, local police, educational institutions, credit bureaus, and employers. Perhaps a better measure was the reported decline in the number of domestic security informants from fifteen hundred in mid-1975 to an estimated six to seven hundred in January 1977, when Attorney General Levi issued new guidelines for the use of informants in domestic security and criminal cases.[16] By 1978, the number of domestic security informants had dropped below one hundred, not counting informants in the Communist party or unpaid sources and contacts.

Moreover, ending rank-and-file cases did not mean that the names and activities of members, supporters, and associates of targeted groups would no longer be included in investigative reports and file indexes. In late 1975 one field office described the established practice as follows: "[Our] informants, after attending meetings of these organizations [under investigation], usually submit reports in which they describe briefly the activities and discussion which took place as well as listing those members and nonmembers in attendance at such meetings. Copies of these informant reports are disseminated to various individuals' files and the names of those in attendance where no individual's file exists, *are indexed to the organization's file*" (emphasis added). FBI headquarters did not disapprove this practice, although it advised all field offices that they should keep no record of statements made in the exercise of a person's right to free speech, and that they should consult headquarters to resolve any question concerning a specific problem. It was considered pertinent to the investigation of an organization "to maintain records concerning membership, public utterings, and/or other activities" of the groups.[17]

The Attorney General's guidelines did not deal with such indexing of information in domestic security cases, but they did limit indexing data contained in FBI reports on civil disorders and demonstrations involving a federal interest. Except when an investigation was specifically requested by the Attorney General, the guidelines limited such reporting to information relating to actual or threatened civil disorders acquired by the FBI from public officials or other public sources in the course of its other investigations; and information relating to demonstration activities that are likely to require the federal government to take action to facilitate the activities and provide health and safety measures with respect to those activities, which is acquired incidentally by the FBI in the course of carrying out its other responsibilities.

The FBI could not undertake investigations to collect this information without the Attorney General's request. However, if past practice were to be a guide for the future, FBI field officials would be particularly alert for such information in the course of their domestic security investigations, and would submit reports to headquarters based on the byproducts of those cases, along with information from such public sources as newspapers and contacts with local police and other public officials. According to the guidelines, reports on civil disorders could include not only the size of an actual or threatened disorder, the potential for violence, and the ability of local officials to handle it, but also such broad factors as "the potential for expansion of the disorder in light of *community conditions* and *underlying causes* of the disorder."[18]

However, the guidelines mitigated the breadth of this reporting standard by limiting indexing of personally identifiable information. Such data could not "be indexed in a manner which permits retrieval . . . by reference to a specific individual unless the individual himself is the subject of an authorized law enforcement investigation." (See Appendix II for the full text of the guidelines on "Reporting on Civil Disorders and Demonstrations Involving a Federal Interest.")

The only civil-disorder type of inquiry requested by Attorney General Levi was a limited thirty-day investigation in May

1976 of the July 4th Coalition, an alliance of 130 groups planning a major demonstration in Philadelphia during the bicentennial celebrations. FBI agents interviewed the coalition's national coordinator and more than a dozen members of its Philadelphia office staff to determine whether federal troops would be required to maintain order. The national coordinator charged that the FBI wanted "to scare people, intimidate us, damage our prestige, drain our energies."[19] Nevertheless, the FBI's investigation made it possible for Deputy Attorney General Harold Tyler to turn down a request from Philadelphia city officials for federal troops to aid in crowd control and to handle any Fourth of July demonstrations.[20] Under the guidelines, the FBI's inquiry was confined to information in the public record, other government agencies, already established informants or confidential sources, and interviews with persons involved in planning the demonstration. The guidelines provided "that in conducting interviews with such persons the FBI shall initially advise them specifically of the authority to make the inquiry and the limited purpose for which it is made."[21]

Overall, the new Domestic Security Section and its counterparts in the field offices ended up with responsibility for three broad classes of investigations: (1) conventional criminal investigations to gather evidence for prosecution in cases of bombings, sabotage, passport and visa violations, offenses under the laws for protection of foreign officials and official guests of the United States, and similar federal criminal violations involving terrorist violence; (2) domestic security investigations under the Attorney General's guidelines, for the purpose of gathering information to "assist in preventing the use of force or violence" and to enable anyone "directly threatened by planned force or violence" to "take appropriate protective safeguards"; and (3) reporting on civil disorders and demonstrations involving a federal interest, under a separate set of Attorney General's guidelines.

After further reorganizations in 1977 and 1978, the renamed Terrorism Section took over the supervision of international and foreign terrorism investigations. In such cases the section operated under the Attorney General's guidelines for FBI foreign counterintelligence investigations, and reported to the Intelligence Division rather than the Criminal Investigative Division. The FBI's Terrorist Research and Bomb Data Center was transferred from the Training Division to the Terrorism Section. The section also had responsibility for interagency coordination and planning efforts to prepare for terrorist incidents. This consolidated FBI counterterrorism efforts that otherwise might have been artificially divided by the 1976 reorganization.

Socialist Workers Party and Communist Party USA Cases

Attorney General Levi's decision to stop the Socialist Workers party (SWP) investigation and his decision to handle the Communist Party USA (CPUSA) investigation under the foreign counterintelligence guidelines were based, in part, on the review unit's analysis of the cases. Levi also consulted other senior department executives before making such major decisions. The unit did not confine itself to considering the materials sent by the FBI and recommending simple approval or disapproval. At times it sought additional information from the Bureau, consulted with the Attorney General's guidelines committee on what they intended by certain standards, and recommended that the Attorney General's statement of written approval include more specific guidance for the future direction of the investigation.

The SWP case was in many ways a test for the domestic security guidelines. Through its informants in the SWP and its youth affiliate, the Young Socialist Alliance, the FBI had kept track of a wide range of antiwar, New Left, and even women's liberation activities in the late 1960s and early 1970s. The SWP's influence in a variety of lawful, nonviolent protest movements had served to justify FBI domestic intelligence reports on the political beliefs and associations of law-abiding Americans who were willing to work or meet with other citizens without asking for proof of their ideological purity.[22]

Among the crucial questions in the review of the Socialist Workers party case were whether its connections with the Trotskyite Fourth International (FI), from which it formally disaffiliated in 1941, constituted technical violation of the Voorhis Act requiring registration of certain foreign-related domestic groups; and whether the party was linked with any violent activities abroad. The SWP had sent delegations of observers to world congresses of Trotskyite groups, but its officers insisted that it was not run by a foreign power or organization. An FBI agent's deposition in the SWP's lawsuit against the Bureau stated that "SWP has conducted a close association with the FI [Fourth International] (a majority of which endorse and supports the current use of violence) and SWP participates and votes as a 'sympathizing group' in FI meetings."[23] In and of itself, the possible technical violation of the Voorhis Act was probably not enough to sustain an intelligence investigation of the SWP without some other element.

According to one account, the political ties with Trotskyite groups abroad involved more than sympathetic association. The FBI also reportedly had evidence that the SWP had been in direct contact with foreign groups engaged in violence, and had contributed small amounts of money to some of them.[24] It was not clear whether this evidence went beyond the FBI's public statement that an expelled minority faction of the SWP favored "the current use of guerilla warfare in Latin America and elsewhere if local conditions indicate that such violence would enhance the revolution," and that some members of this faction had been "reaccepted into the SWP" after agreeing to accept party discipline.[25]

Thus, in the Socialist Workers party case, the guidelines were applied to preclude the investigation of groups adhering to a revolutionary ideology, so long as their activities seem unlikely to involve violence within the United States, or are not subject to foreign control in ways that would harm the security of the nation. The domestic security guidelines did not allow investigation of activities involving violence abroad in violation of foreign laws, and the foreign counterintelligence guidelines appeared to require some form of foreign direction. To some extent this left a gap, with no authority beyond criminal statutes such as the Neutrality Act for the FBI to investigate domestic groups, like some Cuban émigrés, whose activities might involve violence in other countries but not in the United States. This gap made it easier to stop the SWP investigation, even if there was reasonable suspicion that some of its members provided support for violent revolutionary activities overseas.

Terminating such a major investigation was not easy. FBI offices were instructed not to accept any more information about SWP activities from the Bureau informants still in the group, but the directive did not order the informants to leave the party; the decision was up to the individual informant. The SWP was skeptical about taking the FBI's word that it would not receive additional information from these informants, so it insisted upon knowing their names.[26] The Bureau vigorously opposed this demand, on the ground that it would endanger the safety of the informants and would discourage others from becoming informants in lawful investigations. A top FBI executive asserted that more than twenty informants in criminal and security cases had already stopped providing information because of their belief "that the FBI can no longer maintain confidentiality."[27] Attorney General Griffin Bell strongly supported the FBI's position, to the point of defying a court order in 1978 to produce a sample of informant files for examination by SWP attorneys.

Director Kelley's orders raised additional questions because they stated that while each field office should discontinue investigations of the SWP, the Young Socialists Alliance, their chapters, leaders, and members, under the guidelines an FBI office could continue to investigate those members whose activities indicated that they were likely to use force or violence. Both the SWP and some Justice Department officials expressed concern that Kelley's instructions might be interpreted by FBI agents as a covert signal to keep pursuing the party, or as an excuse for footdragging in ending their investigations.[28]

The review of the investigation of the Communist Party USA apparently found indications of direction of the party by agents of the Soviet Union. Therefore, while the Communist party did not fit the domestic security guidelines because its activities were unlikely to result in violence, investigation continued under the classified foreign counterintelligence guidelines.[29] An important question in the Communist party case was whether the FBI investigation would still encompass the party's lawful and open political activities which, as described in the FBI's 1976 appropriations testimony, included supporting detente, "taking advantage of the present economic situation to attack capitalism publicly," trying to influence workers through distribution of publications, and "endeavoring to gain public recognition as a legitimate political party."[30] An alternative was to concentrate on "clandestine intelligence activities," as they came to be defined in legislation on warrantless electronic surveillance. Returning supervision of the Communist party investigation and related cases to the Intelligence Division suggested that these cases would be managed by FBI agents more interested in the threat from Soviet intelligence operations than in the Bureau's traditional concern about the influence of subversive ideology in American political life.

Transferring the Communist party investigations also implied a change in domestic security policies. Before the transfer, Director Kelley said the FBI would investigate not only "domestic organizations oriented toward violence," but also of "basic revolutionary groups dedicated to the overthrow of the Government." Another Bureau official specifically cited the Communist party as "one revolutionary-type organization."[31]

Inclusion of basic revolutionary groups like the Communist party in the domestic security category also affected FBI policies for investigating individuals. Persons could be investigated not only if their activities indicated that they were likely to use force or violence, but also if they held policy-making positions in certain organizations. One reason for this distinction was that individuals with policy-making positions in basic revolutionary groups (as contrasted with groups oriented toward violence) would not necessarily be the persons likely to use force or violence.

The shift of the Communist party investigation into the foreign counterintelligence category meant that the concept of a basic revolutionary group was no longer acceptable, and that domestic security investigations should concentrate exclusively on groups oriented toward violence and the leaders of such groups. The FBI's traditional reliance on the concept of a basic revolutionary group was incompatible with the Attorney General's domestic security guidelines. The Bureau admitted to the GAO that the revolutionary aims of these groups were "not expressed, or likely to be expressed, in imminent violent action." At the most, their "plotting to undermine our institutions" was at the level of "preliminary stages of organization and preparation."[32]

Theoretically, such a group could have fallen within the domestic security guidelines, because they allow the balancing of various factors—the magnitude of the threat, its likelihood, its immediacy, and the danger of the investigation to privacy and free expression. But the threat from basic revolutionary groups was admittedly not imminent, and its likelihood and magnitude were remote and speculative. If there was a serious threat, it arose from a group's links to a hostile foreign power, and thus could be viewed as a foreign counterintelligence problem rather than as a danger from domestic revolutionaries.

According to the GAO report, other cases besides those related to the CPUSA could be handled the same way. At least three additional revolutionary groups were in the category of organizations "in contact with foreign governments considered hostile to the United States," investigated in 1974. The GAO stated: "the investigation of the Venceremos Brigade has concentrated on identifying persons subject to recruitment by foreign intelligence services to carry out intelligence assignments or to foment violence in the United States. Continuing contacts by members of the Revolutionary Communist Party and the October League with the People's Republic of China are a matter of FBI investigative concern."[33] Moreover, the GAO found that the FBI was "monitoring . . . Communists' efforts to infiltrate nonsubversive groups," giving as an example the Vietnam Veterans Against the War, who were "investigated not only because some members and chapters have been involved in militant demonstrations but also because members of the Communist Party-USA . . . were involving themselves in the group's affairs." The GAO framed its recommendations on the assumption that such investigations might be part of the FBI's "counterespionage effort"—a subject technically beyond the GAO's review.[34]

Thus, continuation of the Communist party investigation under the foreign counterintelligence guidelines raised important questions for the future. President Ford's Executive Order on foreign intelligence activities authorized FBI investigations of "foreign subversion." The meaning of this term, as well as such other foreign counterintelligence concepts as "clandestine intelligence activities" adopted in President Carter's Executive Order, was uncertain because the Attorney General's guidelines were classified. Nevertheless, for the first time in forty years the FBI had been forced to reconsider why it was continuing to investigate American Communists.

Director Kelley's reorganization and his imposition of rigorous standards for allocating FBI resources to the most productive or "quality" investigations, combined with Attorney General Levi's decisions in the Socialist Workers party, the Communist party, and other cases, brought FBI domestic security operations down to manageable dimensions. As of September 1976, after termination of the SWP cases, but before the CPUSA case was shifted back to the Intelligence Division, domestic security investigations of 78 organizations and 548 individuals were underway. At the end of 1976, after the Communist party case was reportedly transferred, there were investigations of fewer than 25 groups under the domestic security guidelines.

This number declined even further under Attorney General Bell, who continued his predecessors' basic policies for application of the guidelines in 1977-1978. Bell told the Senate Judiciary Committee in 1978 that the FBI "should not be monitoring the legitimate first amendment activities of our citizens because the views they are expressing are controversial or even antithetical to our constitutional system." He said the FBI would be "branching too far afield" if it were to investigate "legitimate protest groups who speak of violence in the abstract but do not engage in it." Attorney General Bell concluded that FBI domestic security investigations should be based on "information that a group is preparing to commit a violation of law or is engaging in a continuing pattern of federal law violation."[35]

The reduced caseload was less significant than the personnel changes and review procedures designed to establish accountability and encourage credible, objective assessments both inside and outside the Bureau. The new standards for investigation under the guidelines, accompanied by the changes within the FBI itself, and oversight by an Attorney General who weighed the competing interests carefully, produced significant and perhaps lasting reform.

CHAPTER V

Domestic Security and Terrorism Investigations

WHY should the FBI conduct domestic security intelligence investigations? Are criminal investigations for the purpose of prosecution somehow inadequate to the task of protecting the nation against terrorism? What functions do domestic security investigations perform that cannot be served just as well by vigorous criminal investigations and prosecutions? Why do domestic security investigations require special procedural safeguards like those adopted in the 1976 FBI guidelines?

These are crucial questions for assessing the FBI's domestic security mandate. Law enforcement experts have claimed that intelligence gathering is "indispensable . . . in the fight against terrorism." The Task Force on Disorders and Terrorism of the National Advisory Committee on Criminal Justice Standards and Goals recommended in 1976 that there should be "regular and effective collection, processing, storage, retrieval, and exchange of information relating to persons and organizations reasonably suspected of engaging in or likely to engage in certain specified violent, intimidatory, or subversive conduct." Although the Task Force denounced the use of "dirty tricks," it saw a need for carefully controlled covert operations against individuals or groups "likely to engage in criminal activity involving acts of terrorism and political violence." Such operations would include not only the use of paid informants and electronic surveillance to gather intelligence, but also counter-terrorist measures designed to "frustrate or neutralize" terrorism in circumstances where "evidence does not permit immediate legal proceedings against the individual concerned."[1]

The American Civil Liberties Union and other critics have opposed this policy because of the danger that intelligence investigations will intrude into the lawful political activities of citizens. They have rejected preventive action as incompatible with due process of law, and they would confine the FBI to "the investigation of specific acts which violate federal criminal statutes." Thus, no investigation could begin unless there were "a specific allegation that a person has committed, is committing, or is about to commit" a specific criminal act. Investigations of crimes that had not yet occurred would be allowed, on a "reasonable suspicion" standard, for as long as six months; but beyond that time there would have to be "probable cause" to believe that specific criminal acts were "imminent." Where an investigation "may result in the collection of information of First Amendment activity or may pose any danger to First Amendment activity," the Attorney General's written authorization would be required. Judicial warrants would be needed for the FBI to "recruit, place or use an informant or an undercover agent, inspect or obtain access to tax, bank, credit or toll (telephone) records or use mail covers." These procedures would apply to all FBI investigations, not just to those in the domestic security field.[2]

The debate between law enforcement professionals and civil libertarians is likely to go on, in one form or another, for years to come, because each side begins from different premises. Law enforcement officials find it hard to understand why anyone would fear the collection of information about terrorists. Civil liberties advocates are concerned that unpopular, dissenting groups will be labeled "terrorist" without solid justification, and that covert intelligence gathering can easily become covert repression of lawful political activities.

This chapter looks at four aspects of this dispute over domestic security investigations. First, what law enforcement interests are properly served by domestic security intelligence investigations? How do they differ from other types of law enforcement investigations?

Second, what should be the standards for FBI domestic security investigations? Should they rely on criminal law principles, such as the law of conspiracy? Or should the standards have different thresholds geared to intelligence gathering rather than prosecution?

Third, what special procedures are needed for the use of informants and covert infiltration in domestic security investigations? Are judicial warrants the best safeguards? Or can other checks control the risks to privacy and freedom without inhibiting proper investigations?

Fourth, should the FBI ever take preventive action to avert violence? Should it be confined to arrest, the submission of evidence for prosecution, and dissemination of information to other law enforcement agencies? Or are there other ways the Bureau can intervene to prevent a bombing or an assault, consistent with due process of law?

Domestic Security and Law Enforcement

The primary purpose of a criminal investigation is to prepare a criminal case for arrest and prosecution. The FBI conducts its investigations of bank robberies or kidnapings according to a set pattern. An investigation does not begin until the Bureau learns that a specific federal crime has been or is about to be committed. The investigation concentrates on identifying and locating the suspects, and gathering evidence for prosecution. The investigation terminates when the United States Attorney's office either declines to prosecute or carries the case forward to conviction or acquittal.

Domestic security investigations do not fit this model. The most important difference is that the investigation focuses on information other than evidence for prosecution. Consequently, decisions to continue or stop domestic security investigations do not depend on prosecutorial factors. They are based, instead, on an estimate of the value of the intelligence information supplied by the investigation. This ephemeral basis is what makes domestic security investigations so hard to regulate. There is no easy way to measure the quality of intelligence that is comparable to the tests applied in weighing the adequacy of evidence for arrest and prosecution.

The Task Force on Disorders and Terrorism contended that two basic interests are served by domestic security intelligence. Information about persons or groups likely to commit terrorist acts can be used, after a specific crime is committed, to "facilitate the apprehension, processing, and disposition of offenses according to law." In other words, intelligence investigations can be used as a source of leads in criminal cases. In addition, intelligence "can enable those in charge to take preventive measures to protect the lives and property of those threatened by the terrorist."[3]

The users of intelligence are not federal prosecutors, except indirectly, if evidence bearing on a possible prosecution turns up. Instead, the primary users are those law enforcement agencies, including the FBI itself, with responsibilities for apprehending suspects and protecting the targets of violence. The FBI disseminates information to other federal, state, and local authorities for these purposes—sometimes in writing and sometimes through informal discussion.

These two functions—assisting future investigations of specific criminal acts and preventing terrorist crimes—are widely accepted measures of the usefulness of domestic security intelligence. Both the Church committee and the General Accounting Office adopted them as standards for evaluating FBI investigations. To support its conclusion that limited intelligence-gathering authority was justifiable, the Church committee cited examples provided by the FBI. In one instance, intelligence information in Bureau files was used to assist a Secret Service investigation. The Secret Service asked the FBI to conduct a name check of its files on persons applying for press credentials to cover the visit of a foreign head of state. The files disclosed that one applicant had associated with violent groups. Further investigation produced evidence, including weapons, of a plot to assassinate the foreign head of state. In other cases FBI informants reported a plan to ambush police officers and the location of a cache of weapons and dynamite; plans to transport illegally obtained weapons to Washington, D.C.; and plans to dynamite two city blocks. The informant reports made it possible to frustrate all these plans through protective measures or arrests.[4]

However, the overall scope of FBI investigations before 1976 was so broad that the GAO found them to be comparatively unproductive under these standards. Only 1.3 percent resulted in prosecution and conviction; and in only about 2 percent of the cases was advance knowledge of any activity—legal or illegal—obtained. In most of the instances, advance knowledge of an activity involved nonviolent speeches, demonstrations, and meetings.[5] One of the reasons why Director Kelley sought in 1976 to focus the FBI's resources on more productive cases was this relative scarcity of results.

Others have concluded that the low productivity of intelligence investigations makes them unnecessary. The argument is that law enforcement agencies can deal with terrorism by adopting strategies that depend less on advance knowledge than on protective security measures designed in light of past acts of terrorism. Examples include Secret Service protection for U.S. officials and foreign dignitaries, airport security programs to avert hijackings, careful plans for handling political kidnapings and hostage situations, and diplomatic negotiations aimed at eliminating foreign sanctuaries for terrorists. These measures all depend on some form of "intelligence," because there must be a thorough analysis of available information about past crimes and any patterns they exhibit. From this point of view, domestic security intelligence should mean no more than analysis and planning, because the costs to privacy and freedom outweigh the speculative benefits of investigations and covert surveillance.

Eliminating domestic security investigations would not cut off all sources of advance warning, nor would it deprive law enforcement agencies of all background information for investigating specific crimes. In the course of its criminal investigations, the FBI still could learn of impending violence. FBI agents investigating specific crimes for prosecution interview people, develop confidential relationships with sources, sometimes pay for information from informants, and occasionally conduct physical or electronic surveillance—all techniques that may supply warnings of violence as a byproduct. Moreover, with its elaborate system for collating criminal investigative files, the FBI can readily pull together data from different cases and sources. FBI files on criminal cases serve as a resource for other agencies—the Secret Service, for example—seeking to learn whether someone has been involved in or suspected of a federal crime. Access to and storage of this information are matters of deep concern to a society that values personal privacy, but the problems are not the result of intelligence-gathering.

There is, however, a persuasive answer to the argument that the FBI should conduct only criminal investigations aimed at federal prosecution. The absence of intelligence investigations would make it difficult to calm public fears in times of terrorist activity. Those who might be targets of threatened terrorist violence have a compelling right to full protection by their government, consistent with applicable constitutional restrictions. The Supreme Court in the *Keith* case recognized the legitimacy of investigations for "the prevention of unlawful activity," even if the focus of such investigation "may be less precise than that directed against more conventional types of crime."[6] The Court of Appeals, which considered a portion of the Socialist Workers party lawsuit against the Bureau in 1974, stated, "the FBI has a right—indeed, a duty—to keep itself informed with respect to the possible commission of crime; it is not obliged to wear blinders until it may be too late for prevention."[7]

In short, for the FBI to halt all domestic security investigations could undermine public confidence in federal law enforcement, and open the Justice Department to charges that it is neglecting its duty under the Constitution to "insure domestic tranquility" and "take care that the laws be faithfully executed."

What went wrong in the past, and what led to the low productivity of FBI domestic intelligence investigations before 1976, was the Bureau's use of such sweeping terms as "subversion," "sedition," and "overthrow of the government" to define the scope of its inquiries. Instead of concentrating on cases in which individuals or groups had a record of violence or were likely to use violence in the near future, the FBI investigated people because of their adherence to revolutionary or extremist ideologies. The Bureau did so, at least in part, because of the vague and outdated sedition laws that had remained on the books for decades.

The principal law, the Smith Act, was enacted in 1940. The Smith Act punished anyone who "willfully advocates, abets, advises, or teaches the duty, necessity, desirability, or propriety of overthrowing or destroying the government of any state . . . by force or violence," or who joins or attempts to organize a group that does so.[8] The only cases in which the Supreme Court upheld Smith Act convictions involved leaders of the Communist party prosecuted in the 1940s and 1950s.[9]

Seditious action, as well as seditious speech, was also the subject of federal criminal laws. One statute, enacted during the Civil War, made it a crime for two or more persons to "conspire to overthrow, put down, or to destroy by force the Government of the United States . . . or by force to prevent, hinder, or delay the execution of any law of the United States."[10] A parallel law punished anyone who "incites, sets on foot, assists, or engages in any rebellion or insurrection against the authority of the United States or the laws thereof, or gives aid and comfort thereto."[11]

Finally, a provision in the Internal Security Act of 1950

applied the seditious conspiracy concept to those who would replace this nation's form of government with a foreign dictatorship. It imposed criminal penalties upon anyone who conspired "to perform any act which would substantially contribute to the establishment within the United States of a totalitarian dictatorship . . . the direction and control of which is to be vested in, or exercised by or under the domination or control of, any foreign government, foreign organization, or foreign individual."[12] This law extended beyond violence or otherwise illegal conduct to encompass "any act" having the prohibited objective, except proposing a constitutional amendment.

Until 1976, the FBI could rely on these sedition laws as a mandate for sweeping domestic intelligence investigations. They went far beyond looking for information about terrorists, unless the concept of terrorism is stretched to encompass the political beliefs and associates of people who support revolutionary or totalitarian ideologies. It is no wonder that the FBI's investigations failed to contribute very much to the achievement of tangible law enforcement objectives.

However, the small accomplishments of past domestic intelligence investigations, based on outdated standards, do not justify depriving the FBI of a more clearly defined authority to conduct domestic security investigations. The main reason is the organized character of terrorist activity. Like other forms of organized crime, terrorism is clandestine and conspiratorial. Criminal investigations conducted solely for the purpose of prosecution are not adequate to supply the information needed for proper and effective law enforcement.

When specific terrorist acts occur, it is often difficult to identify and locate the offenders. The FBI may find enough information to suspect an individual or group of the crime, but not sufficient evidence for prosecution and conviction. If the Bureau were confined to criminal investigations, it would have to stop there. But domestic security investigations provide a way to keep track of such persons, despite the inability to prosecute, if there is reason to believe they will commit future crimes. In other circumstances, the government may prosecute and convict some of the persons involved, but lack evidence against others who belong to the same group and share objectives with the convicted terrorists. Once again, domestic security investigations make it possible to monitor the activities as long as they remain committed to the use of violence.

Certainly in the field of organized crime, investigations continue regardless of the success or failure of particular prosecutions. These are acknowledged to be "criminal intelligence" investigations; and the Justice Department's Criminal Division established an Intelligence and Special Services Unit for gathering, storing, and retrieving intelligence for use in the effort against organized crime.[13] Domestic security investigations are best understood as another form of criminal intelligence work. As with organized crime intelligence, the information collected is not confined to evidence of a specific federal crime for use in a particular prosecution.

However, there are important differences between organized crime and terrorism. The former involves continuing criminal activities, while acts of terrorist violence are less frequent and more haphazard. Moreover, an integral part of domestic security investigations is the collection of information about the political beliefs, associations, and activities of Americans with grievances against the government. Political advocacy or association, short of indications of preparation for violence, should not start a domestic security investigation; once the investigation is underway there should be restrictions against gathering information that does not relate to the likelihood of violence. But within these outer limits, a wide range of information about political beliefs and activities may appear relevant from the point of view of experienced investigators, who assume that somehow, some day, all the pieces will fall together to reveal a pattern of conspiratorial activity. Organized crime investigators can be more confident that there *is* a syndicate, because they see its lower levels in action every day. Domestic security intelligence lacks comparable signs of criminality.

These two factors—the risks to political freedoms protected by the First Amendment and the absence of normal signs of criminal activity—are the main reasons for concern about domestic security investigations.

Standards for Domestic Security Investigations

The organized, conspiratorial quality of terrorism should determine the threshold for domestic security investigations. The proper purpose of the investigation is to collect intelligence about "the intentions, capabilities, and probable courses of action of terrorist organizations."[14] Sometimes this purpose requires investigations of individuals as well as of groups. The question in each case should be whether the individual plays a leadership role in the group or participates in group activities that involve or are likely to involve terrorist violence.

Isolated individuals do, of course, commit terrorist acts and make threats of violence, but it is doubtful that intelligence investigations would contribute very much more than criminal investigations in such cases. For example, if there were an allegation that a lone individual planned to commit a terrorist crime, the FBI would ordinarily investigate to determine whether a specific crime had been or was about to be committed. Although it might keep information about the person in its files, the FBI would not need to go beyond the bounds of a criminal investigation to gather the facts it would require for confirming the likelihood that the person would carry out the threat. This sort of investigation can focus on establishing the elements of a criminal offense. If the facts indicate the possible violation of a law outside FBI jurisdiction, they can be turned over to another law enforcement agency for further investigation. Without any indication of a wider conspiracy, a domestic security investigation is unnecessary. Law enforcement interests can be served equally well by gathering information directly related to an arrest and prosecution.

There will always be borderline cases. One illustration might involve a former Ku Klux Klan member with a record of arrests and at least one federal conviction for using violence to intimidate black civil-rights activists in a southern state. This person may no longer belong to any organization, but may still advocate violence and make generalized threats of violence against civil-rights leaders. An argument can be made for keeping an individual like this under investigation indefinitely, because of the proven propensity to commit violent acts. But to do so without any specific allegation that a federal law will be violated would raise problems for the FBI. It would substitute national law enforcement for what ought to be, in our federal system, a state or local responsibility.

Another illustration points up the parallel federal jurisdiction of the FBI and the Secret Service in terrorist cases. Where an isolated individual makes threats against the life of the President or other designated officials, the Secret Service has primary responsibility for protection. Under an agreement between the FBI and the Secret Service, the two agencies divide their responsibilities. The Secret Service investigates such threats, unless a specific crime within FBI jurisdiction is involved. However, the Secret Service has looked to the FBI for intelligence information about "persons who may be considered potentially dangerous to individuals protected by the [Secret Service] because of their . . . *participation in groups* engaged in activities inimical to the United States."[15] Similar guidelines for investigating bombing cases have divided authority between the Treasury Department's Bureau of Alcohol, Tobacco and Firearms and the FBI, with the FBI having responsibility for "offenses perpetrated by terrorist/revolutionary organizations."[16]

These policies reinforce the principle that FBI domestic security investigations should concentrate on organized terrorist activity, rather than on individuals who may act alone.

Two types of organizations are the focus of domestic security investigations. The first includes groups, like the Symbionese Liberation Army or the Weather Underground, which have a record of serious acts of terrorist violence. Sometimes they claim credit for bombings or shootings; in other instances their members are convicted of terrorist crimes. The GAO referred to such groups as having "proven ability to commit violent acts," as shown by the "frequency of acts and the time period in which they were committed."[17]

The second type of groups has, to use the GAO's terms, "only shown a likelihood of violence." In such cases there can be strong indications of the likelihood of serious violence. For example, the GAO proposed that such groups should "be of priority interest if they buy and store arms, engage in organized firearms practice, or purchase survival equipment."[18] The likelihood of serious terrorist acts may also be shown by a pattern of less significant criminal acts, in combination with other factors such as the group's discipline, its clandestine operation, and statements of its leaders favoring the use of violence to achieve the group's aims. In such cases, the Attorney General's 1976 guidelines required the FBI to take into account "the magnitude of the threatened harm, the likelihood it will occur, the immediacy of the threat, and the danger to privacy and free expression posed by a full investigation."[19]

The Task Force on Disorders and Terrorism adopted a similar distinction between these two types of domestic security investigations. It labeled as "strategic and tactical intelligence" the gathering of information about "groups *currently* suspected of criminal activity related to extraordinary violence." The other category was "preventive intelligence," dealing with "groups suspected of having *serious potential for future* criminal involvement in acts of disorder and terrorism."[20]

The Task Force recognized that this second category posed difficult problems because "traditional legal tests such as probable cause or reasonable suspicion, designed to be applied in judgments concerning the likelihood that a criminal act *has* taken place or is taking place, can be of only limited help in the search for standards."[21]

Most of the debate over domestic security investigations has focused on standards for opening such "preventive intelligence" investigations. The Church committee recommendations and Attorney General Levi's guidelines paralleled the Task Force Report in adopting a threshold that did not require any indications of current or recent criminal conduct. The guidelines required only a showing that a group is engaged in activities that "will involve" the use of violence and the violation of federal law. The Church committee modified this requirement to include a showing that a group "will *soon* engage in terrorist activity."[22] In neither case did the standard require indications that any federal crime had been committed, even a crime such as conspiracy.[23]

The Committee on Federal Legislation of the Association of the Bar of the City of New York sharply challenged this departure from a criminal standard. It argued that "all necessary investigations" of threatened terrorism would "fall as a practical matter within the mandate to investigate the commission of crimes," because criminal laws dealing with conspiracies or attempts provide sufficient "authority to investigate any conspiracy to commit a crime, or preparation to commit a crime." The bar committee concluded, "we do not believe there can be any reasonable basis for the initiation of a domestic security investigation in the absence of *some* allegation that one or more persons are either planning or preparing to engage in criminal conduct, or that a crime has already been committed."[24] On the other hand, the bar committee thought the ACLU's proposal for limiting investigations to cases where someone "is about to commit a specific act which violates a federal criminal statute" was too restrictive, because investigations of conspiracies do not have to meet a "specific act" standard.[25]

Using federal conspiracy law as the basis for opening domestic security investigations was attractive, from the bar committee's viewpoint. There would be no need to expand the FBI's "mandate to the nebulous and potentially abusive area of an explicit 'intelligence' function."[26] The public could be assured that the FBI was following Attorney General Harlan Fiske Stone's admonition to confine its investigations to violations of federal law. This principle would, in turn, shield the FBI from criticism and make it easier to defend investigations challenged in court. At the same time, however, labeling preventive intelligence investigations as criminal conspiracy cases might diminish pressures to resolve the difficult questions of investigative discretion. As long as the FBI could be said simply to be investigating federal crimes, more Americans might prefer to let the FBI operate on its own without special guidelines or outside supervision.

The bar committee did not go this far. It recognized significant differences between routine criminal investigations and domestic security investigations, which, by the committee's own definition, are "aimed at gathering 'intelligence' on the ongoing activities of individuals and groups where no specific past crime is being investigated." The committee favored special guidelines for any investigations that "cross the line between the 'who done it' solving of particular crimes already committed . . . and the ongoing investigation of the activities of individuals and groups based upon information or belief that the targets of the investigation are or may be regularly involved in particular violations of law, involving use of violence or terrorist tactics, in the domestic security area."[27]

The problem with the bar committee's standard is its reliance on the principle that "preparation to commit a crime is itself a criminal offense."[28] The scope of domestic security investigations based on this standard can be very broad: the law of conspiracy as interpreted by the federal courts allows the use of political expression, otherwise protected by the First Amendment, as evidence of a conspiracy. Moreover, the federal civil rights conspiracy statute can be interpreted to authorize sweeping investigations of criminal conduct ordinarily handled by local police and prosecutors. The Justice Department's Civil Rights Division seldom authorizes FBI criminal investigations for the prosecution of individuals under this statute. But the Attorney General's 1976 guidelines could be interpreted as permitting domestic security investigations of private activities involving violations of the civil rights conspiracy law.

The breadth of this policy is enormous. Potentially, any act of politically motivated violence could justify a domestic security investigation, because it deprives someone of his civil rights. The constitutional framework of federalism, which divides law enforcement power among federal, state, and local governments, would become meaningless. Despite protests to the contrary, the FBI would be a national police force investigating any violent crimes or preparation to commit such crimes.

The Attorney General's guidelines were not carried to these extremes, as indicated by the sharp reduction in the number of domestic security cases in 1976. The guidelines required taking into account "the magnitude of the threatened harm" before opening a full investigation of a conspiracy to violate civil rights. Under this standard, the FBI probably would not investigate isolated incidents or activities confined to a single community. But if a group were active in several states and its members committed less serious violent offenses under state law, a full domestic security investigation could be approved under the civil rights conspiracy theory implicit in the guidelines. Nothing besides the magnitude test governed the exercise of discretion in such cases.

Recognizing this weakness in the guidelines, the New York City bar committee expressed concern about using "as triggering mechanisms such nebulous and hard to define concepts as 'substantially impairing . . . interstate commerce' or 'depriving persons of their civil rights.' " It preferred the Church committee's approach, which was to define terrorism by focusing on "the specific interests to be protected."[29] In effect, this definition would limit domestic security investigations to cases where the FBI has reason to believe someone is likely to violate federal or state criminal statutes concerning assassination, murder, arson, bombing, hijacking, or kidnaping.[30]

Viewed strictly from the law enforcement perspective, this formula may seem inadequate. The Task Force on Disorders and Terrorism agreed that the standards for preventive intelligence should be strict enough "to screen out frivolous potential investigations," and that it should "bar investigations motivated by a mere sense that a potential subject's political rhetoric suggests the possibility of an unspecifiable risk." However, prohibiting investigations unless there is an allegation or information that someone is preparing to commit a particular type of crime would go too far. It might be impossible to meet this standard "in some cases of extreme potential danger—as, for example, when an unsolicited, unverifiable informant's tip warns of a major terroristic attack by a tight-knit political organization that has previously given police no 'specific and articulable grounds' to conduct investigations." The Task Force would merely require a likelihood of "some form of extreme violence" or an "incident of a highly dangerous character." It admitted "the inevitable subjectivity" of such a standard, and proposed added safeguards, including strict standards of relevance for the collection of information and frequent review and purging of preventive intelligence records.[31]

On this issue, Senator Howard Baker, vice-chairman of the Church committee, expressed an equally strong view. "For example," he observed, "an allegation of an assassination attempt on a public figure at an unspecified date in the future could be precluded from investigation; or vague information received by the FBI that there was a plan to obtain some nuclear components, but no indication of when or how, could also be prohibited from investigation. Surely, matters such as these should be the valid subjects of investigation—no matter how vague or piecemeal the information is."[32]

Whatever the standard for assessing the magnitude of the threat—either a general extreme-violence test or a list of particular types of crimes—the crucial issue is whether this type of preventive investigation has to go beyond the scope of a criminal investigation. In other words, what more is needed than an investigation to establish the elements of a crime, including the crime of conspiracy? Where members of a group have a record of federal crimes involving violence, the group deserves wider investigation to determine what it will do next and who may be involved. This requires collecting intelligence information beyond evidence of a crime. But if a group is suspected only of preparing to commit crimes in the future, there is much less justification for broad intelligence gathering. The sole purpose of the investigation should be to find out if, in fact, someone is planning a specific terrorist act.

One way to ensure that FBI investigations of this sort do not become broad intelligence investigations is to require that the results be submitted promptly to the Justice Department. If the facts justify further investigation, the department should direct the FBI to continue gathering evidence that would support a prosecution. If the information is inadequate, then the investigation should stop. This approach satisfies the law enforcement interest in having an investigation to check out allegations or tips that someone is preparing to commit a terrorist act. But it does not allow the FBI to collect information unrelated to verifying or discounting the original information.

These limits on the scope and purpose of purely preventive investigations would confine intelligence gathering to groups such as the Symbionese Liberation Army or the Weather Underground, whose potential for future terrorist acts is clearly established by their track record. The law enforcement interest in extensive information about such groups is compelling: the FBI should investigate their leaders and identify any other individuals who may be closely associated with the group's violent activities. The investigation can encompass the group's sources of financial support, its internal dynamics, the ideology and attitudes of the individuals involved, and any other aspects of the group that may help in evaluating what it will do next, and assist in criminal investigations of any future crimes its members may commit.

On the other hand, for the FBI to gather the same type of intelligence information about a group that has not yet committed a terrorist act, simply to predict when the group will turn to violence, poses a real danger to privacy and First Amendment rights, because the law enforcement justification is far less persuasive.

In short, the standards for domestic security investigations should restrict intelligence gathering only to those groups having a proven propensity to commit acts of terrorism, to the groups' leaders, and to individuals who are reasonably suspected of being involved in the groups' activities related to violence. The FBI should handle allegations about individuals and about groups having only a *potential* for terrorist violence as criminal investigations, limited strictly to establishing whether or not a federal crime (including conspiracy) has been or is about to be committed. These standards permit the FBI to investigate where the law enforcement interest outweighs the risks to privacy and free expression, rather than where the needs of law enforcement are more remote and speculative.

Informants and Covert Infiltration

The Supreme Court has ruled, in the context of criminal investigations, that the use of undercover agents and informants is not such an intrusion into constitutionally protected privacy that it requires a judicial warrant or probable cause of a specific crime. In one leading case, the Court stated, "the risk of . . . being betrayed by an informer or deceived as to the identity of one with whom one deals is probably inherent in the conditions of human society. It is the kind of risk we necessarily assume whenever we speak."[33] The Court has never confronted a case involving the use of informants for intelligence-gathering purposes, rather than in the investigation of specific crimes. As the Church committee's staff report on FBI domestic intelligence informants observed, "no court has seen the overall pattern of FBI intelligence informant coverage of citizens and groups. Consequently, courts have been unable to assess the full impact of the informant system on the exercise of constitutionally protected rights."[34]

Informants and undercover operations raise a combination of constitutional and policy issues. Attorney General Levi's guidelines strongly implied that such techniques were at least comparable to police "stop-and-frisk" practices in their effect on privacy. Levi said the standard for a full domestic security investigation, using informants and other covert techniques, was "the equivalent of the standard for a street stop and frisk enunciated by the Supreme Court in *Terry* v. *Ohio*." The Court held that, under the Fourth Amendment, a police officer "must be able to point to specific and articulable facts which, when taken together with rational inferences from those facts, reasonably warrant the intrusion." The officer is entitled to make "reasonable inquiries" where he "observes unusual conduct which leads him reasonably to conclude in light of his experience that criminal activity may be afoot."[35]

However, the analogy to stop-and-frisk practices is neither complete nor particularly helpful in resolving the issues. Unlike the police officer on the beat, the FBI does not normally make snap judgments in recruiting informants. In rare cases, an FBI agent may unexpectedly discover that someone being interviewed can provide vital information about an imminent meeting to plan a crime; the agent may ask the person to become, in effect, an informant for the particular meeting. But in most instances routine Bureau procedures are followed. A potential informant is subjected to a background check and must be approved by the Special Agent in Charge (SAC) of the field office (in domestic security cases, by FBI headquarters); payments to informants must be authorized by the SAC (if less than $400) or by headquarters (if more than $400); and the informant must undergo a probationary period to establish reliability.[36]

More important, the impact of covert informant surveillance on an American citizen's sense of privacy is probably greater than the effect of an overt police contact. The fear of unknown, secret surveillance was one of the main reasons for the establishment of judicial warrant and probable cause requirements for electronic surveillance. Hence, the Church committee placed the use of informants in the category of "intrusive techniques," along with mail opening, surreptitious entries, and electronic surveillance. It found "that their very nature makes them a threat to the personal privacy and constitutionally protected activities of both the targets and of persons who communicate with or associate with the targets."[37] One legal expert has compared "police spies" and electronic surveillance this way: "The only difference is that under electronic surveillance you are afraid to talk to anybody in your office or over the phone, while under a spy system you are afraid to talk to anybody at all."[38]

Finally, using undercover informants or agents may involve a law enforcement agency in violations of law. An informant or agent may be instructed to participate in a criminal enterprise to get the information desired by the agency or handling agent. Getting the information may involve stealing or photographing documents under circumstances that violate specific legal and constitutional rights. To protect the law enforcement agency, there may be a tacit understanding between the informant and the handling agent that they will not discuss everything the informant is doing or the methods of obtaining documents. The informant's information may be so valuable that the law enforcement agency is not willing to risk exposure through arrest or openly protecting a target of planned violence, and it may look for secret means to avert violence, including unlawful disruptive actions. Attorney General Levi adopted special guidelines designed to control these aspects of FBI informant operations. (See Appendix IV for the full text of the guidelines on "FBI Use of Informants in Domestic Security, Organized Crime, and Other Criminal Investigations.")

To safeguard against the abuses of intelligence informants it uncovered, the Church committee proposed more rigorous standards and review procedures than those contained in the Attorney General's 1976 guidelines. Under these standards, the FBI could use informants at its own discretion only where they were assigned to gather evidence for the prosecution of specific federal crimes. The FBI could not recruit new informants or direct existing informants against a new target for intelligence purposes unless the Attorney General or his designee made "a written finding that (i) he has considered and rejected less intrusive techniques; and (ii) he believes that [informants] are necessary to obtain information for the investigation." Informants could be used on the basis of a "reasonable suspicion" for ninety days, with an option for a sixty-day extension, after they are "in place and capable of reporting." At the end of this period, their continued use would require a written finding by the Attorney General or his designee "that there is probable cause that [an] American will soon engage in terrorist activities."[39]

However, this probable cause standard was not as rigorous as the test under Fourth Amendment warrant procedures for criminal investigations. Under these, to secure a warrant for a physical search or electronic surveillance, there must be probable cause that a specific crime has been, is being, or is about to be committed. The Church committee required only probable cause that an individual or group "will soon engage in terrorist activities." A specific imminent criminal act need not be shown.

The practical problem with this concept was that it multiplied the number of separate decisions the Attorney General's office must make in the course of a single investigation. Although the committee did not require that the Attorney General give prior authorization for every full investigation, prior approval for using informants amounted to the same thing. Another decision had to be made after 90 to 150 days on whether the case had moved beyond reasonable suspicion to probable cause. Then, at the end of a year, still another decision on continuing the investigation was necessary.

The standards for domestic security investigations proposed in the previous section would allow a simpler framework for outside review by "the Attorney General or his designee." Informants are likely to be used in almost every investigation of a proven terrorist group, so it would make sense to incorporate the initial informant-approving duty into a general requirement that the Attorney General's office approve the opening of full investigations and review them yearly thereafter.

In these circumstances, a strong argument can be made that a court, rather than the Attorney General's office, should make the determination of reasonable suspicion or probable cause. The Church committee did not recommend a judicial warrant procedure for informants, but it believed the issue should be "reviewed after two years' experience." Nevertheless, Senator Philip Hart warned that the probable cause standard might prove "illusory" without a judicial check, that informants can "be even more intrusive and more easily abused than electronic surveillance," and that their use "is at the heart of the chilling effect which preventive intelligence has on political dissent."[40]

The Supreme Court has explained the value of the judicial warrant requirement: "it is not an inconvenience to be somehow 'weighed' against the claims of police efficiency. It is, or should be, an important working part of our machinery of government, operating as a matter of course to check the 'well-intentioned but mistakenly over-zealous executive officers who are a part of any system of law enforcement."[41] In the *Keith* case, the Court said, "the Fourth Amendment does not contemplate the executive officers of Government as neutral and disinterested magistrates. Their duty and responsibility are to enforce the laws, to investigate, and to prosecute. But those charged with this investigative and prosecutorial duty should not be the sole judges of when to utilize constitutionally sensitive means in pursuing their tasks. The historical judgment, which the Fourth Amendment accepts, is that unreviewed executive discretion may yield too readily to pressures to obtain incriminating evidence and overlook potential invasions of privacy and protected speech."[42]

When investigative activity focuses on politically motivated groups suspected of criminal plans, First Amendment interests require an especially high standard of investigative care. Up to now the courts have not extended the warrant requirement to undercover informants, on the theory that anyone who discusses criminal actions with another must assume the risk that the other will inform. But the courts now have before them a record of widespread use of such investigative tools as informants to report entirely lawful conversations and private activities, as well as to take lawless disruptive action for the purpose of inhibiting political expression and association.

Therefore, the concept of an "investigative warrant" has become more attractive. In domestic security investigations, a judge would supplement or replace the Attorney General's office in approving the use of informants. The judge could, according to one expert, make the decisions "in light of the totality of the circumstances, including, but not limited to: (1) the reliability of the sources of information on which the government's asserted need is based, (2) the credibility of the information itself, and (3) the reliability of the proposed informant. To test the reliability of the sources on which the application is based, the judge may have to question and therefore know the identity of, other informants or the existence of wiretaps or bugs. To assess the credibility of the information, he may have to examine the factual context in which threats were alleged to have been made, the capabilities of the proposed targets to commit the anticipated crimes, and the gap, if any, between the rhetoric and action of the target group."[43] To a significant degree, the "neutral and disinterested magistrate" would review the management and direction of the investigation.

Attorney General Levi's response went directly to this central point. "Extending the warrant requirement in this way would be a major step toward an alteration in the basic nature of the criminal justice system in America," he told the Edwards subcommittee. "It would be a step toward the inquisitorial system in which judges, and not members of the executive, actually control the investigation of crimes. This is the system used in some European countries and elsewhere, but our system of justice keeps the investigation and prosecution of crime separate from the adjudication of criminal charges. The separation is important to the neutrality of the judiciary, a neutrality which our system takes pains to protect. . . . We must ask ourselves whether the control of human sources of information—which involves subtle, day-to-day judgments about credibility and personality—is something judges ought to be asked to undertake. It would place an enormous responsibility upon courts which either would be handled perfunctorily or, if handled with care, would place tremendous burden of work on federal judges."[44]

Neither the pejorative label—inquisitorial system—nor the workload problem fully disposes of the issue. Attorney General Levi believed he could discharge his duty to oversee domestic security investigations with the help of a three-person review unit; and carving out a limited part of the criminal justice system for exceptional judicial involvement need not impair the overall independence of the judiciary. In fact, with respect to foreign intelligence electronic surveillance, Levi himself proposed giving a handful of specially designed judges the job of issuing warrants according to more complex standards than conventional probable cause of a specific crime.

The more persuasive reason not to adopt investigative warrants is that they would diffuse responsibility in a field where precise accountability is essential. Under the guidelines, the burden rested clearly upon FBI headquarters officials and the Attorney General's office to enforce compliance with the rules. They could not pass the buck to a judge or a magistrate in borderline cases. After examining the history of nearly four decades of "plausible deniabililty" and unregulated growth of domestic intelligence operations, the Church committee concluded that responsibility "must be made clear, formal, and fixed" and that it must ultimately fall upon the Attorney General. "As the chief legal officer of the United States, the Attorney General is the most appropriate official to be charged with ensuring that the intelligence agencies of the United States conduct their activities in accordance with the law."[45] Nevertheless, if further experience demonstrated that the Attorney General's office could not impose sufficiently rigorous review of domestic security investigations, a judicial warrant procedure for opening and periodically approving the continuation of covert investigations would be justified.

Protective Measures and "Preventive Action"

Attorney General Levi withdrew his proposed guidelines for authorizing FBI "preventive action," even though the GAO found them to be "reasonable."[46] However, other guidelines included certain provisions for what the FBI should do when it receives information that violence may occur. The domestic security guidelines allowed the FBI to disseminate information to other law enforcement agencies, and to persons "whose safety or property is directly threatened by planned force or violence, so that they may take appropriate protective safeguards." Separate informant guidelines required instructing informants "to try to discourage the violence."

The question raised by the original preventive action proposal is whether the FBI should itself be allowed to take appropriate protective safeguards beyond dissemination and using informants to discourage violence. There is widespread agreement that the Bureau should not use the clandestine, nonprosecutorial means adopted in its COINTELPRO operations. For example, the Church committee recommended "prohibiting Bureau interference in lawful speech, publication, assembly, organization, or association of Americans . . . [by] mailing fake letters to factionalize a group . . . [or using informants for] manipulating or influencing the peaceful activities of a group on behalf of the FBI." The committee would also bar "harassing individuals through unnecessary overt investigative techniques such as interviews or obvious physical surveillance for the purpose of intimidation."[47] In general, the committee concluded, "a law enforcement agency must not secretly usurp the functions of judge and jury, even when the investigation reveals criminal activity."[48]

In its staff report on COINTELPRO, the Church committee observed that the FBI's disruptive measures were not "directed at specific criminal acts"; instead, the programs were aimed at "preventing possibly violent citizens from joining or continuing to associate with possibly violent groups." It made no difference whether "the particular member [or] the group was violent at the time." Criticizing Director Kelley's defense of COINTELPRO, the report noted, "affirmative legal steps to meet an imminent threat to life or property are, of course, quite proper. The difficulty with the Director's statement . . . is that the threats COINTELPRO purported to meet were not imminent, the techniques used were sometimes illegal, and the purposes went far beyond the prevention of death and destruction." However, Attorney General Levi's more restrictive "preventive action" guidelines were rejected because "it was not possible to frame general language which would permit proper (and indeed ordinary) law enforcement measures such as increased guards around [a] building or traffic control during a demonstration while preventing COINTELPRO type activity."[49]

In any law enforcement organization as large as the FBI,

agents will have strong incentives to act on their own, *sub rosa*, even if their formal authority does not go beyond arrest or warning. There are two drawbacks to reliance exclusively on arrests and warnings. First, such overt action can blow the cover on informants and sources whose continued coverage is vital for advance detection of future violence. Second, an arrest might have to be based on a conspiracy charge, which is difficult to prosecute successfully and raises substantial civil liberties problems. If an arrest is going to stand up in court, it may be necessary to wait until the conspirators have arrived at the scene of the planned crime with weapons or explosives. In such circumstances the risk of a violent clash with law enforcement officers, endangering lives on both sides, is particularly great.

On the other hand, there are legitimate fears of a return to COINTELPRO-type harassment and "dirty tricks." They can be allayed by requiring that protective measures be lawful, by adopting a rigorous probable cause threshold for their use, and by prohibiting the abuses of the past and giving FBI agents advance warning that such activities would make them liable to disciplinary action and to criminal prosecution for willful violation of civil rights.

What, then, are the lawful protective measures that this procedure should cover? Attorney General Levi cited two: "(1) disrupting plans for using force or violence; or (2) preventing access to, or rendering inoperative weapons, explosives, or other instrumentalities of planned violence." He added that the action must be "the minimum necessary to obstruct the force and violence" and "designed and conducted so as not to limit the full exercise of rights protected by the Constitution and laws of the United States." The authorized measures specifically excluded "committing or instigating criminal acts; disseminating information for the purpose of holding an individual or group up to scorn, ridicule, or disgrace; disseminating information anonymously or under a false identity; and inciting violence."[50]

Clearly, measures to prevent access to, or render inoperative, explosives or other instrumentalities of a violent crime are proper. But the broad term "disrupting plans" is too vague, especially if it goes beyond instructing informants to discourage violence by their associates. The standards should specify particular measures for disruption consistent with the rule of law and recognized and accepted law enforcement practice. At least two types of activity fall in this category. The first are measures to provide physical protection to a possible target of violence. The FBI already is authorized by statute to take physical protective measures upon the request of the Secret Service, and it might properly do so in other circumstances with the approval of the Attorney General. The second is more controversial, but nonetheless vital if used with care and precision. It is often called "deterrent interviewing," for the purpose of communicating the desirability of lawful and nonviolent behavior to persons who might commit an act of violence. In a sense, it is the overt counterpart of having undercover informants try to discourage the violence.

One observer contends, "where a terrorist group is intimidating a community, the FBI should be free (with specific authority from the Attorney General and under close Justice Department scrutiny) to conduct deterrent interviewing designed to let suspected terrorists know that they are not anonymous. However, if such interviewing is to be allowed, it must be carried out discreetly, so that employers will not be caused to fire, or neighbors to shun, the suspects."[51] Former Attorney General Nicholas Katzenbach strongly defended this practice as it was used to deter Ku Klux Klan violence in the 1960s. In some respects, it would allow the Bureau, under carefully controlled circumstances, to create the impression among persons planning violence that the FBI knows more about such plans than it actually does.

The standards for deterrent interviewing and for obstructing access to instruments of violence should be more stringent than the proposed preventive action guidelines. They should require that protective measures involving contacts, including interviews with or regarding a person, must be conducted in a manner that will reduce to a minimum any adverse effects on the person. The line should be sharply drawn to prevent harassment or intimidation of law-abiding individuals.

Finally, the requirement that FBI agents instruct informants to discourage violence should be incorporated into such procedures, along with the use of informants or undercover sources to disarm explosives or block access to weapons. However, these procedures should not preclude an informant from initiating lawful protective measures. The discovery of preparation for imminent violence should free an informant "to stuff sawdust into dynamite sticks, defuse bombs, disarm weapons, deactivate ammunition or otherwise deprive the conspirators of the physical capability to commit an imminent attack on life or property."[52]

Attorney General Levi denounced COINTELPRO as allowing activities that "were either foolish or outrageous," and he stressed that his proposed guidelines would not "legitimize such activities." His strongest argument for authorizing protective measures beyond arrest or warnings was that law enforcement officials are "expected to act to save life or protect the functioning of government," and that they "would be condemned if they did not act."[53] Levi was proved correct a year later when the American Civil Liberties Union filed a lawsuit against the FBI for having failed to take adequate measures to protect peaceful civil rights demonstrators from mob violence in the early 1960s. The case involved a situation where local police, to whom the Bureau gave advance warning, chose not to act; the FBI did not have clear authority to make arrests for assaults that violated state, not federal, criminal laws. How else but through some form of preventive action could the Bureau have been expected to satisfy this demand?[54]

Summary

The conclusions growing out of this analysis of FBI domestic security investigations can be summarized as follows:

1. Domestic security intelligence investigations of terrorist

organizations satisfy compelling law enforcement interests. The low productivity of past investigations, based on outdated laws and policies, does not justify abolishing investigations to gather intelligence for use in investigating future terrorist crimes and, where possible, preventing such crimes.

2. The standards for domestic security investigations should limit intelligence gathering to groups with a proven propensity to commit terrorist acts, their leaders, and persons who may be involved in violence-related group activities. In all other circumstances, criminal investigations are sufficient to fulfill domestic security law enforcement requirements.

3. The risks to privacy and the rule of law require special safeguards for using informants and covert infiltration in FBI domestic security investigations. Prior approval of any intelligence investigation by the Attorney General or a designee is likely to provide a sufficient check, although judicial warrants should be considered if review by the Attorney General's office proves inadequate.

4. The FBI should have the authority, within strict limits and with the approval of the Attorney General's office, to take lawful protective measures beyond arrest or the dissemination of information, for the purpose of preventing imminent acts of terrorist violence.

CHAPTER VI

Foreign Counterintelligence Investigations

IN 1976 the FBI received a new presidential charter for counterintelligence investigations. Executive Order 11905 authorized the FBI, under the supervision of the Attorney General, to "detect and prevent espionage, sabotage, subversion, and other unlawful activities by or on behalf of foreign powers through such lawful counterintelligence operations within the United States, including electronic surveillance, as are necessary or useful for such purposes."[1] Classified guidelines issued by Attorney General Levi supplemented this order. President Carter's 1978 order recast the FBI's mandate as authority to "conduct counterintelligence activities," defined as activities "to protect against espionage and other clandestine intelligence activities, sabotage, international terrorist activities or assassinations conducted for or on behalf of foreign powers, organizations or persons."[2]

Foreign counterintelligence investigations pose three broad issues. First, even more than domestic security investigations, they are hard to fit into the framework of ordinary federal criminal investigations. The purpose is seldom prosecution, because presenting the evidence in court risks disclosing more classified information than the spy has already transmitted. Prosecutions also require blowing the cover of counterintelligence sources and methods that are often needed to detect other spies.

Second, where prosecutions are impractical, other techniques may be used to prevent successful espionage. But the law is not clear as to when, if at all, the FBI can go beyond conventional law enforcement measures to combat or neutralize foreign intelligence activities.

The third issue involves the borderline between foreign and domestic intelligence, as illustrated by the FBI's past investigations of Communist party influence in domestic political activities. To what extent should the FBI investigate efforts by foreign powers to "subvert" the United States by exercising improper covert political influence within this country?

Underlying all these issues is the question of whether the FBI should distinguish among individuals and foreign powers in setting its priorities. It might be reasonable to give the FBI wider latitude for investigating foreign government officials or temporary foreign visitors, as opposed to United States citizens or permanent resident aliens. Similarly, the FBI might properly give the highest priority to foreign powers exhibiting an overall pattern of hostility to the United States, in comparison with foreign governments neutral to or allied with this country.

These differences affect how one assesses investigative standards and techniques. The use made of informants—or "assets" in the jargon of counterintelligence—against the intelligence activities of a hostile country need not set a precedent for undercover surveillance of all foreign information-gathering activities in the United States or all efforts by foreign officials to exercise political influence. Those assets might also be used to disrupt a hostile country's espionage operations by means that could not be permitted in any other circumstances.

To be more concrete, the Church committee reported that the Soviet Union and its allies conduct "espionage and 'active measures' or covert action operations on a large scale against its main enemy—the United States," and that the targets include not only U.S. government officials, but also "members of the business, scientific and political communities with access to the U.S. Government, and other influential entities such as youth, journalist, and trade organizations." The objectives are "recruitment of Americans as intelligence assets" and "recruitment and cultivation of 'agents of influence,' or agents who can influence political events or decisions." Soviet intelligence also conducts "technical operations against U.S. installations and personnel."[3]

Despite detente or other diplomatic efforts to reach agreements with the Soviet Union, the secret war between antagonistic intelligence services goes on; FBI counterintelligence operations remain vital for national defense. While respect for the rights of Americans is paramount, the FBI must have the resources and tools to discern the plans and intentions of hostile intelligence services, and to destroy their effectiveness by controlling and manipulating their operations and by deceiving them about our own capabilities and intentions.[4]

Great publicity has also been given to foreign intervention in American affairs by agents of such non-Communist countries as South Korea, Iran, and Chile. These activities have been the subjects of federal criminal investigations; but the FBI's publicly stated counterintelligence priorities focus on the "astronomical" intelligence capabilities of Communist-bloc countries.[5]

Standards for Investigations

The attempt to link counterintelligence investigations to specific federal criminal laws has proved to be one of the most troublesome aspects of FBI intelligence reform. When it considered electronic surveillance legislation, the Congress recognized that ordinary criminal law enforcement standards were inadequate for investigating hostile foreign intelligence activities. In its earlier report, the Church committee strongly urged modernizing the espionage statutes because of the importance of the principle that "intelligence agencies should not investigate activities of Americans which are not federal [crimes]."[6] On the other hand, Attorney General Levi feared widening the espionage laws, and stressed the development of standards for investigation falling short of the requirements for criminal prosecution.

The issue has been debated in terms of the most intrusive techniques, such as electronic surveillance. However, it may be helpful to begin at the other end of the investigative process with a concept of preliminary investigation, similar to the domestic security guidelines. What activities might trigger a preliminary counterintelligence investigation, using techniques such as existing records and sources, interviews, and limited physical surveillance for identification purposes? The next step would be to examine the types of activity requiring full investigation without a clear showing of a specific federal law violation. The standards should confine these investigations within reasonable bounds, so they do not have a chilling effect on other activities of Americans who may fear covert surveillance of their associations with foreigners.

Investigative vs. Prosecutorial Standards

Like the domestic security guidelines, counterintelligence standards should address the investigative process without attempting to resolve all the questions posed by criminal prosecutions. The distinction between investigative and prosecutorial standards is desirable because, in addition to the Espionage Act, there are other federal laws that raise problems of vagueness and overbreadth. These include the foreign agents registration, export disclosures, and neutrality statutes, some of which are rarely, if ever, enforced, but which might serve as the statutory basis for FBI investigations. Just as the Smith Act and the seditions conspiracy law were used for domestic intelligence investigations, federal registration and disclosure laws could perform a similar function for sweeping counterintelligence investigations.

For example, the FBI justified on these grounds its compliance with President Johnson's request for physical surveillance and indirect electronic surveillance of a prominent Republican supporter, Anna Chennault, in the final days of the

1968 presidential election. The purported reason for the surveillance was to determine whether the South Vietnamese were secretly in touch with supporters of presidential candidate Nixon, possibly through Mrs. Chennault. President Johnson apparently suspected that the South Vietnamese were trying to sabotage his peace negotiations in the hope that Nixon would win the election and then take a harder line toward North Vietnam. The FBI told the Church committee that its surveillance of Mrs. Chennault was consistent with its responsibility to determine if her activites violated the Foreign Agents Registration Act and the Neutrality Act.[7]

However, the theory behind Attorney General Levi's domestic security guidelines was that investigative standards do not have to cite particular federal statutes allowing prosecution for sedition or for inchoate crimes like conspiracy. Instead, the guidelines set out certain vital public interests, embodied in numerous laws, that should be served by the investigations. Links to specific criminal statutes were not required until the case reached the stage of a Fourth Amendment search or of arrest and prosecution.

A similar theory makes sense for counterintelligence investigations. The standards should define the national interests to be protected. They should grow out of the body of laws dealing with national defense and foreign affairs, and incorporate policy judgments about the desired purposes of counterintelligence investigations. There should be no need for artificially predicating an investigation on a particular vague registration or disclosure statute.

In addition, defining vital national interests enables the standards to focus on the activities of certain foreign powers that require counterintelligence investigations that go beyond the conventional investigation of specific crimes for purposes of prosecution. Some federal laws already point in this direction. The Export Administration Act of 1969, which restricted the export of technology to other nations, imposed felony (as opposed to misdemeanor) penalties upon persons willfully exporting such information "for the benefit of any Communist-dominated nation."[8]

The question of whether a particular country may be potentially hostile to the United States is not always properly answered in binding legislation. The principle that counterintelligence investigations should be directed primarily against hostile or potentially hostile foreign powers is an essential safeguard for the rights of Americans. It excludes from continuing counterintelligence inquiry the multitude of associations that Americans have with friendly or neutral foreign governments, and with foreign and international organizations or movements that do not pose serious dangers to the United States. There should be regular procedures for determining which foreign powers and entities fall within the scope of broader counterintelligence investigations, and congressional oversight should monitor the application of these procedures.

Similar distinctions can be made for investigating individuals according to their legal status. For example, the Foreign Intelligence Surveillance Act of 1978 set more stringent standards for making U.S. citizens and permanent resident aliens the subjects of surveillance, and imposed fewer restrictions on surveillance of foreigners who act in the United States as officers or employees of a foreign power. The counterintelligence criteria might allow similar leeway for investigating official representatives or visitors from a potentially hostile nation suspected of having intelligence assignments. More rigorous standards in other investigations could then provide greater protection for the privacy of Americans and visitors from other countries.

Counterintelligence investigations demonstrate most clearly why an exclusive emphasis on criminal law standards can distort the issues and detract from a careful weighing of interests. The foreign agents registration and export disclosure laws, combined with the law of conspiracy, could sustain almost any investigation of an American's foreign ties. But to rely on seldom-enforced laws would give a misleading impression of restraint, and discourage efforts to guide the exercise of investigative discretion.

Preliminary Investigations

The basis for opening a preliminary counterintelligence investigation of an American should be information that the person either may be engaged in hostile foreign intelligence activities, or may be a source of information or assistance in an ongoing counterintelligence investigation. The latter standard is consistent with the Church committee's recommendation permitting the CIA to collect information on individuals or organizations, including Americans, "being considered by the CIA as potential sources of information or assistance," although such inquiries were to be limited to a name check of existing information, and "confidential interviews of persons who may know the subject, if the subject is unaware of CIA interest in him."[9] Although the committee did not specifically recommend this standard for the FBI, the same principle applied to both CIA foreign intelligence and FBI counterintelligence operations.

The Church committee gave examples of information that would satisfy the first criterion for opening a counterintelligence investigation of an American, but it did not do so for preliminary investigations of potential sources. Indications that an individual may be engaged in hostile foreign intelligence activities would include:

> information that a member of the National Security Council staff "met clandestinely with a known foreign intelligence agent in an obscure Paris restaurant";
>
> information that an antiwar activist traveling to an international peace conference in Oslo "intended to meet with a person he knew to be a foreign intelligence agent to receive instructions to conduct espionage on behalf of a hostile foreign country";

"information that an atomic scientist has had a number of clandestine meetings with a hostile foreign intelligence agent"; or

"information that an American has been recruited by a hostile intelligence service."[10]

These examples involve either clandestine contacts between known foreign intelligence agents and unwitting Americans having access to valuable information, or contacts (overt or clandestine) in which the Americans know they are meeting with foreign agents to receive intelligence assignments.

There are many other situations in which Americans have open contacts with a hostile foreign intelligence agent, but are unaware that the person with whom they are associating has intelligence assignments. The foreign agent may be assessing an American scientist for a possible recruitment approach, or asking for information that an American business executive does not realize will provide useful intelligence for the hostile service. In these circumstances, opening a preliminary investigation to determine the American's usefulness as a potential source for the FBI would be justified. As the Church committee observed,

> the monitoring of contacts between U.S. government officials and foreign officials who are likely to be carrying out the directions of a hostile foreign intelligence service is a necessary part of the FBI's investigative duties. The subject of the investigation is the foreign official, and any inquiry directed towards the American official can be limited to determining the nature of the foreign official's interests. Frequently, it is desirable that the American official be informed by the Bureau, especially where the contact is overt rather than furtive or clandestine. (The same is also true with respect to overt contacts with American private citizens.)[11]

An American may be the unwitting subject of a recruitment effort by a foreign agent, or his activities may be the target of the foreign agent's intelligence operations. In either case, requiring the FBI to secure consent before any inquiry can jeopardize the Bureau's existing investigative sources.

Greater difficulties arise when the hostile intelligence agent is not a foreign official, but a private foreign citizen visiting the United States. It is here that giving priority to investigations of citizens of hostile nations would be a valuable safeguard against excessive preliminary investigations of Americans.

Few nations mount against the United States an espionage effort comparable to the Soviet Union's. Soviet intelligence practices involving visitors to this country were summarized in a 1973 memorandum that described the CIA project for opening mail between the United States and the Soviet Union:

> The Project is particularly productive in supporting both the Agency and the FBI in pursuing investigative and operational leads to Soviet students, exchange scientists, academicians and intellectuals, trade specialists and experts from organizations such as the USSR Institute of the USA. The basis for exploiting the Project for this purpose is the knowledge we have from every Soviet Bloc intelligence service defector that *each visitor to the West is approved by the respective Security Service*. The Project . . . is basically concerned with individuals the KGB approves because it controls them, their passports, their foreign exchange, their education, etc. Based on KGB and GRU defector information, it is presumed that the visitor is a KGB agent or cooperating with the KGB, i.e., a "cooptee."[12]

The FBI advised the Church committee that during the past decade it had "identified over 100 intelligence officers among the approximately 400 Soviet students who attended American universities during this period," and that "more than 100 American students were the target of Soviet recruitment approaches in the USSR." Aside from exchange students, the number of other Soviet visitors who may have intelligence assignments has risen sharply. East-West commercial exchange visitors increased from 641 in 1972 to 1,500 in 1974. The opening of American deep-water ports to Soviet ships in 1972 allowed more than two hundred vessels with a total complement of 13,000 officers to call at forty ports in 1974. Finally, the number of Soviet immigrants to the United States rose from fewer than 500 in 1972 to 4,000 in 1974.[13] The Soviet threat is multiplied by the presence in the United States of officials and visitors from nations allied with the Soviet Union, including Poland, Czechoslovakia, Romania, Hungary, Bulgaria, East Germany, and Mongolia.[14]

If FBI counterintelligence is to detect the hostile foreign intelligence agents and "cooptees" among potential spies, it needs authority to conduct preliminary investigations of Americans not only when they have clandestine or knowing contacts with suspected agents, but also when their contacts are open or unwitting and they are potential sources. These limited intrusions into privacy are essential if the FBI is to get sufficient information for allocating its resources most effectively against sophisticated adversaries.

Full Investigations

Sometimes the exact purpose of a hostile foreign intelligence agent's activities cannot easily be determined. It is not hard to justify a full investigation if there is reasonable suspicion that the agent's objective is to secure valuable information. But sometimes all the FBI may have to go on is reasonable suspicion that the person is a conscious member of a clandestine foreign intelligence network. As a study prepared by the Fund for the Republic stated more than twenty years ago, "the problems of crime detection in combatting espionage are not ordinary ones. Espionage is a crime which succeeds only by secrecy. Moreover, spies work not for themselves or private organized crime 'syndicates,' but as agents of national states. Their activities are therefore likely to be carefully planned, highly organized, and carried on by techniques skillfully designed to prevent detection."[15]

Some of the most serious espionage threats are posed by "illegals," counterintelligence jargon for foreign intelligence agents who have no overt, formal, "legal" connection with a foreign government. The FBI has stated, "The illegal is a highly trained specialist in espionage tradecraft. He may be a [foreign] national and/or professional intelligence officer dispatched to the United States under a false identity. Some illegals [may be] trained in the scientific and technical field to permit easy access to sensitive areas of employment. . . . Once they enter the United States with either fraudulent or true documentation, their presence is obscured among the thousands of legitimate émigrés entering the United States annually."[16] The most notorious example of a Soviet "illegal" who operated undetected for many years in the United States was Colonel Rudolf Abel, whose activities were discovered in the late 1950s only when one of his fellow agents defected. The extent to which Colonel Abel's espionage network included Americans was never established.[17] The FBI admits that its most difficult counterintelligence task is "the detection, identification, and neutralization of the so-called illegals," because they "maintain no open contact with official foreign establishments in this country, and their activities are directed from abroad."[18]

Americans who are recruited by legal or illegal foreign agents in the United States pose the same problems as illegals. In addition, Americans who travel overseas may be recruited by Soviet bloc intelligence officers in other countries. An FBI official has observed, "an operation might begin in the home country with recruitment of an American visitor; transfer to the United States with his return; and again, even later, might be transferred to a third country where the American agent may be met outside the normal reach of United States counterintelligence coverage."[19]

One example shows the dimensions of the problem. In 1976, James Frederick Sattler, an American political scientist engaged in research for the Atlantic Council, an organization devoted to the study of the common concerns of NATO countries, filed a registration statement with the Justice Department under the 1956 "Spy Registration" statute.[20] His statement admitted that he had been recruited in 1967 by an East German intelligence officer and had thereafter "transmitted to my principals in Berlin, GDR, information and documents which I received from the North Atlantic Treaty Organization and from individuals in institutions and government agencies in the Federal Republic of Germany, United States, Great Britain, Canada, and France." His last assignment, given in 1975 on a visit to East Berlin, was "to attempt to obtain a position in the United States government with access to classified information." He had previously received instructions in the use of "codes and ciphers, microphotography, radio and mail communications, clandestine meetings, concealment devices," and he had already sent "microdisc" photographs of documents by mail "to West Germany which I know were subsequently received by my principals in Berlin, GDR."[21]

The Justice Department did not give any official explanation for not prosecuting Sattler on a charge of conspiracy to commit espionage. One reason may have been the government's desire to avoid exposing its own counterespionage practices and sources of information. In addition, until he received a specific assignment in 1975 to obtain classified U.S. government information, his activities may not have constituted a violation of the Espionage Act. There is no indication that he had previously transmitted or agreed to transmit *secret* information obtained from U.S. government agencies; many of his targets were foreign governments and institutions. Indeed, the FBI may not have known exactly what assignments Sattler had received until he made the voluntary disclosures contained in his registration statement.

Because of the difficulties in determining the purpose of an agent's activities, the Foreign Intelligence Surveillance Act of 1978 recognized the occasional need to make an American the target without probable cause of a specific crime. The standard was, instead, probable cause to believe that the person "knowingly engages in clandestine intelligence gathering activities for or on behalf of a foreign power, which activities involve or may involve a violation of the criminal statutes of the United States." The Senate Intelligence Committee concluded that this "may involve" standard was necessary "to investigate adequately in cases such as those where Federal agents have witnessed 'meets' or 'drops' between a hostile foreign intelligence officer and a citizen who might have access to highly classified or similarly sensitive information; information is being passed, but the Federal agents have been unable to determine precisely what information is being transmitted. Such lack of knowledge would of course disable the Government from establishing that a crime was involved or what specific crime was being committed."[22]

Thus, by implication, the FBI could conduct a full counterintelligence investigation of an American if there were reasonable suspicion that he was a conscious member of a hostile foreign intelligence network, and it could seek approval for electronic surveillance if there were probable cause that the American's activities involved clandestine transmission of information to a hostile intelligence service.

In addition to the problems of identifying the assignment of currently active agents, another issue is raised by so-called "sleepers" who are not currently engaged in intelligence activities. Sleeper agents are those not immediately used by a hostile intelligence service, but instructed to await an assignment at some future time. In these cases, an investigation based on contacts with a hostile intelligence service might not uncover any signs of current clandestine intelligence activity.

The Church committee recommendations would preclude a continuing investigation (even a low-level preliminary investigation) in such cases. They require reasonable suspicion that an American "will *soon* engage in hostile foreign intelligence activity." In most cases the Church committee standard is appropriate, in order to keep the FBI from long-term monitoring of the lawful activities of Americans merely because they have not renounced political beliefs or associations that might have led to their initial clandestine contacts with hostile intelligence agents.

Nevertheless, in unusual cases where the evidence of recruitment is strong, a continuing investigation using less intensive means is justified to keep track of the person's whereabouts and employment. For instance, if the FBI has a reliable informant who reports that a hostile intelligence service considers someone to be a sleeper, then the grounds for continuing investigation would be much stronger than information simply that the person had a suspicious contact with an intelligence officer.

The threat of sleepers also justifies different standards for the retention of counterintelligence investigative files for future access. While domestic security case files should be purged or sealed within a reasonably short time, counterintelligence files should be accessible for a much longer period, so that they are available for name checks under the federal employee security program.

Employee Security Requirements

The employee security program performs a vital counterintelligence function, even though many of its features are outdated and lack clearly defined objectives. The Church committee endorsed Attorney General Levi's position that the program should not be used as the basis for conducting any FBI investigations beyond background investigations of federal employees or employees of federal contractors. The committee also saw a need to reexamine the standards of Executive Order 10450, which governs the program, so as to "modify criteria based on political beliefs and associations unrelated to suitability for employment," and to "make those criteria consistent with judicial decisions regarding privacy of political association."[23]

Any revision should sharply distinguish between the counterintelligence objectives of an employee *security* program and the broader purposes of assessing *suitability* for employment. Suitability inquiries belong in the hands of the Civil Service Commission or the employing agency, and should not involve access to FBI files on closed cases. Dissemination of information from the FBI's files through name checks greatly magnifies the adverse impact of the Bureau's initial investigations on individual privacy. In fiscal year 1974, for example, the FBI received more than 367,000 requests for name checks on prospective federal employees. The Bureau disseminates data from its files in response to these requests without making any recommendations and without any evaluation (except for a statement on the reliability of the source), partly because it is not equipped to judge the differing suitability requirements of the employing agencies. On the other hand, personnel officers and other executives in the employing agencies are not always prepared to evaluate the implications of the information supplied by the FBI.[24]

Therefore, except for a small number of sensitive positions (presidential appointees and certain jobs involving access to classified information), the Bureau's closed files should not be used as a source of suitability data. The costs to the privacy of hundreds of thousands of Americans holding ordinary government jobs outweigh the possible benefits.

By contrast, the FBI has significant experience with the counterintelligence aspects of federal employment decisions. It has an appreciation of the tactics of hostile foreign intelligence services, and the implications of these activities for the employment of persons in jobs having access to sensitive information. In this area, the Bureau should draw conclusions and make recommendations on the basis of both its background investigations and any data already in its files. If it avoids doing so and seeks to pass responsibility on to the employing agency, the government sacrifices an important counterintelligence resource. Evaluation of the significance of various kinds of information depends less on the requirements of the particular sensitive job than on the characteristics of long-term hostile intelligence operations. Counterintelligence investigations and the employee security program should be two sides of the same coin; they must complement each other if the United States is to counter hostile foreign intelligence activities effectively.

As long as the FBI's role in federal employment decisions is confined to jobs involving access to sensitive information, it need not affect the privacy of the vast majority of government workers. By assigning to the Bureau a duty to assess only the counterintelligence aspects of employment decisions, the employing agency would still retain the final decision and sole authority to evaluate suitability factors not directly related to hostile intelligence activities.

Preventive Techniques

When the Justice Department issued its report on the FBI's COINTELPRO operations in 1974, it stated that such activities were "continuing today" in connection with the Bureau's "counterintelligence efforts against hostile foreign intelligence services."[25] The department committee, chaired by Assistant Attorney General Henry Petersen, which studied COINTELPRO for Attorney General Saxbe, made "a sharp distinction between FBI activities in the area of foreign counterintelligence and those in the domestic field." Its proposed restrictions against "disruptive action" applied only to the FBI's "investigative responsibilities involving domestic based organizations."[26] The FBI itself has stated that its counterintelligence duties include not only detecting hostile activities by foreign intelligence services, but also combatting such activities and neutralizing them. These operations also extend to terrorist activities "by persons acting in behalf of foreign powers, groups, or movements."[27]

Therefore, it must be recognized that the Justice Department has claimed authority for FBI foreign counterintelligence activities that may depart from conventional law enforcement procedures. To some extent, this authority was ratified by Executive Order 11905, which directed the FBI to use "lawful counterintelligence operations" both to detect and to *prevent* "unlawful activities by or on behalf of foreign powers." Executive Order 12036 simply changed "prevent" to "protect."[28] The central question is whether preventive or protective measures going beyond conventional techniques may be lawful for foreign counterintelligence purposes.

Federal court decisions on electronic surveillance have allowed departures from ordinary criminal procedures for collecting foreign counterintelligence information, but these legal standards address only the use of surveillance techniques that normally require a judicial warrant. Legal standards for the use of preventive measures are not necessarily the same as those for intelligence collection techniques. Certain activities can be less harmful to constitutionally protected interests than the search and surveillance methods covered by the Fourth Amendment, while other types of actions are much more harmful to those interests.

Reliance of FBI officials on the specific approval of the Attorney General or the President, and even on clear legislative authority, would not be enough to justify some actions. This must be so in any system of free government under law, except in the most extreme emergency. The standard should, at the very least, be one of fundamental fairness under the due process clause of the Fifth Amendment, which protects every individual—citizen, alien visitor, or foreign official. For instance, the Rockefeller Commission reported that a foreign defector was held for years "in solitary confinement under extremely spartan living conditions," and that another defector was "physically abused." Under any standard of fundamental fairness, the commission was correct in its conclusion that "such treatment by an agency of the United States is unlawful."[29]

On the other hand, if actions are significantly less harmful to constitutionally protected interests than Fourth Amendment search or surveillance, Congress or the President might lawfully delegate discretion in their use to the FBI, although such delegation should be accompanied by precise standards and internal reporting procedures. Those standards should permit actions directed only against foreigners who are officers of a hostile intelligence service.

What, then, are the permissible kinds of preventive actions against hostile foreign intelligence officers, under authority delegated by the President or by Congress? Among the techniques the FBI used under the COINTELPRO rubric were "anonymous mailings for the purpose of disrupting activities of a suspected agent of a foreign intelligence service."[30] In addition, the Church committee described other accepted features of counterespionage work. One is deception, described as "an attempt to give the enemy a false impression about something, causing him to take action contrary to his own interests." Hence, double agents are recruited to "serve both as collectors of positive intelligence and channels for deception." Another method for disruption of the enemy service is provocation, which amounts essentially to "harassment of the opposition, such as publishing the names of his agents."[31]

Like the lawful protective measures that may be a part of domestic security law enforcement—such as deterrent interviewing, or disarming weapons and explosives, or having informants discourage violence—these counterintelligence operations are designed to restrict the illegal activities of the person under investigation; they are a means to the same end as prosecution, where the latter would be either impractical or counterproductive.

Justification of these measures is based not only on the magnitude of the hostile intelligence threat and the sophistication of foreign intelligence services (which may not hesitate to use even more aggressive methods), but also on the limited usefulness of criminal prosecution as a counterespionage weapon. Prosecution risks exposing U.S. counterespionage practices and secret information, and, in the case of foreigners who are legal agents in the United States under diplomatic cover, expulsion allows substitutes to be sent in their place, and risks retaliation against U.S. officials abroad. The Church committee observed, "since foreign agents are replaceable, it may be a better defense not to expel them from the country or otherwise halt their activities, but rather to maintain a constant watch on their operations."[32]

Any authorization for using preventive techniques, beyond just watching the agents, should be strictly confined to the most serious foreign espionage threats. This has not been the case in the past. The Petersen committee reported that the FBI's targets included "foreign Communist organizations and individuals connected with them."[33] A later report disclosed that "a foreign nationality group in the United States" was targeted.[34] These activities came perilously close to, if they did not in fact cross, the line between counterintelligence and covert political action. The FBI has no business taking or facilitating covert action operations in the United States. Even if the CIA may do so abroad in extraordinary circumstances, for the Bureau to become involved inevitably risks contaminating the American political process, and damaging public confidence in the FBI.

Foreign "Subversion" Investigations

The criminal investigation in the late 1970s of South Korean KCIA influence on members of Congress showed that federal criminal laws could serve as the basis for investigating certain kinds of "foreign subversion," such as bribery or blackmail. In addition, the Foreign Agents Registration Act of 1938 applies where a concealed agent-principal relationship exists and the agent is engaged in propaganda or other specified political activities in behalf of a foreign government. There should be substantial evidence of an agent-principal relationship for the Justice Department to approve an investigation under the Registration Act. These criminal investigations differ from FBI counterintelligence investigations, which are conducted primarily not to gather evidence for federal prosecutions, but to find out as much as possible about what a hostile intelligence service is doing and to ensure a minimum of damage.

In the past, FBI intelligence investigations went far beyond the direct influence of foreign intelligence services; they encompassed indirect foreign influence exercised through such "subversive" groups as the Communist party. For example, the GAO found that one of the reasons that the FBI investigated members of "subversive" groups was its concern that they might "at some future time, gain responsible positions not only in Government but also in industry and education."[35]

The origins of this policy go back to the 1930s. When President Roosevelt instructed Director Hoover to investigate "subversive activities" in 1936, he did so largely on the basis of Hoover's report that "activities have recently occurred with[in] Governmental service inspired by Communists, particularly in some of the Departments and in the National Labor Relations Board." Hoover also warned that Communists "planned to get control of" the West Coast longshoremen's union, the United Mine Workers, and the Newspaper Guild, and that "the Communist Internationale in Moscow had recently issued instructions for all Communists to vote for President Roosevelt and against Governor Landon" in the forthcoming election. According to Hoover's memorandum of their meeting, Roosevelt asked the FBI to gather intelligence on such Communist and Fascist "activities as may affect the economic and political life of the country as a whole."[36]

Through the succeeding decades, the FBI continued to report to high Executive Branch officials on Communist influence on the economic and political life of the country. It told the Kennedy White House in 1961 that Communists had attempted to take advantage of racial disturbances in the South, and had endeavored to bring pressure to bear on government officials through the press, labor unions, and student groups. At that time, the Bureau was investigating "two hundred known or suspected Communist front and Communist-infiltrated organizations." In 1965, it reported to President Johnson on the Communist party's attempts to encourage domestic dissent by "a crescendo of criticism aimed at negating every effort of the United States to prevent Vietnam from being engulfed by Communist aggressors." Director Hoover's reports discussing Communist influence also provided the White House with a considerable amount of extraneous information about domestic politics, including lobbying activities in support of civil rights legislation and the political activities of senators and congressmen.[37]

The FBI investigations of Communist influence consistently overemphasized the role of Communists in domestic protest and dissent, especially during the 1960s. According to the Church committee, the Bureau "exaggerated the strength of the Communist Party and its influence over the civil rights and anti-Vietnam War movement." An examination of the FBI's confidential reports and testimony by a former head of the Intelligence Division supported this conclusion. The committee found it "impossible to measure the full effect of this distorted perception at the very highest policymaking level."[38]

In the late 1960s, FBI attention shifted away from the Communist party to the possibility of foreign influence over the New Left and black militants; White House pressures brought the CIA into the picture. Together, the FBI and the CIA began looking for signs that foreign governments were providing financial support or guidance for antiwar protest activities. Neither of the two agencies uncovered significant evidence of foreign control over domestic dissent. A former head of the FBI Intelligence Division told the Church committee that foreign financial support for the antiwar movement was unnecessary because the "credit card revolutionaries" had ample resources of their own. Leaders of the peace movement did attend international conferences held under Communist auspices, but the only significant result was agreement on the timing of demonstrations to coincide with protests abroad.[39]

In retrospect, the Church committee found that the scope of FBI-CIA investigations to discover foreign influence continually broadened, because no thought was given "to terminating the program in the face of negative findings." Only by demonstrating that they "had investigated *all* antiwar persons and *all* contacts between them and any foreign person could CIA [and the FBI] 'prove the negative' that none were under foreign domination."[40] The Rockefeller Commission, appointed by President Ford to investigate the CIA's role in these investigations, arrived at the same conclusion.[41]

The Church committee and the Rockefeller Commission disagreed on their recommendations for the future. The Rockefeller Commission still saw a need for intelligence about foreign-directed "subversive activities"; it concluded that the CIA's "mission of gathering intelligence abroad as to foreign influence on domestic dissident activities was proper," so long as the information "directly related to the question of the existence of foreign connections." By clear implication, the commission supported a similar mission for the FBI to collect information "on domestic dissident activities in order to assess fairly whether the activities had foreign connections."[42]

By contrast, the Church committee proposed moving decisively away from the foreign subversion concept. It recognized that there are hostile foreign intelligence efforts "to influence the U.S. policymaking structure" or to develop "agents of influence" in American politics, but the committee believed that although there is "a compelling need to investigate *all* the activities of hostile foreign intelligence services, including their efforts to recruit 'agents of influence,' " these investigations should focus on "the foreign agents themselves." Therefore, the committee suggested that FBI counterintelligence investigations "should be confined solely to learning more about the overall mission of the hostile service and the particular assignments of its officers." It found "no compelling reason for intensive investigations of U.S. officials (or private citizens) simply because they are targets of foreign 'influence.' "[43]

The Senate Judiciary Committee report on the Foreign Intelligence Surveillance Act of 1978 pointed out the dangers of such investigations to First Amendment interests. It excluded from the meaning of "clandestine intelligence activity" any activity involving "the lawful exercise of first amendment rights of speech, petition, assembly, and association." The report specifically excluded "activities, even though not public and conducted for a foreign power, [that] involve *lawful* acts such as lobbying or the use of confidential contacts to influence public officials, directly or indirectly, through the dissemination of information." The report declared, "individuals exercising their right to lobby public officials or to engage in political dissent from official policy may well be in contact with representatives of foreign governments and groups when the issues concern foreign affairs or international economic matters. They must continue to be free to communicate about such issues and to obtain information or exchange views with representatives of foreign governments or with foreign groups, free from any fear that such contact might trigger the Government's power to conduct electronic surveillance."[44]

These concerns led the House and Senate Intelligence Committees to adopt a higher standard in the 1978 act for surveillance of Americans suspected of covert political action for a foreign power. Citizens and resident aliens who engage in "clandestine intelligence-*gathering* activities" could be targeted for surveillance if their activities "may involve" a federal crime. But the standard for "*other* clandestine intelligence activities," such as political influence, required that the person act "pursuant to the direction of an intelligence service or network of a foreign power" and that the activities "involve or are about to involve" a federal crime. The committees also added a provision stating that a United States person (including citizens, resident aliens, and domestic groups) could not "be considered a foreign power or an agent of a foreign power solely upon the basis of activities protected by the first amendment to the Constitution of the United States."[45]

Strict limits to prevent interference with First Amendment freedoms can be reconciled with counterintelligence requirements, so long as Americans are not labeled as foreign agents because they have political contacts with foreigners and share common goals. An American citizen's activities are the proper object of FBI counterintelligence inquiry when there is reason to suspect recruitment by a hostile foreign intelligence service; but only if the American is engaged in spying or clearly illegal conduct like bribery, rather than just "influence," should the investigation use intrusive techniques to monitor his or her activities.

In every case, the dissemination of personally identifiable information about the activities of Americans who are not believed to be foreign agents should be kept to a minimum and prohibited whenever possible, unless this incidentally acquired information is needed to investigate spying or imminent criminal acts.

These restrictions are especially important for intelligence about foreign government officials in the United States who have contacts with Americans. Information about their attempts to influence our domestic affairs may be valuable foreign intelligence information, contributing to an overall assessment of the country's intentions. However, the Church committee found this type of information to be a long-standing source of political abuse.[46]

Clearly, if there is to be more latitude for FBI intelligence collection activities aimed at foreign officials, there must be restrictions upon disseminating incidentally acquired information about Americans. Intelligence about foreign influence on domestic affairs can be a potent weapon in the arsenal of an administration seeking either to discredit its opponents or to achieve its constructive goals. Today, with international economic affairs at the forefront of national policy, the desire of the Executive Branch for intelligence about the foreign contacts of American businessmen and corporations may match or exceed past concern about domestic protest and dissent.

Foreign efforts to influence American executives of multinational corporations and domestic firms with extensive international dealings are commonplace, not merely speculative. Some would argue that there is a sharp difference between economic intelligence and intelligence about the legislative process or political dissent. Nevertheless, the risks to privacy and to the integrity of the FBI are great whenever its resources are used, even indirectly, to supply information about the lawful activities of Americans who are not foreign agents engaged in spying or other illegal conduct on behalf of a foreign intelligence service. There must be safeguards to ensure that "foreign intelligence information" pertains solely to "the capabilities, intentions and activities of foreign powers, organizations or persons."[47]

The need to detect hostile foreign intelligence operations in the United States requires a careful analysis of the specific interests to be served by FBI counterintelligence investigations. Criminal law standards do not help very much in setting priorities. The fundamental principles of the rule of law can govern FBI operations if they are regulated by standards that the Attorney General and the Congress (through oversight or legislation) adopt after weighing the competing interests and reducing unnecessary intrusions into the privacy of American citizens.

Summary

This chapter has attempted to suggest how limits can be placed on a wide range of FBI foreign counterintelligence activities. In this field more than any other, responsible officials have an obligation to examine FBI operations with the greatest care. Questions about counterintelligence activities often cannot be answered in public without revealing valuable information that would allow an adversary to take evasive action. The absence of the normal scrutiny of the press and of interested groups and citizens is a substantial handicap in the policy-making process. Neither the secrecy of Bureau operations nor the magnitude of the claimed threats should stand in the way of setting clear standards for the FBI, monitoring its performance, and ensuring that counterintelligence operations adhere to the rule of law. Specifically, those standards should be based on the following principles:

1. Investigative standards should not be the same as standards for prosecution, because of the vagueness of existing statutes and the need to give priority to the hostile intelligence activities of certain foreign powers.

2. Preliminary counterintelligence investigations of Americans should be limited to persons who may be engaged in hostile foreign intelligence activities, or who may be sources of information or assistance in current counterintelligence investigations. Indications of hostile intelligence activity include clandestine contacts with known intelligence agents. Potential sources include persons who may be the unwitting targets of recruitment efforts or intelligence operations of foreign agents.

3. Full investigations of Americans should be conducted only when there is reasonable suspicion that a person is a conscious member of a hostile foreign intelligence network. His or her activities need not involve a specific criminal act, so long as they are covert and under the direction of a hostile intelligence service. Where the activities are not current or imminent, as in the case of a suspected sleeper, the FBI should not use intrusive investigative techniques.

4. The FBI should play a role in the counterintelligence aspects of federal employment decisions for jobs involving ac-

cess to valuable information. However, its closed files should not be used to assess the general suitability of persons for federal employment, except for a small number of sensitive positions.

5. The FBI should have the authority, subject to clear standards and reporting procedures, to take preventive counterintelligence measures against foreign nationals who are officers of a hostile intelligence service. Such measures should not violate standards of fundamental fairness, but they may include deception and disruption for the purpose of frustrating illegal intelligence efforts.

6. The FBI should not investigate Americans suspected of involvement in foreign "subversion," such as foreign efforts to influence domestic political or economic activities, unless the investigation is based on specific criminal acts for the purpose of prosecution. The demonstrated abuses of "subversion" investigations outweigh the need to monitor possible covert foreign intervention, unless the subject of the investigation is a foreign intelligence officer.

7. To reduce the risks of political abuse, the dissemination of personally identifiable information about Americans not believed to be foreign intelligence agents should be strictly limited, unless the information is needed to investigate spying or imminent criminal acts.

CHAPTER VII

Professional Responsibility

IN 1975 Attorney General Levi established an Office of Professional Responsibility within the Justice Department "to ensure that Departmental employees continue to perform their duties in accord with the professional standards expected of the Nation's principal law enforcement agency."[1] The following year, Director Kelley created the Bureau's own Office of Professional Responsibility in a reorganized FBI Planning and Inspection Division. The new FBI office reported directly to the FBI director and was assigned to handle "complaints and investigations of an internal nature."[2] In addition, Executive Orders 11905 and 12036 authorized an Intelligence Oversight Board, appointed by the President, to monitor activities of the U.S. intelligence community "that raise questions of legality or propriety." FBI foreign counterintelligence operations fell under its jurisdiction.

The Special ABA Committee on Federal Law Enforcement Agencies praised the formation of the Attorney General's Office of Professional Responsibility as "an important first step in providing a place to which individuals, in government or out, may go with complaints or allegations of abuse or misuse of power by employees of the Department of Justice."[3] The Church committee proposed that the office be recognized in statute, and have wider jurisdiction.[4] A coalition of civil liberties groups recommended a presidentially appointed Inspector General for the FBI, who would have statutory authority to investigate complaints and conduct field audits, with unrestricted access to Bureau information.[5]

This internal executive machinery for uncovering improper conduct and looking into allegations of misconduct is vital for public confidence in the FBI.

Procedures such as these are essential to ensure that improper conduct will be fully investigated and remedied with fairness to the parties concerned. They should make top executives aware of problems in the organization that may require changes in policy or personnel. They can also be a check against improper actions authorized by high officials, although this task may be difficult to perform without some form of congressional involvement.

Although, traditionally, the FBI has viewed its inspection process mainly as a management tool, providing the FBI Director with information about the efficiency of Bureau operations, Director Kelley gave greater emphasis to the function of investigating departures from legal and professional standards, in response to serious allegations of past misconduct. Under those arrangements, however, there was a danger that the professional responsibility function would lose its effectiveness once the latest furor had subsided.

The duties, respectively, of the Attorney General's Office of Professional Responsibility, the FBI Director's Professional Responsibility Office, the President's Intelligence Oversight Board, and the Justice Department's prosecuting divisions were not clearly defined. Among the questions that arose were: (1) who should conduct investigations of alleged misconduct? (2) what procedures should be followed for handling citizen complaints, including grievances reflected in requests under the Privacy and Freedom of Information Acts? (3) how could improper behavior be uncovered and grievances redressed where there was no citizen complaint? (4) how could top policymakers use information about patterns of misconduct to institute reforms that would prevent their recurrence?

The Attorney General's Office of Professional Responsibility

The appointment of a Counsel for Professional Responsibility, reporting directly to the Attorney General and the Deputy Attorney General, and heading an office devoted to maintaining high professional standards in the Justice Department, had two rationales. First, the Attorney General needed a unit for investigating alleged misconduct, separate from the internal inspection units of the various bureaus and the prosecutors in the Criminal and Civil Rights Divisions. Second, a unit was needed to oversee the investigations undertaken by these other divisions, and to evaluate the department's policies for dealing with unprofessional conduct.

These two roles sometimes conflict. Oversight is best performed by a small unit: the larger an office gets, the more likely it is to have its own bureaucratic interests to defend. A smaller office focuses accountability and encourages candid judgments. On the other hand, investigating serious allegations of misconduct requires a staff of field investigators and attorneys. But the more people involved and the more complex the inquiry, the more likely the staff is to have a special interest in the outcome. It becomes less capable of detached and objective assessments, and this evaluation responsibility is passed back to the Attorney General.

Attorney General Levi, Attorney General Bell, and the first Counsel for Professional Responsibility, Michael E. Shaheen, reconciled these conflicts by delegating investigative duties to special task forces. Whenever the counsel decided that substantial allegations of misconduct deserved an independent investigation, he recommended that the Attorney General form a task force composed of investigators and attorneys from other parts of the department. Thus, his office remained small (three or four attorneys) and concentrated on oversight rather than detailed supervision of investigations.

During its first year, the Office of Professional Responsibility devoted most of its time to the Justice Department's investigative agencies. A precedent for the office, and one of the reasons for establishing it, was an inquiry into alleged improprieties in the Drug Enforcement Administration (DEA). But the office's most visible work involved the FBI, including the formation of task forces to investigate alleged administrative corruption, to review the FBI's activities with respect to Dr. Martin Luther King, Jr., and to notify victims of COINTELPRO abuses. The composition of the task forces varied. The group examining FBI conduct regarding Dr. King was composed exclusively of department attorneys and research analysts under the direction of an experienced criminal lawyer. The panel to notify COINTELPRO victims included a representative of the FBI's Legal Counsel Division as well as department attorneys.

The task force on FBI administrative corruption needed greater investigative resources, and Attorney General Levi wanted to give the FBI an opportunity to show it was capable of impartial inquiry into its own activities. This was particularly important because an initial investigation of corruption charges by the FBI Inspection Division was found to be inadequate. Consequently, the corruption task force included both department attorneys and FBI agents carefully selected by Director Kelley for their records as field investigators. A senior attorney from the Criminal Division was placed in charge; and the FBI team was headed by the assistant director for the Identification Division. The FBI agents were instructed to report solely through the task force and not through regular FBI channels.

Later, the Civil Rights Division's investigation of FBI break-ins attempted to follow this model. FBI agents were initially assigned to a task force, headed by a senior attorney in the Civil Rights Division. Assistant Attorney General Stanley Pottinger announced that the task force findings were "not disseminated to other persons in the FBI." Director Kelley endorsed this special arrangement because he and Pottinger wanted "to see that the thoroughness and objectivity of this inquiry is preserved both in fact and appearance."[6] However, department attorneys eventually conducted most of the criminal investigation. Upon its completion in 1978, Director William H. Webster formed a Bureau task force to investigate disciplinary matters assigned to him by Attorney General Bell.

Several aspects of the work of the Office of Professional Responsibility deserve special attention. The first is the Attorney General's use of disclosure as an instrument of dealing with certain types of alleged misconduct, including the COINTELPRO notification program and publication of findings regarding the FBI and Dr. King. Second are the relationships between the office and its institutional competitors, the Justice Department's prosecuting divisions. Third, questions arise about the propriety of having an investigative agency like the FBI investigate itself. Fourth is the duty of the office to advise the Attorney General on the broader policy implications of the patterns of misconduct it may discover.

The Disclosure of Misconduct

Ordinarily, when an agency of government infringes upon the rights of a citizen, the citizen, aware of the wrongdoing, can complain to Congress, to the courts, or to some other body. But covert intelligence activities like the FBI's COINTELPRO operations were designed to achieve their objectives under the cover of secrecy. When the existence and broad dimensions of COINTELPRO were made public by Attorney General Saxbe and later, in more detail, by the Church committee, the question arose of how the victims might be informed of the wrongful acts committed against them.

Attorney General Levi decided that the Justice Department had an obligation "to notify individuals who may have been personally harmed by improper COINTELPRO activities that they were the subjects to such activities, and to advise them that they may seek further information from the Department if they wish." He set up a three-member review committee for this purpose within the Office of Professional Responsibility, and he formed an advisory group composed of two Assistant Attorneys General and the FBI legal counsel "to pass upon those instances where the committee is uncertain as to whether notification should be given, and otherwise advise the committee as requested." The standard for notification was whether the action was "improper" and there was reason to believe it "caused actual harm" to an individual. The committee was to resolve doubtful cases "in favor of notification," but it was not to notify "individuals who are known to be aware that they were the subjects of COINTELPRO activities."[7]

At the end of six months, the counsel for the Office of Professional Responsibility reported that notification had been approved in 225 cases. The procedure was to give a notification letter to the U.S. Marshals Service for delivery; in some instances delivery was delayed or impossible because of incorrect addresses. Out of at least 36 deliveries by November 1, 1976, 24 individuals had requested further information from their files.[8]

The COINTELPRO notification program had certain limitations. Because it was confined to instances where the targets were individuals who actually may have been harmed, it excluded the great majority of the more than two thousand actions directed against groups and designed to deter people from associating with those groups. Nevertheless, it marked what the Church committee staff report on COINTELPRO described as "an important step toward redressing the wrongs done."[9] It established a precedent for future disclosures to the victims wherever internal executive inquiries may uncover FBI activities that could harm people because of improper actions taken in secret.

The other instance of disclosure, publication of the report of the Task Force to Review the FBI Martin Luther King, Jr., Security and Assassination Investigations, was intended for Congress and the general public. The task force's main assignment was to determine whether the FBI investigation of the King assassination was thorough and honest, and whether there was any new evidence in the case. It also considered whether there should be legal or disciplinary action against past or present FBI officials in cases where the Bureau had attempted to discredit and harass Dr. King. Attorney General Levi rejected a proposal by Assistant Attorney General Pottinger, whose Civil Rights Division attorneys had made a preliminary review of these matters, that an advisory committee of distinguished citizens be formed to work with the task force.[10]

The report detailed the results of the FBI investigation of the King assassination. It found no fault with the technical competence of the investigation, nor did it uncover any new evidence bearing on the crime. Its findings on FBI efforts to intimidate Dr. King confirmed the report of the Church committee, and added some other facts: the FBI conducted a series of illegal surreptitious entries to photograph information about Dr. King; and the Bureau took no action when it learned that one of its informants in the Southern Christian Leadership Conference had embezzled SCLC funds.[11] The statute of limitations precluded criminal prosecution of Bureau personnel for possible criminal harassment of Dr. King, and disciplinary measures against current FBI agents who had been involved were rejected because "they did not make command decisions and merely followed orders," in circumstances where the standard of proper behavior was "undefined."[12] As noted later, the task force made important recommendations for changes in Justice Department policy to prevent some of the improprieties it discovered.

Attorney General Griffin Bell's decision to publish the task force report, with its full summary of the FBI investigation of the King assassination, is a more questionable precedent for the future than the COINTELPRO notification program. Bell had little choice in the matter, because his predecessor had already sent copies to certain congressional committee chairmen, and some of the findings had appeared in the press. Nevertheless, as a general practice, internal Justice Department reviews of the adequacy of FBI criminal investigations should not be made public in such detail. Disclosure of this kind is likely to invade the privacy of citizens about whom information is gathered, or who may cooperate with federal investigators. The COINTELPRO notification program was designed to give citizens whose rights may have been violated the option of making public any information about FBI behavior in their cases. But the attractiveness of disclosure as a remedy for misconduct should not lead officials to compound the harm by ill-considered publicity affecting individual privacy.

Institutional Rivals

The Office of Professional Responsibility has a precarious position in the Justice Department because it threatens the prerogatives of the prosecuting divisions, who may view the task forces as usurping their jurisdiction. Some may argue that the office was a short-run expedient established in response to Watergate, and that, in the long term, all that is needed is an Attorney General committed to the highest standards of professional conduct. If that commitment is clear to the bureau heads and the prosecuting divisions, they can do the job themselves without a separate office looking over their shoulders. An Attorney General may find this argument persuasive because of his power to select his subordinates. He may want to give the bureau heads and Assistant Attorneys General full responsibility, and they may demand it for themselves. Should this happen, the Office of Professional Responsibility might as well be abolished. A counsel who does not have a special relationship of trust with the Attorney General cannot expect to survive the departmental infighting.

In addition to the Civil Rights Division, another serious competitor for the job of the Office of Professional Responsibility is the Public Integrity Section in the Criminal Division. Created in January 1976, the Public Integrity Section handled all federal offenses involving official corruption. When he announced its establishment, Attorney General Levi stated that it would "be available to assist the Office of Professional Responsibility in monitoring responsibilities with the various Inspectors General who now inquire into possible corruption in the Federal executive departments."[13]

The Public Integrity Section may be an appropriate body to

supervise criminal prosecutions of corruption within the Justice Department, but its jurisdiction does not encompass all criminal misconduct by department personnel, because of the Civil Rights Division's authority to prosecute violations of the civil rights statutes. Aside from this divided jurisdiction, there are at least four reasons why these prosecutorial bodies should not supplant the Office of Professional Responsibility.

First, the office can inquire into improprieties and ethical lapses which fall short of a criminal offense. For example, after an inquiry by the Office of Professional Responsibility, the Deputy Attorney General rendered an official apology to a newspaper publisher for remarks an FBI official made about him in 1976. Departmental integrity means more than not violating the law; it involves adherence to the highest professional standards.

Second, the office has oversight duties with respect to department practices going beyond specific cases. The counsel is required to submit an annual or semiannual report "reviewing and evaluating the activities of internal inspection units within the Department," and he may recommend "changes in policies and procedures that become evident during the course of his inquiries."[14]

Third, the office is a check against prosecutorial as well as investigative misconduct. The ABA Committee stressed the need "to assure that decisions in criminal cases are made professionally and untainted by politics." Although it proposed a mechanism for triggering appointment of a temporary Special Prosecutor, its overall view was that the Attorney General has the primary duty to prevent conflicts of interest and the misuse of law enforcement power.[15] Both the Office of Professional Responsibility and the Public Integrity Section are needed, and they complement each other. Former Assistant Attorney General Richard Thornburgh admitted that federal efforts to prosecute official corruption are "controversial," and that concern is often voiced that these prosecutions are "undertaken for partisan interests by a particular administration to embarrass its political opponents."[16] Thus it is all the more important to have a separate office where complaints can be addressed, and where both prosecutorial and investigative practices can be measured with a degree of detachment.

Finally, without a Counsel for Professional Responsibility, there is likely to be greater intradepartmental conflict between the FBI and other components of the Justice Department on the one hand, and the prosecuting divisions on the other. The counsel can play a vital role in easing the burdens on the Attorney General and the Deputy Attorney General, who would otherwise have to devote much more of their time and influence to mediating these conflicts. Therefore, the Attorney General should resist the argument that an Office of Professional Responsibility is unnecessary, and he should view the counsel as one of his principal aides.

Other department executives must perceive a close relationship of mutual trust between the Attorney General and the Counsel for Professional Responsibility, but this relationship should allow the counsel sufficient independence to inquire, if necessary, into the conduct of the Attorney General himself. During the investigation of corruption in the FBI, for instance, one major question was whether Director Kelley had improperly received personal benefits from his subordinates. A similar question was then raised about security arrangements made for Attorney General Levi and gifts he had received. The charter for the Office of Professional Responsibility recognized the possibility that the Attorney General may be the subject of its inquiry by allowing the counsel to report to either the Deputy Attorney General or the Solicitor General where referral to the Attorney General "would be inappropriate."

Investigating the Investigators

The department-wide Office of Professional Responsibility did not replace the FBI's own internal inspection unit, nor did it foreclose the use of FBI agents to investigate other Bureau personnel. The Attorney General's regulations provided that the heads of the bureaus and divisions of the department had "primary responsibility for assuring the maintenance of the highest standards of professional responsibility" by their employees; investigations of alleged unprofessional conduct were normally to be conducted by the bureau head or internal inspection unit. The one major exception was where "the conduct appears to constitute a violation of law." In that case responsibility for investigation normally rested with "the head of the investigative or prosecutive agency having jurisdiction over the subject matter involved."[17]

Apart from these normal procedures, the Counsel for Professional Responsibility could recommend "any special arrangements that appear warranted," including assignment of the matter to a task force or to another individual or organization. Both the counsel and the various internal inspection units might initially receive allegations of improper conduct, and the counsel had to be informed by other department officials of any "major investigations that they are conducting" in this area. In other words, the Office of Professional Responsibility need not be advised of *every* instance of alleged FBI misconduct. The regulations brought the office into the process only where it received the original charge or where a "major investigation" was contemplated. The office might subsequently learn of minor internal FBI inquiries in the course of its preparation of annual or semiannual reports "reviewing and evaluating the activities of internal inspection units within the Department."[18]

This framework was consistent with the concept of the Office of Professional Responsibility as primarily an oversight body, rather than a full-scale inspector general for the department. But there were several problems with viewing the office solely in terms of oversight. The lack of any permanent investigative resources limited the office's ability to handle certain cases. More generally, there may be inherent conflicts of interest in having FBI agents investigate other Bureau employees, either through the FBI's own Professional Responsibility Office or as part of task forces under the direction of prosecuting attorneys.

The first problem has a simple remedy. While task forces work for major investigations, they do not help the office in the early stages of a case. Having no investigative staff, the counsel cannot easily make preliminary inquiries into allegations, and must rely almost exclusively on the various inspection units. The attorneys in the office can ask pointed questions and propose lines of inquiry, but they lack the resources to verify independently the reports they receive. Therefore, a small number of experienced investigators might be assigned to the office. If their work is confined to preliminary investigations, they could strengthen the detachment and objectivity of the office. Major investigations and most routine inquiries may still belong outside the office, in task forces or internal inspection units. But effective and credible oversight depends on the ability of the counsel to make inquiries in certain cases, so that task forces are not hastily or unnecessarily created.

The general problem of having FBI agents investigate their colleagues cannot be fully resolved. One of the most perceptive observers of American police, Yale sociologist Albert J. Reiss, Jr., has discussed the issue of "accountability of police bureaucracies to external units" in the following terms:

> Any system whereby complaints are lodged with the guardian of the offending parties inevitably coerces many clients against their interest. Many citizens are reluctant to complain against agencies that hold power over them and could respond with punitive action. . . . In short, the agency is not a disinterested party. Since in our system of justice, justice depends upon "disinterest" in the outcome of the case, it seems obvious that no citizen should be required to make and pursue his complaint through an agency that has a stake in the outcome.[19]

On the other hand, Reiss found "grounds for questioning whether a disinterested agency should also process complaints and decide about sanctions," because it would run counter to the goals of law enforcement professionalism. He stressed that "professionals will cooperate more fully with internal investigations" and that "change is more likely to result if the administration and staff of an organization are involved." Despite the risks of agency manipulation and citizen mistrust, Reiss concluded,

> The interests of professionals and administrators in the agency to make decisions about the quality of work and to sanction deviation from professional standards must be balanced with citizen concern for proper practice and a right to hold practitioners accountable to them. One way to balance these interests is to lodge the responsibility for investigation of the complaint, sanctioning of any offending parties, and adjudication in the agency against which the complaint is lodged, while an independent agency would receive all complaints, transmit them to the appropriate agency, and be given a full transcript and report of decisions as to the outcome of investigations.[20]

This is essentially the arrangement adopted by the Office of Professional Responsibility, except for the most serious cases, where the task forces were formed. Even then, some task forces included FBI agents on special assignment to work under the supervision of department attorneys.

The assignment of FBI agents to the task force on administrative corruption in the Bureau raised fewer questions than did their initial role in the Civil Rights Division's task force on break-ins. In the first case, the investigation focused on past and present headquarters administrators and not field agents. But there are greater difficulties where FBI agents on a task force must investigate their colleagues at the field office level. When they are reassigned, it may affect their career prospects and the way they are treated by their fellow agents. However, the FBI is a sufficiently large organization that agents could be found to investigate their peers without bias, especially where the inquiry is directed by department attorneys.

The problem may be more of appearance than of reality of conflict of interest, but it is no less a problem. The appearance of impartiality is essential for public confidence in the result, especially where an investigation leads to a conclusion that an allegation of misconduct is unfounded.

One possible solution is to rely on agents from other investigative agencies, but this remedy probably would engender interagency conflicts and resentments. Another answer is to transform the Attorney General's Office of Professional Responsibility into a chief inspection unit with a large permanent investigative staff, in effect replacing the FBI Professional Responsibility Office. This, too, has serious drawbacks, because it would undermine the sense of responsibility within the Bureau for uncovering improper behavior in its own ranks.

Indeed, there is no perfect solution to the problem of investigating the investigators. During the 1960s the idea of a civilian police review board was widely proposed as an answer to police misconduct. But almost every attempt to institute some form of independent body foundered, either because of lack of public support in cities such as New York, where the voters defeated Mayor John Lindsay's civilian police review board plan, or because reform-minded police administrators developed more workable alternatives within their departments. Temporary investigations of police corruption by prosecuting attorneys do occur, but continuing inquiries into corruption are usually the responsibility of internal police units.

For example, as New York City Police Commissioner, Patrick V. Murphy emphasized the need for structural and psychological change within the department to combat corruption. This meant creating a strong internal affairs bureau trained to recognize patterns of possible impropriety, and to take measures to uncover it. It also meant acting decisively to hold every manager and supervisor answerable for misconduct by his subordinates. Murphy has written, "the most effective way to instill integrity in a department is through leadership and a system of accountability at all levels which motivates officers to be honest, i.e., encourages honest officers to do their duties as they deem right and discourages other officers from resorting to corruption for fear of being caught. The critical factor . . . is the controls within the department and the climate which prevails."[21]

Those who would set up a permanent outside inspection unit to investigate misconduct within the FBI may end up defeating their own ends. It could discourage the internal reforms needed to make the maintenance of high professional standards a vital element of the Bureau's own operations.

In the past, the FBI has been viewed as a monolith, both by outsiders and by FBI officials themselves.[22] This misconception has blinded reformers and FBI old-liners alike to the diversity inside the Bureau. With scores of offices and divisions spread across the country, in communities with widely differing law enforcement problems, the FBI has room for many kinds of people.[23] Some may succumb to pressures to disregard professional and legal standards; most prize those standards as the key to the FBI's reputation and their own self-esteem. For more than thirty years the FBI has gathered evidence for federal prosecutions of local law enforcement officers for corruption, police brutality, and other crimes. Now it is learning that it must sometimes investigate its own personnel. Every law enforcement agency has to face this problem; and there is no simple answer. But to act as if the FBI is incapable of investigating itself would be as unrealistic as to rely on the traditional assumption that the FBI does not need investigating.

Professional Responsibility and Reform Measures

The mandate of the Counsel for Professional Responsibility was not just to review specific cases of misconduct, but also to "submit recommendations to the Attorney General and the Deputy Attorney General for changes in policies or procedures that become evident during the course of his inquiries." A good example is the recommendations made by the task force on FBI activities regarding Dr. Martin Luther King, Jr.

On the assassination investigation, the task force found that the FBI's "lack of coordination and cooperation" with the Attorney General and federal prosecutors was "highly improper," although it attributed some of the blame to the failure of department executives to "insist on their prerogatives." It made three recommendations:

> 1. The progress of such sensitive cases as the King murder investigation and the development of legally sufficient evidence to sustain prosecution are properly the ultimate responsibility of the Division of the Department having supervision of the kind of criminal prosecution involved. The Division head should delineate what progress reports he wishes. The Bureau should not be permitted to manipulate its submission of reports to serve its purposes, such as the protection of its public relations efforts, or the prevention of the responsible Division of the Department from causing the Bureau to pursue a line of inquiry which the Bureau does not approve. The Attorney General and his Assistants are the officers most accountable to the electorate and they, not the police agency, must maintain effective supervision.
>
> 2. As a corollary of our espousal of tighter Department authority over the FBI, we recommend that the Bureau's public relations activities and press relations be controlled by the Attorney General's Office of Public Information. Clear directives to prevent the development of personality cults around particular Bureau Directors and officials should be drawn. Bureau press releases should be cleared through the Office of Public Information.

3. The task force recommends that in sensitive cases no criminal action be instituted by the Bureau without the closest coordination and consultation with the supervising Division of the Department. This supervision by the Department should be as tight as the control and consultation the Bureau had with its Field Offices as exhibited in our review of the assassination investigation.[24]

The task force also noted that the absence of black FBI agents and officials in the 1960s "undoubtedly had the effect of limiting not only the outlook and understanding of the problems of race relations, but also must have hindered the ability of investigators to communicate fully with blacks during the murder investigation."

With respect to FBI harassment of Dr. King in its domestic security investigation of his activities, the task force stressed the importance of departmental and congressional oversight as safeguards against "the potential for abuse by the individual occupying the office of Director of the FBI which has been amply demonstrated by our investigation." It proposed, "both the Office of Professional Responsibility and the Senate Select Committee on Intelligence should be expressly designated in their respective enabling regulations and resolutions to be a place to which Bureau subordinates may complain, confidentially and with impunity, of orders which they believe to threaten a violation of the civil rights and liberties of citizens and inhabitants of the United States." It suggested that "unauthorized malicious dissemination of investigative data from FBI files" should be made a felony, rather than just a misdemeanor.

New regulations were also proposed to make "clear that it is improper (but not criminal) for the Bureau to by-pass the Attorney General and deal directly with the White House." Finally, the task force recommended "that the FBI have no authority to engage in COINTELPRO type activities which involve affirmative punitive action following Star Chamber decisions with respect to citizens or inhabitants."[25]

These recommendations show the kinds of reforms that may grow out of internal investigations. They demonstrate how, as Professor Reiss contends, an independent review body can use "knowledge gained from complaints to change practices of agencies." As important as the findings in a particular investigation, he suggests, are the overall data on cases investigated by the agency's own internal inspection unit. The independent body should receive full reports on every complaint and inquiry and on any actions taken by the agency. "Acquisition of the input and output information is one of the most powerful monitoring devices available over an organization. Whoever has that information has the potentiality to assess where the problems of the organizations lie. The power of aggregative information is considerable. The patterns exhibited in matters surrounding the complaint and its processing provide useful information for changing the organization." By looking for "the structural sources of misconduct," the review body may "propose changes in the bureaucracy to forestall future occurrences." Reiss argues strongly against the exclusive emphasis by "legalists, journalists, and moral entrepreneurs" on trying to change an organization by making "a case" for sanctions against particular officials for a specific offense. "That may be good public relations; it is hardly good organizational practice. All too often it leaves the agency and its practices unchanged."[26]

These observations underscore the importance of the Office of Professional Responsibility as one of the Attorney General's main instruments for holding the FBI accountable and for evaluating its practices and the need for reforms. The key, of course, is the independence and stature of an Attorney General who is committed to the highest standards for the administration of justice.

The FBI Professional Responsibility Office

Traditionally, the FBI Inspection Division served as a management tool for the FBI director. The Bureau's annual reports and other publications seldom, if ever, discussed the citizen complaint function. The Church committee found that the inspection process was, in the past, tied more to FBI policy than to any independent standards of legality or propriety. The Inspection Division's "responsibility was simply to ensure that FBI policy, as defined by J. Edgar Hoover, was effectively implemented and not to question the propriety of the policy." Consequently, it "became an active participant in some of the most questionable FBI programs," such as annually reviewing "all memoranda relating to illegal break-ins prior to their destruction under the 'Do Not File' procedure."[27] One of Director Kelley's major objectives in establishing a new FBI Professional Responsibility Office in 1976 was to rebuild public confidence in the Bureau's internal inspection process.

Broadly considered, this process covers more than the investigation of specific complaints. It includes measures taken to inform agents of the standards governing their conduct, and procedures for agents to report improprieties that might not otherwise come to light through citizen complaints. Moreover, the process is not simply a matter of formal rules and procedural arrangements. Its effectiveness depends on leadership, administrative style, choice of the right people, and intangible rewards. There must be substantial incentives to make the process work, and corresponding costs if it does not.

Nor can the inspection process be viewed in isolation from the FBI as a whole and its relationship with its environment. The extent to which the Bureau is centralized or decentralized, autonomous or closely supervised, monolithic or open to diverse ideas, admired or feared by segments of the public, all affect the handling of possible misconduct. With respect to domestic intelligence operations, the most significant factor is whether influential voices call upon the FBI to protect the nation's security without regard for the means it may use.

Assuming that the FBI Professional Responsibility Office will continue to have the primary duty to handle complaints about misconduct by Bureau personnel falling short of criminal offenses, under the oversight of the Attorney General's Office of Professional Responsibility, the following analysis presents a framework for evaluating the inspection process. It points out the types of questions that responsible authorities should ask in conducting such an evaluation, and it suggests answers to some of them.

Citizen Complaints

The normal source of information about possible improper conduct by a law enforcement agency is citizen complaint. In the past the FBI Manual provision on disciplinary matters stated: "Any investigation necessary to develop complete essential facts regarding any allegation against Bureau employees must be instituted promptly, and every logical lead which will establish the true facts should bc completely run out unless such action would embarrass the Bureau or might prejudice pending investigations or prosecutions in which event the Bureau headquarters will weigh the facts, along with the recommendation of the division head." When this provision was criticized by members of the Church committee, the FBI advised that the "phraseology" regarding embarrassment to the Bureau would be removed from the manual, although its intent was only to place headquarters "on notice" so that it "could direct the inquiry, if necessary."[28] Besides this brief provision, additional information is needed for a full understanding of how the FBI handles complaints.

First, what forms do public complaints generally take? Where are they addressed? To what extent are they generalized or specific? If allegations are made publicly and reported in the press, but not submitted formally to the FBI or the Justice Department, are they still investigated? Are allegations made in the course of criminal or civil litigation investigated?

Second, what factors determine the level and scope of the inquiry? Are all allegations, whether received in the field or at headquarters, referred to the Professional Responsibility Office? In what circumstances is the inquiry conducted by field office personnel only? By the Professional Responsibility Office only? Or by the field office initially and the Professional Responsibility Office later? What considerations enter decisions not to institute an immediate inquiry where such action "might prejudice pending investigations or prosecutions"? In what ways do other factors, similar to the concern for "embarrassment," result in postponement or limitation of an inquiry?

Third, what actions are taken regarding a complainant or an alleged victim of improper conduct? In what circumstances is the person interviewed? Is the person given a written explanation of the disposition of the complaint? Is he informed that the Attorney General's Office of Professional Responsibility is also authorized to receive allegations of impropriety?

Finally, the purpose and effect of a request for information under the Freedom of Information Act or the Privacy Act may also be to discover possible misconduct. For example, the FBI's response to a request from a prominent political figure disclosed that an apparently improper name check had been conducted on him for a White House aide in 1969.[29] Is the unit that handles Freedom of Information and Privacy Act requests instructed to be alert for information or allegations concerning misconduct, either in requests or in materials reviewed in response to requests? Are such allegations or information referred to the Professional Responsibility Office or elsewhere for any further inquiry and disposition beyond the required review of FBI files?

In this respect, a significant aspect of the process is public knowledge of the channels for complaining about misconduct. Freedom of Information Act and Privacy Act procedures have been widely publicized. But neither the FBI nor the Justice Department has issued for easy reference a description of how they handle complaints. Consequently, persons who have grievances (real or imagined) against the FBI have no clear place to turn. This may be one reason for the high volume of Freedom of Information and Privacy Act requests, because that procedure may be seen as the only route available for redress. Similarly, the absence of a well-known complaint channel may encourage resort to civil suit, either with private counsel or with the aid of groups like the ACLU.

Knowledge of complaint procedures may not be enough to instill confidence in their fairness and objectivity, but it is an essential step toward that goal. At the very least, it can help establish stable expectations for those who have complaints. The ability of the Justice Department and the FBI to publish a useful description of complaint procedures depends, of course, on whether appropriate procedures are in effect. If the Bureau normally responds to each complaint promptly and explains the disposition clearly, there is every reason to publicize these practices.

Complaint data may also indicate certain common questions of public concern which could also be addressed in a publication on complaint procedures. For example, if they reveal substantial apprehension about political surveillance, the material might explain how FBI domestic security investigations are conducted under public guidelines issued by the Attorney General and reviewed by congressional oversight committees. Heretofore, the FBI has attempted to answer such questions in ways that, to be generous, can be characterized as public relations efforts. There have been few attempts to address clearly and directly the issues most troubling to persons who may fear they have been treated improperly by the Bureau.

Information from within the Bureau

In addition to citizen complaints, another source of information about misconduct is FBI personnel themselves. Under Attorney General Levi, FBI officials and agents were ordered to report "any requests made of the Bureau or practices within the Bureau which may be improper or which present the appearance of impropriety."[30] Similarly, Executive Orders 11905 and 12036 directed the Inspectors General and General Counsels within the intelligence community to "formulate practices and procedures to discover and report to the Intelligence Oversight Board activities that raise questions of legality or propriety." All senior officials of the intelligence community had to "provide for a strong and independent organization for identification and inspection of, and reporting on, unauthorized activity."[31]

Hence, FBI regulations are needed to instruct its personnel where to report possible misconduct. While in most instances this should be the Bureau's Professional Responsibility Office, or the Attorney General's Office of Professional Responsibility, alternative channels must be available, along with firm guarantees against reprisal. An FBI agent who suspects that an improper order originated with high FBI executives, or even with the Attorney General or the President, should know that there is recourse outside the Executive Branch, particularly to the congressional committees having specific authority to oversee FBI activities. FBI regulations should specify that an employee who communicates such information in confidence to an appropriate legislative body does not violate secrecy obligations to the Bureau.

A strong internal directive to report illegal conduct poses problems under the Fifth Amendment. The coercive effect of such a directive could make it impossible to use incriminating evidence in a criminal trial. If agents are told that they must come forward with information about their activity that raises questions of illegality, or else risk administrative sanctions, their privilege against self-incrimination may be violated. However, the alternative is not to make the reporting requirement purely voluntary, but rather to divorce the inspection process from administrative decisions on personnel matters until after final disposition of the case. In short, there may be ways to induce FBI personnel to report their possible illegal conduct without having the effect of immunizing them from prosecution.

As important as encouraging agents to come forward with information are the affirmative steps taken by the FBI's Professional Responsibility Office to discover unreported misconduct. This can be done at least two ways. The first is through the audit type of inspections conducted regularly by the other components of the Planning and Inspection Division. A second technique involves special professional responsibility inquiries, which neither respond to specific allegations nor serve other management purposes.

When Director Kelley formed the Planning and Inspection Division in 1976, he set in motion significant changes in the FBI's traditional audit-inspection practices. Under the system established by J. Edgar Hoover, the Inspection Division conducted routine annual audit-inspections of every FBI field office and headquarters division. According to the Inspector's Manual, the general purpose was to "report on whether or not applicable laws, regulations, and instructions have been complied with; resources are used in an economical and efficient manner; desired results and objectives are being achieved effectively." The Inspection Division staff examined the files on the most important pending cases, as well as "any other files deemed necessary to resolve any apparent weaknesses." It reviewed all files pending more than one year to determine if there had been "unwarranted, harmful, or extensive delays in investigation or reporting."[32]

However, as a practical matter, audit-inspections often were a matter of bargaining between the inspectors and the Special Agent in Charge. One informed observer found that "the content of the inspection report often seems to depend upon the status of the particular SAC, and in some instances it is the product of delicate negotiation, almost collusion, between him and the chief of the inspection team."[33]

Director Kelley abandoned this system, with the aim of "radically changing the orientation and thrust of our inspections to meet the needs of the FBI today." Kelley said that the new inspection program would "be tailored to the individual management needs of each division and field office and to the law enforcement priorities of each." Inspections would no longer "be annual or automatic or at all routine," but instead "designed to address specific problems." In line with the department-wide Management By Objectives system, the Bureau was "moving from fiscal auditing into program auditing—appraising results." Finally, the new policies emphasized "pre-evaluation—review of field office activities as reflected in our Headquarters records—so that we can preserve our major personnel inspection resources for on-site problem solving."[34]

This type of inspection can play a constructive role in decisionmaking and in monitoring compliance with new policies. For example, inspections during 1974 and 1975 discovered that field offices had "not adhered to the 90-day time limitation or to restrictions on sources" in preliminary domestic security investigations. These findings (reinforced by a similar report on the General Accounting Office) led to changes in FBI policy "to insure adequate Headquarters control over the duration and scope of preliminary inquiries."[35]

However, unless improprieties are recorded in the files, they are not likely to be uncovered by conventional audit procedures. Additional steps should be considered to discover misconduct other than minor rules infractions reflected in the files. Assessments of the most frequent types of improprieties discovered should be made in order to anticipate where future problems may arise. There may be indirect signs of likely sources of misconduct, growing out of the pressure on particular offices or agents to get results in certain kinds of cases. As far as intelligence operations are concerned, these special professional responsibility inspections might focus on those few offices that handle the heaviest workload.

Most important, inspections and the complaint procedures discussed earlier must not take responsibility away from Bureau officials in the regular chain of command. The Special Agents in Charge of the field offices and their principal deputies should have a continuing duty to monitor the conduct of the agents in their offices, to investigate complaints of unprofessional behavior, and to recommend reasonable and equitable sanctions. According to Director Kelley, the aim of the Professional Responsibility Office was "not centralizing disciplinary responsibility," but instead providing a "formalized function to insure that *every* FBI member assumes a primary responsibility to prevent corruption, and to maintain professional discipline."[36]

Disposition of Cases

Although the source of allegations or information about misconduct may be citizen complaints, internal reporting, or inspections, in every instance there must be a disposition of the case at some level. Where the disposition is made at the field office level, it should be reported to the Professional Responsibility Office. This office, like the Attorney General's Office of Professional Responsibility, should do more than just ensure that the disposition in each case is justified by the facts. In order to plan for the use of special inspection techniques and to recognize broader policy implications, the office should compile overall information on the way cases are being handled. Hence, the following categories are suggested as the basis for collecting aggregate data:

Source of Allegation or Information

Citizen complaint, press report, civil or criminal litigation, Freedom of Information or Privacy Act request, FBI field agents, FBI supervisory officials, audit-inspections, professional responsibility inspections.

Nature of Inquiry

No inquiry, inquiry postponed, inquiry by field office only, inquiry by Professional Responsibility Office only, inquiry by field office initially and Professional Responsibility Office later.

Scope of Inquiry

Agent explanation only, interview of complainant or victim, file review, multiple interviews with agents, complainant, victim, and witnesses.

Type of Misconduct Alleged

Unauthorized use of investigative or surveillance techniques, harassment or intimidation, improper use of force, dissemination of improper or inaccurate information, mishandling of financial matters, violation of other standards of professional conduct, law violation under federal or state statute.

Disposition

Pending, letter of censure, personnel reassignment, other administrative sanctions, referral for outside investigation or criminal prosecution, allegations unfounded.

Reporting

Complainant or victim advised of disposition; notification to FBI director, FBI legal counsel, Office of Professional Responsibility, Attorney General and Deputy Attorney General, Intelligence Oversight Board.

Even more than the Attorney General's Office of Professional Responsibility, the FBI office should examine cases of possible misconduct carefully to see if they disclose practices or policies that encourage impropriety. Assuming, for instance, that there are cases where agents have inadequately investigated illegal wiretapping by local police, there may be reason to consider assigning such investigations in the future to agents who have not dealt regularly with the police department involved. Another example might be the discovery, through professional responsibility inspections, that FBI agents in a number of cases reported information as coming from informants or confidential sources when, in fact, it came from an unauthorized technique such as surreptitious entry, theft, mail opening, or an electronic listening device. Apart from the question of whether these are violations, one larger policy result might be to adopt new procedures to verify the identity of sources, if previous policies allowed sources to be so thoroughly disguised that agents had an open opportunity to use information obtained from unauthorized techniques.

The duty to analyze the policy implications arising from the professional responsibility process is shared with the Attorney General's Office of Professional Responsibility and, in the foreign intelligence field, with the President's Intelligence Oversight Board. Nevertheless, because the FBI itself has the greatest expertise in the organization and management of investigative operations, it should take the lead in developing measures that reinforce adherence to high professional standards. Above all, this requires addressing problems as the agents in the field see them, not just as FBI headquarters officials view them. No system of rules, inquiries, and sanctions will work adequately unless the members of the organization share the values that system represents

In his study of police behavior in western Europe and America, George Berkley concluded,

> Legal limitations on police power, while important, will not in themselves ensure that restriction on police activities is sufficient to be compatible with a democracy. Often the problem is not so much a question of adhering to restrictions in letter, but adhering to them in spirit. Thus, for a police force to operate in a manner fully consistent with democratic principles,

> its members must not only work under legal restrictions but must genuinely accept them. Realizing the problems which police power presents to a democratic society, democratic policemen will tolerate the limitation placed upon them.[37]

The significance of the FBI's adherence to constitutional principles and the highest standards of professional responsibility goes far beyond the Bureau itself. For decades it has been a model for other law enforcement agencies, at home and abroad. Its achievements often have been the result of the willingness of citizens to cooperate with it in solving crimes; that cooperation has been based, in turn, on the FBI's unquestioned reputation for integrity and respect for the law in its own operations. Thus, restoration of confidence in those qualities is vital if the FBI is to combat effectively the crimes under its jurisdiction and to encourage other agencies to maintain their own standards.

CHAPTER VIII

Conclusion

THE five years after J. Edgar Hoover's death was a time of transition for the FBI. An Acting Director resigned in disgrace, disclosures of secret activities tarnished the Bureau's reputation, and it lost its traditional immunity from outside supervision. In this atmosphere, Director Clarence M. Kelley found it difficult to restore confidence in the FBI's intelligence programs. He and Attorneys General Edward H. Levi and Griffin Bell attempted to overcome the legacy of the past by discarding outdated practices and building safeguards against them. One after another, new allegations of misconduct kept national attention focused on what had happened years earlier. They made it all but impossible to improve public understanding of how and why properly controlled intelligence investigations can serve the national interest without infringing individual rights.

The principal conclusion of this study is that FBI intelligence programs *are* necessary to achieve compelling law enforcement and national security objectives, and that they *can* do so without violating constitutional rights. Before 1976, it would have been much harder to reach this conclusion. Neither the FBI nor any Attorney General had yet demonstrated the ability to strike a reasonable balance between intelligence demands and individual liberties. FBI resources were being devoted to unproductive investigations of "subversives," which contributed little to protecting the American people against tangible threats. Even where FBI intelligence operations were aimed at real dangers of foreign espionage, no Attorney General had devised adequate legal procedures to distinguish between proper and improper foreign counterintelligence measures. The same unexamined theory of presidential power that permitted the FBI to conduct warrantless electronic surveillance of foreign spies allowed wiretaps on journalists and critics of the President.

The reforms in FBI intelligence policies placed greater emphasis on investigating violent activities and hostile foreign intelligence operations in this country. The FBI and the Justice Department worked more closely to develop guidelines for exercising investigative discretion, procedures for review by the Attorney General, and machinery to investigate allegations of misconduct. The underlying principles were sound, even if some details could be improved. The domestic security guidelines brought an end to forty years of FBI investigations of lawful political activities, conducted in the name of protecting the government from remote, speculative threats of revolutionary overthrow. Legislation was enacted to bring foreign counterintelligence electronic surveillance techniques within the rule of law. The Justice Department investigated alleged FBI abuses vigorously, and FBI agents themselves participated in some of the most controversial inquiries. These were not cosmetic reforms, but significant changes in the FBI's priorities and in its relationships with the Justice Department.

The most important reform was the abandonment of intelligence investigations based on federal sedition laws such as the Smith Act and the seditious conspiracy statutes. The sedition concept almost inevitably had allowed the FBI to look into the political activities of anyone who proclaimed a revolutionary ideology. But the domestic security guidelines stressed, instead, the need for specific and articulable facts indicating that someone is engaged in activities that involve or will involve serious violence.

Breaking with the long and unhappy tradition of sedition investigations has great symbolic significance for the nation, both at home and abroad. It announces that the government of the United States is fully confident of its security against threats to its existence from its own citizens. It expresses our belief in the essential strength of our form of government. Yet it does not deprive law enforcement agencies of the authority to conduct more carefully defined intelligence investigations. The American people can support efforts to apprehend terrorists and prevent serious violence without acting as if domestic unrest is ever likely to shake the foundations of constitutional government in the United States.

Nevertheless, intelligence investigations of terrorism still are susceptible to abuse. Covert surveillance through informants and undercover agents is an intrusion into individual privacy that requires a substantial law enforcement justification. It also creates incentives to seek covert means for preventing violence, instead of such open measures as arrest and prosecution. Law enforcement agencies fear that arrests will blow the cover of informants, possibly endangering their safety and sacrificing their warnings of violence in the future. The pressures toward covert repression are even greater when prosecutions fail because there is not enough evidence for conviction, or because probative evidence is excluded under stringent constitutional rules. A study for the National Commission on the Causes and Prevention of Violence in 1969 warned of the inherent risks of relying on covert operations. Their control "is at best difficult"; and the task is "even more complex and troublesome" because surveillance agencies often "develop the conception that to collect information is not enough." These are agencies tempted to "begin spreading distrust" within the organizations under investigation.[1]

The way to counter these pressures within the FBI is not to abolish covert infiltration or blindly to prohibit preventive action. Using undercover informants to gather intelligence about groups with a proven record of violence—and taking lawful protective measures to disarm explosives or persuade individuals to respect the law—are fully justified law enforcement activities. They do not mean adopting the inexcusable features of COINTELPRO, or the efforts to discredit Dr. Martin Luther King, Jr. With proper standards and outside supervision, they need not raise the specter of a return to the unsavory tactics of the past.

The scope of intelligence investigations also poses continuing dangers to the rights of Americans. The fact that the FBI is in the business of monitoring American citizens who participate in politically motivated groups linked to violence makes domestic security investigations a constant threat to our system of political liberty. This is why the threshold for investigations must be high enough to ensure that only groups with a record of violence are targeted for domestic security *intelligence* gathering.

The law of conspiracy and the civil rights statutes may permit criminal investigations before a specific act of terrorist violence is committed. But investigations based on such broad criminal law standards should be confined to looking for specific information to corroborate the initial signs of preparation to commit terrorist acts. Their purpose should not be to compile information on a group's political activities, membership, finances, ideology, publications, or internal dynamics, unless the facts relate directly to plans for violence. This distinction between extensive intelligence investigations and criminal investigations limited to establishing the elements of a crime is a crucial safeguard for the privacy of political beliefs and associations protected by the First Amendment.

Foreign counterintelligence investigations raise different issues. The techniques are similar, but the risks to constitutional rights take other forms. Preventive measures, rather than arrest and prosecution, are the norm because prosecution is impractical in most espionage cases. Protecting secret or sensitive information is more important than bringing prosecutions, which often add to the disclosures and may reveal sources and methods needed for other investigations. To provide adequate protection against hostile foreign intelligence activities, the FBI must investigate in circumstances where individuals are not suspected of committing a specific criminal act. If the individual is a potential source who might be able to assist the FBI in monitoring a foreign intelligence agent's activities, a limited inquiry is justified. Where specific and articulable facts indicate that an American is a member of a hostile foreign intelligence network, there are grounds for a continuing investigation regardless of whether or not all the elements of an Espionage Act offense can be established. These standards are closely tied to the criminal law—but they take account of the needs of the investigative process, which differ from the requirements for prosecution.

An important safeguard against unjustified FBI foreign counterintelligence investigations is the focus on hostile intelligence services and their agents. The foreign agents registration laws extend far more broadly. Just as the law of conspiracy and the civil rights statutes might sustain sweeping domestic security intelligence investigations where no specific act of terrorist violence has been committed, the foreign agents registration laws could allow the FBI to intrude into a wide range of political contacts between Americans and foreigners. The answer is the same in both areas: distinguishing intelligence investigations from criminal investigations designed to prepare cases for prosecution. Where an investigation does not involve hostile intelligence-gathering activities, the FBI should conduct foreign agents registration investigations only to gather evidence for prosecution.

Foreign counterintelligence investigations of political influence—as opposed to spying—by foreign intelligence services are potentially the most controversial of all FBI responsibilities. Unless there is clear evidence of a criminal violation, the FBI should target its counterintelligence investigations only against foreign intelligence officers and against Americans engaged in spying. An assignment to investigate Americans because they are engaged in or subjects of foreign political influence would give the FBI too broad a mandate to monitor the political process.

These conclusions indicate why Attorney General Harlan Fiske Stone's policy of confining the FBI to the investigation of federal crimes is only the beginning of the search for intelligence standards. Investigating crimes is a complex and difficult enterprise. The criminal laws supply minimum criteria for prosecutions, arrests, and searches or surveillance based on Fourth Amendment principles of probable cause. However, criminal statutes are less helpful when it comes to the exercise of investigative discretion generally. All crimes are not equally serious nor equally worthy of investigative attention.

FBI domestic security and foreign counterintelligence investigations differ from ordinary investigations because of the nature of the crimes involved. Although in each instance broad criminal statutes are on the books, they do not tell the FBI when to investigate for the purpose of preparing a case for prosecution and when to conduct an intelligence investigation. Both are investigations of crimes; but an intelligence investigation gathers more information than evidence of specific criminal acts, and continues regardless of decisions made to prosecute or not to prosecute particular criminal cases. The seriousness of terrorism and foreign espionage, the clandestine and conspiratorial character of the criminal activity, the need for a body of information to use in investigating future crimes, and the importance of protecting the targets of such crimes justify these differences in investigative policy.

Whatever the standards for intelligence investigations, they are no more effective than the means adopted to enforce them. The Attorney General and the FBI director share this responsibility. In an organization as large as the FBI, maintaining high standards requires positive incentives as well as punitive sanctions. Internal inspection procedures should reinforce, not replace or impair, the accountability of each supervisory official. FBI officials must be held responsible when standards are violated, and they should be rewarded for responding promptly to complaints or internal signs of misconduct. Above all, the Attorney General and the FBI Director need to realize how the pressures on FBI agents may lead to improper actions, so they can adopt policies to prevent departures from professional standards.

There are powerful incentives for FBI agents to act without proper authority if they believe secrecy can be assured. Their desires to prevent violent crimes and to secure information that may supply vital leads in a major investigation are understandable, but the result may be actions in violation of constitutional rights. This is particularly true for intelligence operations which, like certain police patrol practices, are immune from normal judicial scrutiny because their objective is frequently not criminal prosecution.[2] Therefore, it is vital to eliminate those practices that allow for "plausible denial" and permit agents or officials to escape accountability.

Finally, the best deterrent against official lawlessness is for FBI agents and all other law enforcement officials to recognize that their adherence to the law is part of a compact between citizens and their government. If the government breaks that compact, it weakens the ties that bind the members of a free society together. The FBI should never forget the warning expressed fifty years ago by Supreme Court Justice Louis D. Brandeis:

> Decency, security and liberty alike demand that government officials shall be subjected to the same rules of conduct that are commands to the citizen. In a government of laws, existence of the government will be imperiled if it fails to observe the law scrupulously. Our Government is the potent, the omnipresent teacher. For good or ill, it teaches the whole people by its example. Crime is contagious. If the Government becomes a lawbreaker, it breeds contempt for the law; it invites every man to become a law unto himself; it invites anarchy. To declare that in the administration of the criminal law the end justifies the means—to declare that the Government may commit crimes in order to secure the conviction of a private criminal—would bring terrible retribution.[3]

APPENDIX I

Attorney General's Guidelines for FBI Domestic Security Investigations, March 10, 1976

I. Bases of Investigation

A. Domestic security investigations are conducted, when authorized under Section II(C), II(F), or II(I), to ascertain information on the activities of individuals, or the activities of groups, which involve or will involve the use of force or violence and which involve or will involve the violation of federal law, for the purpose of:

1. overthrowing the government of the United States or the government of a State;
2. substantially interfering, in the United States, with the activities of a foreign government or its authorized representatives;
3. substantially impairing for the purpose of influencing U.S. government policies or decisions:
   (a) the functioning of the government of the United States;
   (b) the functioning of the government of a State; or
   (c) interstate commerce.
4. depriving persons of their civil rights under the Constitution, laws, or treaties of the United States.

II. Initiation and Scope of Investigations

A. Domestic security investigations are conducted at three levels—preliminary investigations, limited investigations, and full investigations—differing in scope and in investigative techniques which may be used.

B. All investigations undertaken through these guidelines

shall be designed and conducted so as not to limit the full exercise of rights protected by the Constitution and laws of the United States.

Preliminary Investigations

C. Preliminary investigations may be undertaken on the basis of allegations or other information that an individual or a group may be engaged in activities which involve or will involve the use of force or violence and which involve or will involve the violation of federal law for one or more of the purposes enumerated in IA(1)-IA(4). These investigations shall be confined to determining whether there is a factual basis for opening a full investigation.

D. Information gathered by the FBI during preliminary investigations shall be pertinent to verifying or refuting the allegations or information concerning activities described in paragraph IA.

E. FBI field offices may, on their own initiative, undertake preliminary investigations limited to:
   1. examination of FBI indices and files;
   2. examination of public records and other public sources of information;
   3. examination of federal, state, and local records;
   4. inquiry of existing sources of information and use of previously established informants; and
   5. physical surveillance and interviews of persons not mentioned in E(1)-E(4) for the limited purpose of identifying the subject of an investigation.

Limited Investigations

F. A limited investigation must be authorized in writing by a Special Agent in Charge or FBI Headquarters when the techniques listed in paragraph E are inadequate to determine if there is a factual basis for a full investigation. In addition to the techniques set forth in E(1)-E(4) the following techniques also may be used in a limited investigation:
   1. physical surveillance for purposes other than identifying the subject of the investigation;
   2. interviews of persons not mentioned in E(1)-E(4) for purposes other than identifying the subject of the investigation, but only when authorized by the Special Agent

in Charge after full consideration of such factors as the seriousness of the allegation, the need for the interview, and the consequences of using the technique. When there is a question whether an interview should be undertaken, the Special Agent in Charge shall seek approval of FBI Headquarters.

G. Techniques such as recruitment or placement of informants in groups, "mail covers," or electronic surveillance, may not be used as part of a preliminary or a limited investigation.

H. All preliminary and limited investigations shall be closed within 90 days of the date upon which the preliminary investigation was initiated. However, FBI Headquarters may authorize in writing extension of a preliminary or limited investigation for periods of not more than 90 days when facts or information obtained in the original period justify such an extension. The authorization shall include a statement of the circumstances justifying the extension.

Full Investigation

I. Full investigations must be authorized by FBI Headquarters. They may only be authorized on the basis of specific and articulable facts giving reason to believe that an individual or a group is or may be engaged in activities which involve the use of force or violence and which involve or will involve the violation of federal law for one or more of the purposes enumerated in IA(1)-IA(4). The following factors must be considered in determining whether a full investigation should be undertaken:

1. the magnitude of the threatened harm;
2. the likelihood it will occur;
3. the immediacy of the threat; and
4. the danger to privacy and free expression posed by a full investigation.

Investigative Techniques

J. Whenever use of the following investigative techniques are permitted by these guidelines, they shall be implemented as limited herein:

1. use of informants to gather information, when approved

by FBI Headquarters, and subject to review at intervals not longer than 180 days; provided,

(a) when persons have been arrested or charged with a crime, and criminal proceedings are still pending, informants shall not be used to gather information concerning that crime from the person(s) charged; and

(b) informants shall not be used to obtain privileged information; and where such information is obtained by an informant on his own initiative no record or use shall be made of the information.

2. "mail covers," pursuant to postal regulations, when approved by the Attorney General or his designee, initially or upon request for extension; and

3. electronic surveillance in accordance with the requirement of Title III of the Omnibus Crime Control and Safe Streets Act of 1968.

Provided that whenever it becomes known that person(s) under surveillance are engaged in privileged conversation (e.g., with attorney), interception equipment shall be immediately shut off and the Justice Department advised as soon as practicable. Where such a conversation is recorded it shall not be transcribed, and a Department attorney shall determine if such conversation is privileged.

NOTE: These techniques have been the subject of strong concern. The committee is not yet satisfied that all sensitive areas have been covered (e.g., inquiries made under "pretext," "trash covers," photographic or other surveillance techniques).

III. Terminating Investigations

A. Preliminary, limited, and full investigations may be terminated at any time by the Attorney General, his designee, or FBI Headquarters.

B. FBI Headquarters shall periodically review the results of full investigations, and at such time as it appears that the standard for a full investigation under II(I) can no longer be satisfied and all logical leads have been exhausted or are not likely to be productive, FBI Headquarters shall terminate the full investigation.

C. The Department of Justice shall review the results of full domestic intelligence investigations at least annually, and shall determine in writing whether continued investigation is warranted. Full investigations shall not continue beyond one year without the written approval of the Department. However, in the absence of such notification the investigation may continue for an additional 30 day period pending response by the Department.

IV. Reporting, Dissemination, and Retention

A. *Reporting*

1. Preliminary investigations which involve a 90-day extension under II(H) and limited investigations under II(F), shall be reported periodically to the Department of Justice. Reports of preliminary and limited investigations shall include the identity of the subject of the investigation, the identity of the person interviewed or the person or place surveilled, and shall indicate which investigations involved a 90-day extension. FBI Headquarters shall maintain, and provide to the Department of Justice upon request, statistics on the number of preliminary investigations instituted by each field office, the number of limited investigations under II(F), the number of preliminary investigations that involved 90-day extensions under II(H), and the number of preliminary or limited investigations that resulted in the opening of a full investigation.
2. Upon opening a full domestic security investigation the FBI shall, within one week, advise the Attorney General or his designee thereof, setting forth the basis for undertaking the investigation.
3. The FBI shall report the progress of full domestic security investigations to the Department of Justice not later than 90 days after the initiation thereof, and the results at the end of each year the investigation continues.
4. Where the identity of the source of information is not disclosed in a domestic security report, an assessment of the reliability of the source shall be provided.

B. *Dissemination*

1. *Other Federal Authorities*

   The FBI may disseminate facts or information obtained during a domestic security investigation to other federal authorities when such information:

   (a) falls within their investigative jurisdiction;

   (b) may assist in preventing the use of force or violence; or

   (c) may be required by statute, interagency agreement approved by the Attorney General, or Presidential directive. All such agreements and directives shall be published in the *Federal Register*.

2. *State and Local Authorities*

   The FBI may disseminate facts or information relative to activities described in paragraph I(B) to state and local law enforcement authorities when such information:

   (a) falls within their investigative jurisdiction;

   (b) may assist in preventing the use of force or violence; or

   (c) may protect the integrity of a law enforcement agency.

3. When information relating to serious crimes not covered by paragraph I(A) is obtained during a domestic security investigation, the FBI shall promptly refer the information to the appropriate lawful authorities if it is within the jurisdiction of state and local agencies.

4. Nothing in these guidelines shall limit the authority of the FBI to inform any individual(s) whose safety or property is directly threatened by planned force or violence, so that they may take appropriate protective safeguards.

5. The FBI shall maintain records, as required by law, of all disseminations made outside the Department of Justice, of information obtained during domestic security investigations.

C. *Retention*

1. The FBI shall, in accordance with a Records Retention Plan approved by the National Archives and Records

Service, within ____ years after closing domestic service investigations, destroy all information obtained during the investigation, as well as all index references thereto, or transfer all information and index references to the National Archives and Records Service.

NOTE: We are not yet certain whether empirical data exists to help define a period of retention for information gathered in preliminary or full investigations. Whatever period is determined should take into account the retention period for other categories of information (e.g., general criminal, organized crime, and background checks); since we have not yet considered these areas we cannot fix a period for retention at this time.

NOTE: It may also be possible to establish a sealing procedure to preserve investigative records for an interim period prior to destruction. After being sealed, access would be permitted only under controlled conditions.

2. Information relating to activities not covered by paragraph I(A) obtained during domestic security investigations, which may be maintained by the FBI under other parts of these guidelines, shall be retained in accordance with such other provisions.
3. The provisions of paragraphs one (1), and two (2) above apply to all domestic security investigations completed after the promulgation of these guidelines, and apply to investigations completed prior to promulgation of these guidelines when use of these files serves to identify them as subject to destruction or transfer to the National Archives and Records Service.
4. When an individual's request pursuant to law for access to FBI records identifies the records as being subject to destruction or transfer under paragraph one (1), the individual shall be furnished all information to which he is entitled prior to destruction or transfer.

APPENDIX II

Attorney General's Guidelines for FBI Reporting on Civil Disorders and Demonstrations Involving a Federal Interest, March 10, 1976

I. Basis for Reports and Investigations

The Federal Bureau of Investigation is responsible for reporting information on civil disturbances or demonstrations in four categories:

A. Investigating
   1. violations of federal criminal law directed explicitly at civil disorders (e.g., 18 U.S.C. 231, 2101); and
   2. violations of federal criminal law of general applicability occurring during civil disorders.

B. Providing information and assistance, upon request of the Secret Service, to aid in carrying out its protective responsibilities under 18 U.S.C. 112, 970, 3056 and P.L. 90-331. NOTE: Under 18 U.S.C. 112 and 3056 the Secret Service is assigned responsibility to provide protection to certain U.S. Government officials and foreign officials and visitors. P.L. 90-331 provides Secret Service protection for candidates for office and authorizes Secret Service to call on any federal agency to assist in this regard. Responsibility for protection of foreign missions is assigned to the Executive Protection Service under the direction of the Secret Service. This accounts for the reference to 18 U.S. C. 970 dealing with damage to foreign missions.

C. Providing information concerning actual or threatened

civil disorders which may require the presence of federal troops to enforce federal law or federal court orders (10 U.S.C. 332, 333) or which may result in a request by State authorities to provide federal troops in order to restore order (10 U.S. C. 331).

NOTE: The statutes cited provide three bases for the use of troops in connection with civil disorders. Section 332 authorizes troops, at Presidential initiative, to enforce federal law and was the basis for the use of troops to protect the mail in the Pullman strike. Section 333 deals with the use of troops to protect civil rights and enforce court orders and was the basis for using troops at Little Rock and Oxford. Section 331 permits the President to send troops at the request of a State when State authorities cannot restore order, e.g., the Detroit Riot.

D. Providing information relating to demonstration activities which are likely to require the federal government to take action to facilitate the activities and provide public health and safety measures with respect to those activities.

NOTE: While there is no specific statutory authority for collection of information in these circumstances, the Second Circuit recognized in *Fifth Avenue Peace Parade Committee* v. *Kelley*, 480 F. 2d 326, cert. denied, 415 U.S. 948, that the federal government has a legitimate need for information concerning demonstrations planned at federal facilities in order to provide services in connection with the demonstration. For example, considerable information was needed in order to fashion an appropriate permit for the November 1971 moratorium march in Washington, D.C.

II. Criminal Offenses

A. Investigation of criminal offenses referred to in paragraph I.A. shall be undertaken in the manner provided for in guidelines relating to criminal investigations generally.

B. Information concerning criminal offenses within the investigative jurisdiction of the FBI which is acquired incidentally in the course of implementing parts III through V, shall be handled in the manner provided for in guidelines relating to the criminal investigations generally.

C. Information concerning criminal offenses within the investigative jurisdiction of another federal agency which is acquired incidentally in the course of implementing parts II through V shall be reported to the agency having jurisdiction.

D. Information concerning serious criminal offenses within the investigative jurisdiction of State or local agencies which is acquired incidentally in the course of implementing parts II through V shall be reported to the appropriate lawful authorities.

NOTE: Using the criteria now applied by NCIC, the reference to serious offenses would exclude such matters as: drunkenness, vagrancy, loitering, disturbing the peace, disorderly conduct, adultery, fornication, and consensual homosexual acts, false fire alarm, non-specific charges of suspicion or investigation, traffic violations, and juvenile delinquency.

E. Information relating to criminal offenses acquired in the course of implementing parts II through V shall be retained and indexed as provided for in guidelines relating to criminal investigations generally.

III. Assisting the Secret Service

A. Information relating to the protective responsibilities of the Secret Service described in Paragraph I.B., which is acquired incidentally by the FBI in the course of carrying out its responsibilities, shall be reported to the Secret Service. The FBI shall not undertake specific investigations for the purpose of assisting the Secret Service in its protective responsibilities without a specific request from the Director of the Secret Service or his designee, made or confirmed in writing.

NOTE: The Department should undertake to review with the Secret Service existing agreements on the dissemination of information from the FBI to the Secret Service. The draft report of the General Accounting Office indicates that very little information reported by the FBI is actually retained by Secret Service.

B. A record shall be made of all information reported to the

Secret Service pursuant to paragraph III.A. and the record shall be retained by the FBI for five years.

NOTE: This is the standard Privacy Act accounting requirement.

C. Information reported to the Secret Service may be retained by the FBI for a period of ____ years.

NOTE: The retention period for this information will be considered in a general review of retention under all the guidelines.

IV. Civil Disorders

A. Information relating to actual or threatened civil disorders acquired by the FBI from public officials or other public sources or in the course of its other investigations, shall be reported to the Department of Justice.

B. The FBI shall not undertake investigations to collect information relating to actual or threatened civil disorders except upon specific request of the Attorney General or his designee. Investigations will be authorized only for a period of 30 days but the authorization may be renewed, in writing, for subsequent periods of 30 days.

C. Information shall be collected and reported pursuant to paragraphs A and B above for the limited purpose of assisting the President in determining whether federal troops are required and determining how a decision to commit troops shall be implemented. The information shall be based on such factors as:

1. The size of the actual or threatened disorder—both in number of people involved or affected and in geographic area;
2. The potential for violence;
3. The potential for expansion of the disorder in light of community conditions and underlying causes of the disorder;
4. The relationship of the actual or threatened disorder to the enforcement of federal laws or court orders and the likelihood that State or local authorities will assist in enforcing those laws or orders;
5. The extent of State or local resources available to handle the disorder.

D. Investigations undertaken, at the request of the Attorney General or his designee, to collect information relating to actual or threatened civil disorders shall be limited to inquiries of:

1. FBI files and indices;
2. Public records and other public sources of information;
3. Federal, state and local records and officials;
4. Established informants or other established sources of information.

Interviews of individuals other than those listed above, and physical or photographic surveillance shall not be undertaken as part of such an investigation except when expressly authorized by the Attorney General or his designee.

E. Information relating to civil disorders, described in paragraph C above, shall be reported to the Department of Justice and may also be reported to federal, state or local officials at the location of the actual or threatened disorder who have a need for the information in order to carry out their official responsibilities in connection with such a disorder.

F. Information acquired or collected pursuant to paragraphs A through D above may be retained by the FBI for a period of ____ years but may not be indexed in a manner which permits retrieval of information by reference to a specific individual unless the individual himself is the subject of an authorized law enforcement investigation.

NOTE: Retention period to be fixed later; indexing limit to be implemented immediately.

V. Public Demonstrations

A. Information relating to demonstration activities which are likely to require the federal government to take action to facilitate the activities and provide public health and safety measures with respect to those activities, which is acquired incidentally by the FBI in the course of carrying out its responsibilities, shall be reported to the Department of Justice.

B. The FBI shall not undertake investigations to collect information with respect to such demonstrations except upon specific request of the Attorney General or his designee.

C. Information collected and reported pursuant to paragraphs A and B above shall be limited to that which is necessary to determine:
   1. The date, time, place and type of activities planned;
   2. The number of persons expected to participate;
   3. The intended mode of transportation to the intended site or sites and the intended routes of travel;
   4. The date of arrival in the vicinity of the intended site and housing plans, if pertinent;
   5. Similar information necessary to provide an adequate federal response to insure public health and safety and the protection of First Amendment rights.

   NOTE: Clause 5 above is intended to encompass such additional facts affecting the federal responsibility as unusual health needs of participants, counter-demonstrations planned which may increase safety needs, or possible inability of participants to arrange return transportation.

D. Investigations undertaken to collect information relating to demonstrations pursuant to paragraph B above shall be limited to determining the information described in paragraph C. Such information shall be collected only by inquiries of:
   1. FBI files and indices,
   2. Public records and other public sources of information,
   3. Federal, state and local records and officials,
   4. Persons involved in the planning of the demonstration, provided that in conducting interviews with such persons the FBI shall initially advise them specifically of the authority to make the inquiry and the limited purpose for which it is made.

E. The FBI shall not undertake to photograph any demonstration or the preparation therefor in carrying out its responsibilities under paragraph V.

F. Information acquired or collected pursuant to paragraphs A through D above may be retained by the FBI for a period of ____ years but may not be indexed in a manner which permits identification of an individual with a particular demonstration or retrieval of information by reference to a specific individual, unless the individual himself is the subject of an authorized law enforcement investigation.

NOTE: Retention period to be fixed later; indexing limit to be implemented immediately.

APPENDIX III

Draft Attorney General's Guidelines for FBI White House Personnel Security and Background Investigations, March 10, 1976

I. Collection of Information

A. *Initiation of Investigation*

1. White House investigations involving file reviews or field investigations conducted by the FBI shall be initiated only to ascertain facts and information relevant to the suitability of persons being considered for Presidential appointment; staff of the Executive Office; clearance for access to classified information; granting clearance for access to or service at the White House or other places under the protection of the U.S. Secret Service in connection with its duties to protect the President and the Vice President of the United States.

2. White House investigations involving file reviews or field investigations shall be initiated as follows:

a. The President of the United States, and the Counsel or Associate Counsel to the President or the Attorney General may initiate investigations directly with the FBI.

b. The Secretary of State and the Director of the National Security Counsel may request the FBI to conduct White House investigations when authorized by formal agreements with the Attorney General. These agreements shall designate by title all persons authorized to request White House inquiries, shall be consistent with the provisions of these guidelines, and are to be published in the Federal Register.

3. Requests for White House investigations involving file reviews shall be made or confirmed in writing; specify the official initiating the request; identify the person under investigation for appointment, clearance or service; and the purpose of the investigation as described in A(1) above.
4. Requests for White House investigations involving field investigations shall be made or confirmed in writing; specify the official initiating the investigation, and identify the person under investigation for appointment, clearance, or service. The request shall be accompanied by a statement signed by the subject of the investigation acknowledging that he has consented to the investigation with the knowledge that facts or information gathered shall be retained consistent with the FBI Records Retention Plan. The requesting official must certify the subject of the investigation has been apprised of the provisions of Section (e)3 of the Privacy Act of 1974.

B. *Investigation*

1. White House investigations involving file reviews or field investigations must be thorough, precise, and fair.
2. Persons interviewed during White House field investigations shall be told that the individual under investigation is being considered for a position of trust involving the Government. The name of the official or agency initiating the investigation, or the position for which the individual is being considered shall not be disclosed unless specifically authorized by the requesting official.
3. Subject to the Freedom of Information Act and Privacy Act of 1974, persons interviewed during White House field investigations may be assured that, to the extent permitted by law, information identifying such persons will be kept confidential.
4. Where a person is the subject of a subsequent White House field investigation, information contained in the earlier report reflecting adversely on the person shall be

re-investigated, where such inquiry is likely to yield information relevant to the current investigation and where such inquiry is practicable.

C. *Reporting*

1. Information obtained during White House file reviews or field investigations shall be furnished to the initiating authority and/or the White House. The FBI shall retain a record of persons to whom such information is furnished.
2. Any investigative efforts to determine the truth or falsity of reported derogatory allegations or information shall be reported.
3. Where the identity of the source of information is not reported in a White House file review or field investigation, an assessment shall be provided of the reliability of such source.

II. Dissemination and Retention of Information

A. *Retrieval*

1. The FBI shall retain a record of all relevant information gathered during the course of White House investigations consistent with these guidelines.
2. Information obtained during these investigations may be indexed in such a manner as to assist in its subsequent retrieval.

B. *Access*

1. The Director of the FBI shall insure that access to White House investigative files under his control is restricted and that stringent controls are maintained over such files limiting their use to official purpose.
2. Officials outside the FBI to whom White House file review and field investigations reports are furnished shall insure that internal access thereto is restricted to persons directly involved in making Presidential appointments; determining Executive Office staffing; granting clearance to classified information; approving access to or service at the White House or other place under the protection of the U.S. Secret Service as described in these guidelines. A record shall be maintained of the identity and organizational unit of officials requesting

access to White House investigative files, as well as the dates these files are issued and returned.

C. *Dissemination*

1. Where during the course of a White House field investigation the FBI finds some indication that the person under investigation may have committed a crime or other violation of law the FBI shall notify the initiating official thereof; and either investigate the crime if within its jurisdiction or refer the facts or information of the possible violation to appropriate authorities for determination.
2. No subsequent dissemination shall be made by the FBI of the results of White House field investigations or file reviews, conducted for the incumbent Administration, without the express approval of the President, Counsel, or Associate Counsel to the President, except as expressly required by federal statute or as part of an investigation of a violation of law.
3. No one receiving FBI reports of White House file reviews or field investigations shall reproduce or disseminate these materials other than in accord with B(2) above without the express consent of the FBI. Such dissemination must be predicated upon the request of an official authorized by or in accordance with these guidelines to initiate a White House investigation, and only for a purpose authorized by these guidelines.
4. The FBI and officials receiving reports of White House file reviews or field investigations shall maintain a record of all dissemination of these materials to other agencies.

D. *Retention of Information*

1. Information obtained during White House file reviews or field investigations shall be retained at FBI Headquarters and at FBI field offices as prescribed by the FBI Records Retention Plan.
2. Results of White House investigations maintained by the FBI shall be destroyed ____ years after completion of the investigation subject to the following conditions:
   a. files and information determined by the Archivist of

the United States to be of historic interest shall be transferred to the custody of the National Archives and Records Service ____ years after the completion of the investigation.

b. files and information relating to persons who have been re-investigated may be retained ____ years from the date of the latest investigation.

3. Anyone receiving FBI reports of White House file reviews or field investigations shall destroy such reports within ninety (90) days after receiving them, unless notice in writing is given to the FBI that an additional period of time, not exceeding ninety (90) days, is needed to complete a decision relating to the White House investigation.
4. The provisions of paragraphs two (2) and three (3) above apply to all inquiries completed after the promulgation of these guidelines. The provisions of paragraph two (2) apply to inquiries completed prior to promulgation of these guidelines when use of these files serves to identify them as subject to destruction or transfer to the National Archives and Records Service.
5. When an individual's request pursuant to law for access to files pertaining to him identifies files as being subject to destruction or transfer under paragraph two (2), he shall be furnished all information to which he is entitled prior to destruction or transfer.

   NOTE: The primary reference of "pursuant to law" in this paragraph is to the Privacy Act of 1974, which specifically authorizes access to background investigation files.

APPENDIX IV

Attorney General's Guidelines for FBI Use of Informants in Domestic Security, Organized Crime, and Other Criminal Investigations, December 15, 1976

TO: Clarence M. Kelley
Director
Federal Bureau of Investigation

FROM: Edward H. Levi
Attorney General

Courts have recognized that the government's use of informants is lawful and may often be essential to the effectiveness of properly authorized law enforcement investigations. However, the technique of using informants to assist in the investigation of criminal activity, since it may involve an element of deception and intrusion into the privacy of individuals or may require government cooperation with persons whose reliability and motivation may be open to question, should be carefully limited. Thus, while it is proper for the FBI to use informants in appropriate investigations, it is imperative that special care be taken not only to minimize their use but also to ensure that individual rights are not infringed and that the government itself does not become a violator of the law. Informants as such are not employees of the FBI, but the relationship of an informant to the FBI imposes a special responsibility upon the FBI when the informant engages in activity where he has received, or reasonably thinks he has received, encouragement or direction for that activity from the FBI.

To fulfill this responsibility, it is useful to formulate in a single document the limitations on the activities of informants and the duties of the FBI with respect to informants, even though many of these limitations and duties are set forth in individual instructions or recognized in existing practice.

As a fundamental principle, it must be recognized that an informant is merely one technique used in the course of authorized investigations. The FBI may not use informants where it is not authorized to conduct an investigation nor may informants be used for acts or encouraged to commit acts which the FBI could not authorize for its undercover Agents. When an FBI informant provides information concerning planned criminal activity which is not within the investigative jurisdiction of the FBI, the FBI shall advise the law enforcement agency having investigative jurisdiction. If the circumstances are such that it is inadvisable to have the informant report directly to the agency having investigative jurisdiction, the FBI, in cooperation with that agency, may continue to operate the informant.

A. Use of Informants

In considering the use of informants in an authorized investigation, the FBI should weigh the following factors—

1. the risk that use of an informant in a particular investigation or the conduct of a particular informant may, contrary to instructions, violate individual rights, intrude upon privileged communications, unlawfully inhibit the free association of individuals or the expression of ideas, or compromise in any way the investigation or subsequent prosecution.
2. the nature and seriousness of the matter under investigation, and the likelihood that information which an informant could provide is not readily available through other sources or by more direct means.
3. the character and motivation of the informant himself; his past or potential involvement in the matter under investigation or in related criminal activity; his proven reliability and truthfulness or the availability of means to verify information which he provides.
4. the measure of the ability of the FBI to control the informant's activities insofar as he is acting on behalf of the Bureau and ensure that his conduct will be consistent with applicable law and instructions.

5. the potential value of the information he may be able to furnish in relation to the consideration he may be seeking from the government for his cooperation.

B. Instructions to Informants

The FBI shall instruct all informants it uses in domestic security, organized crime, and other criminal investigations that in carrying out their assignments they shall not:

1. participate in acts of violence; or
2. use unlawful techniques (e.g., breaking and entering, electronic surveillance, opening or otherwise tampering with the mail) to obtain information for the FBI; or
3. initiate a plan to commit criminal acts; or
4. participate in criminal activities of persons under investigation, except insofar as the FBI determines that such participation is necessary to obtain information needed for purposes of federal prosecution.

   Whenever the FBI learns that persons under investigation intend to commit a violent crime informants used in connection with the investigation shall be instructed to try to discourage the violence.

C. Violations of Instructions and Law

1. Under no circumstances shall the FBI take any action to conceal a crime by one of its informants.
2. Whenever the FBI *learns* that an informant used in investigating criminal activity has violated the instructions set forth above *in furtherance of his assignment*, it shall ordinarily notify the appropriate law enforcement or prosecutive authorities promptly of any violation of law, and make a determination whether continued use of the informant is justified. In those exceptional circumstances in which notification to local authorities may be inadvisable, the FBI shall immediately notify the Department of Justice of the facts and circumstances concerning the investigation and the informant's law violation, and provide its recommendation on reporting the violation and on continued use of the informant. The Department shall determine:
   (a) when law enforcement or prosecutive authorities should be notified of the law violation;
   (b) what use, if any, should be made of the information

gathered through the violation of law, as well as the disposition and retention of such information; and

(c) whether continued use should be made of the informant by the FBI.

NOTE: Since the FBI has a special responsibility to control the activity of informants collecting information for the Bureau, and is ordinarily familiar with these activities, a comparatively minimal degree of certainty on the part of the FBI (i.e., "learns") is required before the FBI must report informant misconduct to the appropriate law enforcement authorities.

3. Whenever the FBI has *knowledge of the actual commission* of a serious crime by one of its informants *unconnected with his FBI assignment*, it shall ordinarily notify the appropriate law enforcement or prosecutive authorities promptly and make a determination whether continued use of the informant is justified. In those exceptional circumstances in which notification to local authorities may be inadvisable, the FBI shall promptly advise the Department of Justice of the facts and circumstances concerning the investigation and the informant's law violation, and provide its recommendation on reporting the violation and on continued use of the informant. The Department of Justice shall determine:

(a) when law enforcement or prosecutive authorities should be notified of the law violation; and

(b) whether continued use should be made of the informant by the FBI.

NOTE: Because the criminal activity described in this provision is independent of any government assignment, and since the FBI will have no special knowledge to determine such informant malfeasance, a substantial degree of certainty on the part of the Bureau is required before it must report to other authorities. The standard of certainty is derived from the federal Misprision of Felony statute, 18 U.S.C. 4, "Whoever, having *knowledge of the actual commission* of a felony cognizable by a court of the United States, conceals and does not as soon as possible make known the same to some judge or other person in civil or military authority under the

United States, shall be fined not more than $500 or imprisoned not more than three years, or both."

4. In determining the advisability of notifying appropriate law enforcement and prosecutive authorities of criminal activity by FBI informants the FBI and the Department of Justice shall consider the following factors:
   (a) whether the crime is completed, imminent or inchoate;
   (b) seriousness of the crime in terms of danger to life and property;
   (c) whether the crime is a violation of federal or state law, and whether a felony, misdemeanor or lesser offense;
   (d) the degree of certainty of the information regarding the criminal activity;
   (e) whether the appropriate authorities already know of the criminal activity and the informant's identity; and
   (f) the significance of the information the informant is providing, or will provide, and the effect on the FBI investigative activity of notification to the other law enforcement agency.

Abbreviations

ABA Committee Report: American Bar Association, Special Committee to Study Federal Law Enforcement Agencies, *Preventing Improper Influence on Federal Law Enforcement Agencies* (Washington, D.C.: American Bar Association, 1976).

Disorders and Terrorism: National Advisory Commission on Criminal Justice Standards and Goals, Task Force on Disorders and Terrorism, *Final Report: Disorders and Terrorism* (Washington, D.C.: U.S. Government Printing Office, 1977).

FBI Oversight: United States House of Representatives, Committee on the Judiciary, Subcommittee on Civil and Constitutional Rights, *Hearings*: *FBI Oversight*, Serial No. 2, Parts 1-3, 94th Cong., 1st and 2d sess., 1975-1976.

GAO Report: Comptroller General of the United States, *FBI Domestic Intelligence Operations—Their Purpose and Scope: Issues that Need to Be Resolved* (Washington, D.C.: General Accounting Office, February 24, 1976).

SSC Hearings: United States Senate, Select Committee to Study Governmental Operations with respect to Intelligence Activities, *Hearings: Intelligence Activities*, Volumes 2-6, 94th Cong., 1st sess., 1975.

SSC Report: United States Senate, Select Committee to Study Governmental Operations with respect to Intelligence Activities, *Final Report*, Books I-IV, 94th Cong., 2d sess., 1976.

Notes

Chapter I

1. Archibald Cox, "Reflections upon Watergate," Louis D. Brandeis Memorial Lecture, Brandeis University, April 24, 1974.

2. *United States* v. *United States District Court*, 407 U.S. 297 (1972), referred to as the *Keith* case, after the name of the U.S. District judge whose ruling was appealed by the government.

3. *Id.* at 320.

4. *Id.* at 322-23.

5. *Id.* at 309, 391.

6. *Id.* at 313-14.

7. 28 U.S.C. 533 (1).

8. Prepared statement of FBI Director Clarence M. Kelley before the Select Committee on Intelligence, United States Senate, September 22, 1976.

9. 28 U.S.C. 533 (3). See also *SSC Report*, Book III, 379, 389-90, 395-96, 400-407.

10. Executive Order No. 11905, sections 4(g) and 5(h)(2).

11. Executive Order No. 12036.

Chapter II

1. Max Lowenthal, *The Federal Bureau of Investigation* (New York: William Sloane Associates, 1950); Fred J. Cook, *The FBI Nobody Knows* (New York: Macmillan and Company, 1964).

2. Alpheus T. Mason, *Harlan Fiske Stone: Pillar of the Law* (New York: Viking Press, 1956), 149-53.

3. Harold L. Wilensky, *Organizational Intelligence: Knowledge and Policy in Government and Industry* (New York: Basic Books, 1967), 117.

4. Harry Howe Ransom, *The Intelligence Establishment* (Cambridge, Mass.: Harvard University Press, 1970), 196.

5. Sir Ronald Howe, *The Story of Scotland Yard* (New York: Horizon Press, 1966), 55-63, 72-74, 82-87, 134-42.

6. David Wise and Thomas B. Ross, *The Espionage Establishment* (New York: Random House, 1967), 78-131.

7. Edward Crankshaw, *Gestapo* (New York: Pyramid Books, 1957), 9.

8. Robert Jackson, "The Federal Prosecutor," *Journal of the American Judicature Society*, June 1940, p. 18.

9. Frank Murphy, quoted in *The New York Times*, October 1, 1939, 38, col. 3.

10. Statement of President Franklin D. Roosevelt, September 6, 1939.

11. *Proceedings* of the Federal-State Conference on Law Enforcement Problems of National Defense, August 5-6, 1940.

12. The Truman Administration secretly approved an FBI program for this

purpose in 1948, and it disregarded the act in subsequent plans that anticipated suspension of habeas corpus rather than the administrative hearing procedure of the law. *SSC Report*, Book III, 436-47.

13. *Pennsylvania* v. *Nelson*, 350 U.S. 497 (1956), 504-05.

14. *Communist Party* v. *Subversive Activities Control Board*, 367 U.S. 1 (1961), 147, dissenting on other grounds.

15. Director Hoover's 1961 report to the White House on the "Status of U.S. Internal Security Programs" did state, however, that the FBI also conducted security investigations of such predominantly domestic groups as the Nationalist Party of Puerto Rico, the Nation of Islam, and the Socialist Workers Party. *SSC Report*, Book III, 465-66.

16. Otto Kirchheimer, *Political Justice: The Use of Legal Procedure for Political Ends* (Princeton, N.J.: Princeton University Press, 1961), 204.

17. *SSC Report*, Book II, 116-22.

18. *Ibid.*, 165-219.

19. *Ibid.*, 265-88.

20. *Ibid.*, 137-63.

21. *SSC Report*, Book III, 550.

22. *FBI Oversight*, 11-12.

23. Kirchheimer, *Political Justice*, 202-04.

24. *FBI Oversight*, testimony of Attorney General Edward H. Levi, February 11, 1976.

25. *SSC Hearings*, Vol. 6, 314.

26. *SSC Report*, Book II, 318.

27. *GAO Report*, 138-47, 158-61.

28. *ABA Committee Report*, 21-22.

29. *SSC Report*, Book II, 359-60.

30. *Ibid.*, 21, 319.

31. *GAO Report*, 158.

32. *Ibid.*

33. *SSC Report*, Book II, 291.

34. *GAO Report*, 147.

35. *SSC Hearings*, Vol. 6, 207.

36. United States House of Representatives, Committee on Appropriations, *Hearings: Departments of State, Justice, and Commerce, the Judiciary, and Related Agencies*, Part 4, *Appropriations for 1977*, 94th Cong., 2d sess., 1976, 571.

37. *SSC Report*, Book I, 176.

38. Attorney General Edward H. Levi, address before the American Law Institute, May 21, 1976.

39. *SSC Hearings*, Vol. 6, 314-15.

40. *SSC Report*, Book II, 294, 316, 332.

41. *Ibid.*, 23.

42. Robert Jackson, "The Federal Prosecutor," *Journal of the American Judicature Society* (June 1940), 18.

43. *ABA Committee Report*, 48-53, 130-33.

44. Jessica Mitford, *The Trial of Dr. Spock* (New York: Vintage Books, 1971), Foreword.

45. *United States* v. *Spock*, 416 F. 2d 165, 172-74 (1st Cir. 1969).

46. *Brandenburg* v. *Ohio*, 395 U.S. 444, 447-48 (1969).

47. *Foreign Agents Registration Act*, 22 U.S.C. 611-21.

48. 45 U.S.C. 951.

49. 50 U.S.C. 851-57.

50. *Marchetti* v. *United States*, 390 U.S. 39 (1968); *Albertson* v. *Subversive Activities Control Board,* 382 U.S. 70 (1965).

51. United States Senate, Committee on the Judiciary, *S.1566: Foreign Intelligence Surveillance Act of 1977*, Report No. 95-604, 95th Cong., 1st sess., 1977, 23; United States Senate, Select Committee on Intelligence, *S.1566: Foreign Intelligence Surveillance Act of 1978*, Report No. 95-701, 95th Cong., 2d sess., 1978, 29; United States House of Representatives, Permanent Select Committee on Intelligence, *H.R.7308: Foreign Intelligence Surveillance Act of 1978*, Report No. 95-1283, 95th Cong., 2d sess., 1978, 40-42.

52. *SSC Report*, Book II, 339-41.

53. Levi, American Law Institute address.

54. Kenneth Culp Davis, *Police Discretion* (St. Paul, Minn.: West Publishing Co., 1975), 52.

55. *Ibid.*, 169.

Chapter III

1. Executive Order No. 12036, section 2-201.

2. Memorandum from Hoover to Mitchell, July 27, 1970, in *SSC Hearings*, Vol. 2, Exhibit 40, 315.

3. Memorandum from Belmont to Tolson, in *SSC Hearings*, Vol. 6, Exhibit 71-2, 832.

4. *SSC Report*, Book III, 64.

5. *Ibid.*, 548.

6. *Ibid.*, 512-26.

7. *Ibid.*, 542-44.

8. *SSC Hearings*, Vol. 6, Exhibits 60-2 and 60-3, 655-58.

9. *SSC Report*, Book III, 454-57.

10. Memorandum from Hoover to Kleindienst, February 25, 1972, in *SSC Report*, Book III, 549.

11. Sanford J. Ungar, *FBI: An Uncensored Look behind the Walls* (Boston: Atlantic-Little, Brown, 1976).

12. *SSC Report*, Book III, 549-50.

13. *Ibid.*, 551; *SSC Hearings*, Vol. 6, Exhibit 60-1, 645-51.

14. *The Smith Act*, 18 U.S.C. 2383-85.

15. United States House of Representatives, Committee on Internal Security, *Hearings: Domestic Intelligence Operations for Internal Security Purposes*, 93d Cong., 2d sess., 1974, 3569-70. Emphasis added.

16. 18 U.S.C. 241.

17. *SSC Report*, Book III, 552.

18. Interviews with FBI field supervisors, January 1975.

19. Executive Conference memorandum, October 29, 1970; *SSC Hearings*, Vol. 2, Exhibits 41-43, 317-27.

20. Richard D. Cotter, "Notes toward a Definition of National Security," *The Washington Monthly*, December 1975, pp. 4-16.

21. Memorandum from Kelley to Richardson, August 7, 1973; *SSC Hearings*, Vol. 6, Exhibit 53, 544-45; *SSC Report*, Book III, 552-53.

22. Ungar, *FBI*, 568.

23. *SSC Report*, Book III, 553-54.

24. *Ibid.*, 75-76.

25. Memorandum from Kelley to All Special Agents in Charge, December 5, 1973; *SSC Hearings*, Vol. 4, Exhibit 17, 232.

26. United States House of Representatives, Committee on the Judiciary, Subcommittee on Civil and Constitutional Rights, *Hearings: FBI Counterintelligence Programs*, 93d Cong., 2d sess., 1974, testimony of Clarence M. Kelley, 39, 44-47.

27. Executive Order No. 10540, section 8(a)(5).

28. Executive Order No. 11605, July 2, 1971; *SSC Report*, Book III, 538.

29. *SSC Report*, Book III, 538.

30. Executive Order No. 11785, June 4, 1974.

31. Memorandum from Pommerening to Kelley, November 19, 1974; *SSC Hearings*, Vol. 6, Exhibit 66-2, 706-08. Emphasis added.

32. Memorandum from Clark to Hoover, September 14, 1967; *SSC Hearings*, Vol. 6, Exhibit 66-1, 703-05.

33. *SSC Report*, Book III, 515.

34. Memorandum from Petersen to Kelley, October 22, 1974; *SSC Hearings*, Vol. 6, Exhibit 66-1, 703-705.

35. *SSC Report*, Book III, 556.

36. *Ibid.*, 74.

37. *FBI Counterintelligence Programs*, Kelley, 3.

38. *FBI Oversight*, 8-11.

39. Fred D. Thompson, *At That Point in Time: The Inside Story of the Senate Watergate Committee* (New York: Quadrangle Books, 1975), 126-244.

40. *FBI Oversight*, 11-12.

41. *SSC Hearings*, Vol. 6, esp. 158-65.

42. *FBI Oversight*, 12.

43. *Ibid.*, 14.

44. Attorney General Edward H. Levi, address before the American Bar Association, August 13, 1975.

45. *Ibid.*

46. Attorney General Edward H. Levi, address before the Los Angeles County Bar Association, November 18, 1976.

47. Executive Order No. 11905.

48. Levi, Los Angeles address.

49. *Ibid.*

50. Memorandum from Dixon to Richardson, June 26, 1973; United States

Senate, Committee on the Judiciary, Subcommittee on Constitutional Rights, *Staff Report: Surveillance Technology—1976*, 94th Cong., 2d sess., 1976, 422.

51. 18 U.S.C. 2511(3).

52. Letter from Richardson to Senator William Fulbright, September 12, 1973; *Surveillance Technology—1976*, 418-19.

53. United States Senate, Subcommittees on Criminal Laws and Procedures and Constitutional Rights, *Joint Hearings: Warrantless Wiretapping and Electronic Surveillance—1974*, 93d Cong., 2d sess., 1974, 484-90.

54. *Ibid.*, 17.

55. United States Senate, Committee on the Judiciary, Subcommittees on Criminal Laws and Procedures and Constitutional Rights, *Joint Hearings: Electronic Surveillance for National Security Purposes*, 93d Cong., 2d sess., 1974, 234, 236, 253.

56. *SSC Hearings*, Vol. 5, 6, 10, 12.

57. Memorandum from Gayler to Mitchell and Laird, January 26, 1971; *SSC Hearings*, Vol. 5, Exhibit 5, 156-57.

58. Letter from Richardson to Allen, October 1, 1973; *SSC Hearings*, Vol. 5, Exhibit 7, 160-61.

59. Letter from Allen to Richardson, October 4, 1973; *SSC Hearings*, Vol. 5, Exhibit 8, 162-63.

60. *SSC Hearings*, Vol. 5, 107.

61. United States Department of Justice, *Report of the Department of Justice Concerning Its Investigation and Prosecutorial Decisions with Respect to Central Intelligence Agency Mail Opening Activities in the United States* (Washington, D.C.: Department of Justice, January 14, 1977), 50-52.

62. *Ibid.*, 29, 32.

63. *Ibid.*, 28-29, 34-35.

64. Levi, Los Angeles address, 6.

65. *SSC Hearings*, Vol. 5, 24.

66. *SSC Report*, Book III, 370.

67. *Report of the Department of Justice*, 25-26, n. 9.

68. Executive Order No. 11905, section 5(b)(2) and (3).

69. Executive Order No. 12306, sections 2-2 and 4-106.

70. *Youngstown Sheet and Tube Co.* v. *Sawyer*, 343 U.S. 579, 637-38 (1952).

Chapter IV

1. Statement of FBI Director, August 11, 1976.
2. *SSC Report*, Book III, 471-72.
3. *Ibid.*, 18-19.
4. *Ibid.*, 470-71, 492-93.
5. *Ibid.*, 535-36.
6. *Ibid.*, 472.
7. *SSC Hearings*, Vol. 2, Exhibit 1, 159-60.
8. Richard H. Blum, ed., *Surveillance and Espionage in a Free Society* (New York: Praeger, 1972), 78.

9. Shortly before his forced resignation in 1971, FBI executive William C. Sullivan proposed that there be two separate divisions—one for domestic intelligence and one for counterespionage and foreign intelligence. For budgetary reasons, Hoover did not approve. *SSC Report*, Book III, 534-35.

10. *SSC Hearings*, Vol. 2, Exhibits 32-34, 273-380.

11. United States House of Representatives, Committee on Internal Security, *Hearings: Domestic Intelligence Operations for Internal Security Purposes*, 93d Cong., 2d sess., 1974.

12. *SSC Report*, Book III, 558.

13. *GAO Report*, 150.

14. Prepared statement of FBI Director Clarence M. Kelley before the Subcommittee on Intelligence and the Rights of Americans, Select Committee on Intelligence, United States Senate, September 22, 1976.

15. *Ibid.*

16. *SSC Report*, Book III, 260; John M. Goshko, "Strict Guidelines on FBI Informers Issued by Levi," *The Washington Post*, January 6, 1977.

17. *SSC Report*, Book III, 263, nn. 59, 60.

18. Emphasis added. See Appendix II.

19. Margot Hornblower, "FBI Probes Coalition Planning July 4 Rally," *The Washington Post*, May 29, 1976.

20. The Associated Press, "U.S. Bars Troops for Philadelphia," *The New York Times*, June 22, 1976.

21. Department of Justice, *Guidelines for Reporting on Civil Disorders and Demonstrations Involving a Federal Interest*, Section V, D, 4.

22. *SSC Report*, Book II, 180.

23. United States House of Representatives, Select Committee on Intelligence, *Hearings: U.S. Intelligence Agencies and Activities: Domestic Intelligence Programs* [hereafter, *House Intelligence Hearings*], 94th Cong., 1st sess., 1975, Part 3, 1153.

24. John M. Goshko, "FBI Can Continue Probe of Communists," *The Washington Post*, November 10, 1976.

25. *House Intelligence Hearings*, Part 3, 1142.

26. Jerry Oppenheimer, "Kelley Cuts Ties to Left Informers," *The Washington Star*, September 17, 1976.

27. John M. Crewdson, "FBI Reports Losing 20 Informers over Fear of Disclosures of Names," *The New York Times*, October 25, 1976.

28. John M. Goshko, "Socialist Workers Party Assails FBI on Inquiry," *The Washington Post*, November 10, 1976.

29. Goshko, "FBI Can Continue Probe of Communists."

30. United States House of Representatives, Committee on Appropriations, *Hearings: Departments of State, Justice, and Commerce, the Judiciary, and Related Agencies*, Part 4, *Appropriations for 1977*, 94th Cong., 2d sess., 1976, 153.

31. Testimony of FBI Deputy Associate Director James B. Adams before the Subcommittee on Intelligence and the Rights of Americans, Select Committee on Intelligence, United States Senate, September 22, 1976.

32. *GAO Report*, 213.

33. *Ibid.*, 46.

34. *Ibid.*, 46, 151.

35. Statement of Attorney General Griffin B. Bell before the Committee on the Judiciary, United States Senate, April 20, 1978.

Chapter V

1. *Disorders and Terrorism*, 90-96.

2. Committee for Public Justice, *et al.*, "A Law to Control the FBI" (New York: 1977).

3. *Disorders and Terrorism*, 31.

4. *SSC Report*, Book II, 18, n. 105.

5. *GAO Report*, 138-47.

6. *United States* v. *United States District Court*, 407 U.S. 297, 322 (1972).

7. *Socialist Workers Party* v. *Attorney General*, 510 F.2d 253 (1974).

8. *The Smith Act*, 18 U.S.C. 2385.

9. At the height of the Cold War tension, the Supreme Court took judicial notice of the special features of the Communist party that made it seem a serious danger to the existence of the government. The party, the Court found, was "a highly organized conspiracy, with rigidly disciplined members subject to call when the leaders . . . felt that the time had come for action." Equally important were "the inflammable nature of world conditions, similar uprisings in other countries, and the touch-and-go nature of our relations with [Soviet bloc] countries with whom [the party leaders] were in the very least ideologically attuned." *Dennis* v. *United States*, 341 U.S. 494, 510-11 (1951). No one has been prosecuted under the Smith Act since the 1950s.

10. 18 U.S.C. 2384.

11. *Id.* at 2383.

12. 50 U.S.C. 783.

13. *1977 Annual Report of the Attorney General.*

14. Christopher H. Pyle, "Terrorism, Crime Control, and Civil Liberties," paper presented before the Panel on Civil Liberties and Social Control, American Political Science Association, Chicago, September 4, 1976, 35.

15. *SSC Report*, Book II, 85, n. 4.

16 *Ibid.*, 86.

17. *GAO Report*, 161.

18. *Ibid.*, 150, 160.

19. Department of Justice, *Guidelines for Domestic Security Investigations*, Section II (I).

20. *Disorders and Terrorism*, 144.

21. *Ibid.*, 147.

22. *SSC Report*, Book II, 320.

23. *Ibid.*, 347.

24. Association of the Bar of the City of New York, Committee on Federal Legislation, *Legislative Control of the FBI*, 12.

25. *Ibid.*

26. *Ibid.*, 15.
27. *Ibid.*, 22.
28. *Ibid.*, 16.
29. *SSC Report*, Book II, 341.
30. *Disorders and Terrorism*, 147-48.
31. *SSC Report*, Book II, 382.
32. *Hoffa* v. *United States*, 385 U.S. 293 (1966).
33. *SSC Report*, Book III, 232.
34. *Terry* v. *Ohio*, 392 U.S. 1, 30 (1968).
35. *SSC Report*, Book III, 261-62.
36. *SSC Report*, Book II, 183.
37. Anthony Amsterdam, "Perspectives on the Fourth Amendment," 58 *Minn. L. Rev.* 349, 407 (1974). For a contrasting view of the role of informants in FBI criminal investigations, see James Q. Wilson, *The Investigators: Managing FBI and Narcotics Agents* (New York: Basic Books, 1978).
38. *SSC Report*, Book II, 325-29.
39. *Ibid.*, 325, 361.
40. *Coolidge* v. *New Hampshire*, 403 U.S. 443, 481 (1971).
41. *United States* v. *United States District Court*, 407 U.S. 297, 316-17 (1972).
42. Pyle, "Terrorism, Crime Control, and Civil Liberties," 53.
43. *FBI Oversight*, testimony of Attorney General Edward H. Levi, February 11, 1976.
44. *SSC Report*, Book II, 294, 332.
45. *GAO Report*, 157.
46. *SSC Report*, Book II, 317.
47. *Ibid.*, 212.
48. *SSC Report*, Book III, 6, 14, 76.
49. *GAO Report*, 226-28.
50. *Ibid.*
51. Pyle, "Terrorism, Crime Control, and Civil Liberties," 16.
52. *Ibid.*
53. *FBI Oversight*, testimony of Attorney General Edward H. Levi, February 11, 1976.
54. For other recent assessments of FBI domestic security investigations, see Comptroller General of the United States, *FBI Domestic Intelligence Operations: An Uncertain Future* (Washington, D.C.: General Accounting Office, November 9, 1977); and Richard E. Morgan, *Domestic Intelligence: Monitoring Dissent in America* (New York: Twentieth Century Fund, forthcoming).

Chapter VI

1. Executive Order No. 11905, section 4(g).
2. Executive Order No. 12036, sections 1-14 and 4-202.
3. *SSC Report*, Book I, Appendix III, 557, 561.
4. *Ibid.*, 163, 178, 439.
5. United States House of Representatives, Committee on Appropriations,

Hearings: Departments of State, Justice, Commerce, the Judiciary, and Related Agencies, Part 4, *Appropriations for 1977*, 94th Cong., 2d sess., 1976, 575.

6. *SSC Report*, Book II, 340 n. 74.
7. *SSC Hearings*, Vol. 6, 164.
8. *Export Administration Act of 1969*, 50 U.S.C. 2402, 2405.
9. *SSC Report*, Book II, 303.
10. *Ibid.*, 322-23.
11. *SSC Report*, Book I, 176.
12. *SSC Hearings*, Vol. 2, Exhibit 59, 374, emphasis added.
13. *SSC Report*, Book I, 163-64.
14. *1977 Appropriations Hearings*, 575-76.
15. Fund for the Republic, *Digest of the Public Record of Communism in the United States* (New York, 1955), 29.
16. *SSC Report*, Book I, 164.
17. Louise Bernikow, *Abel* (New York: Trident Press, 1970).
18. *1977 Appropriations Hearings*, 575.
19. *SSC Report*, Book I, 165.
20. *Foreign Agents Registration Act of 1956*, 50 U.S.C. 851-57.
21. James F. Sattler, Registration Statement No. 115, United States Department of Justice, March 23, 1976.
22. United States Senate, Select Committee on Intelligence, *Report on S.1566: Foreign Intelligence Surveillance Act of 1978*, Report No. 95-701, 95th Cong., 2d sess., 1978, 23.
23. *SSC Report*, Book II, 323-24.
24. *Ibid.*, 254, 261-62.
25. United States House of Representatives, Committee on the Judiciary, Subcommittee on Civil and Constitutional Rights, *Hearings: FBI Counterintelligence Programs*, 93d Cong., 2d sess., 1974, 15.
26. *SSC Report*, Book III, 75-76.
27. *1977 Appropriations Hearings*, 571-75.
28. Executive Order No. 11905, section 4(g); Executive Order No. 12036, section 4-202.
29. Commission on CIA Activities within the United States, *Report to the President* (Washington, D.C.: U.S. Government Printing Office, 1975), 170.
30. *FBI Counterintelligence Programs*, 15.
31. *SSC Report*, Book I, 168-69, 620.
32. *Ibid.*, 175.
33. *FBI Counterintelligence Programs*, 15.
34. *SSC Report*, Book III, 14.
35. *GAO Report*, 36.
36. *SSC Report*, Book II, 393-94.
37. *Ibid.*, 49, 51, 251.
38. *Ibid.*, 249-52.
39. *SSC Hearings*, Vol. 2, 104.
40. *SSC Report*, Book II, 101-02, 180-81.
41. *Commission on CIA Activities*, 24-25, 131.

42. *Ibid.*, 6-7, 13, 24-25.

43. *SSC Report*, Book I, 176-77.

44. United States Senate, Committee on the Judiciary, *Report on S.1566: Foreign Intelligence Surveillance Act of 1977*, Report No. 95-604, 95th Cong., 1st sess., 1977, 22-23.

45. *Foreign Intelligence Surveillance Act of 1978*, 92 Stat. 1783, Public Law 95–511, Sec. 101(b)(2), 105(a)(3).

46. *SSC Report*, Book III, 313-15.

47. Executive Order No. 12036, section 4-205.

Chapter VII

1. 28 C.F.R. O.39.

2. Statement of FBI Director Clarence M. Kelley, August 11, 1976.

3. *ABA Committee Report*, 57.

4. *SSC Report*, Book II, 335.

5. Committee for Public Justice, *et al.*, "A Law to Control the FBI" (1977), 21-22.

6. Statement of Assistant Attorney General J. Stanley Pottinger, June 30, 1976.

7. Statement of the Attorney General, April 1, 1976; *SSC Report*, Book III, 76-77.

8. Letter from Michael E. Shaheen, Counsel for Professional Responsibility, to Representative Bella S. Abzug, November 1, 1976.

9. *SSC Report*, Book III, 76.

10. *Report of the Department of Justice Task Force to Review the FBI Martin Luther King, Jr., Security and Assassination Investigations* (Washington, D.C.: January 11, 1977), 3-6.

11. *Ibid.*, 137-39; *SSC Report*, Book III, 79-184.

12. *Task Force Report*, 145-46.

13. *Report of the Watergate Special Prosecution Force*, October 1975, 139.

14. 28 C.F.R. O.39.

15. *ABA Committee Report*, 53-57.

16. Richard Thornburgh, "Priorities in Federal Law Enforcement," September 24, 1976.

17. 28 C.F.R. O.39.

18. *Ibid.*, O.39a-O.39b.

19. Albert J. Reiss, *The Police and the Public* (New Haven: Yale University Press, 1971).

20. *Ibid.*, 189-93.

21. Patrick V. Murphy, "Corruptive Influences," in Bernard Garmire, ed., *Local Government Police Management*, Institute for Training in Municipal Administration, Municipal Management Series (Washington, D.C.: International City Management Association, 1977), 65-86.

22. See Victor Navasky, *Kennedy Justice* (New York: Atheneum, 1971), Part I.

23. Sanford J. Ungar, *FBI: An Uncensored Look behind the Walls* (Boston: Atlantic-Little, Brown, 1976), chapters IV-X.

24. 5 U.S.C. 522a(i)(1).
25. *Task Force Report*, 110-12, 243-49.
26. Reiss, *The Police and the Public*, 193-97.
27. *SSC Report*, Book II, 155.
28. *SSC Hearings*, Vol. 5, 124, 164-65.
29. *SSC Report*, Book II, 230-31.
30. *SSC Hearings*, Vol. 6, 316.
31. Executive Order No. 11905, sections 4(a)(4) and 6(b)(5); Executive Order No. 12036.
32. *GAO Report*, 41-42.
33. Ungar, *FBI*, 177.
34. Clarence M. Kelley, "The FBI—Today and Tomorrow," address at the 83rd Annual Conference of the International Association of Chiefs of Police, Miami, September 28, 1976, 11-12.
35. *GAO Report*, 214-15.
36. Kelley, IACP address, 12.
37. George Berkley, *The Democratic Policeman* (Boston: Beacon Press, 1969), 121.

Chapter VIII

1. Morris Janowitz, "Patterns of Collective Racial Violence," in H. H. Graham and T. R. Gurr, eds., *Violence in America* (New York: Signet Books, 1969), 414.
2. Cf. *Terry* v. *Ohio*, 392 U.S. 1 (1968).
3. *Olmstead* v. *United States*, 277 U.S. 438 (1928), Brandeis dissenting.

Selected Bibliography

Congressional Publications

United States House of Representatives

Committee on Appropriations. *Hearings: Departments of State, Justice, Commerce, the Judiciary, and Related Agencies*. Part 4. *Appropriations for 1977*. 94th Cong., 2d sess., 1976.

Committee on Governmental Operations. *Hearings: Notification to Victims of Improper Intelligence Activities*. 94th Cong., 2d sess., 1976.

———. *Justice Department Internal Investigation Policies*. 95th Cong., 1st sess., 1977.

Committee on Internal Security. *Hearings: Domestic Intelligence Operations for Internal Security Purposes*. Part 1. 93d Cong., 2d sess., 1974.

Committee on the Judiciary. Subcommittee on Civil and Constitutional Rights. *Hearings: FBI Oversight*. Serial No. 2, Parts 1-3. 94th Cong., 1st and 2d sess., 1975-1976.

———. *Hearings: FBI Counterintelligence Programs*. 93d Cong., 2d sess., 1974.

Permanent Select Committee on Intelligence. *H.R.7308: Foreign Intelligence Surveillance Act of 1978*. Report No. 95-1283. 95th Cong., 2d sess., 1978.

Select Committee on Intelligence. *Hearings: U.S. Intelligence Agencies and Activities: Domestic Intelligence Programs*. 94th Cong., 1st sess., 1975.

United States Senate

Committee on Appropriations. *Hearing: Review of Secret Service Protective Measures*. 94th Cong., 1st sess., 1975.

Committee on the Judiciary. Subcommittee on Administrative Practice and Procedure. *Hearings: Warrantless Wiretapping*. 92d Cong., 2d sess., 1972.

———. Subcommittee on Constitutional Rights. *Staff Report: Surveillance Technology—1976*. 94th Cong. 2d sess., 1976.

Committee on the Judiciary. Subcommittees on Criminal Laws and

Procedures and Constitutional Rights. *Joint Hearings: Electronic Surveillance for National Security Purposes*. 93d Cong., 2d sess., 1974.

———. ———. *Joint Hearings: Warrantless Wiretapping and Electronic Surveillance—1974*. 93d Cong., 2d sess., 1974.

———. Subcommittee on FBI Oversight. *Hearing: Ten-Year Term for the Director*. 93d Cong., 2d sess., 1974.

———. Subcommittee on Internal Security. *Hearing: Terroristic Activity: Hostage Defense Measures*. Part 5. 94th Cong., 1st sess., 1975.

———. ———. *Hearing: The Nationwide Drive against Law Enforcement Intelligence Operations*. 94th Cong., 1st sess., 1975.

Committee on the Judiciary. *S.1566: Foreign Intelligence Surveillance Act of 1977*. Report No. 95-604. 95th Cong., 1st sess., 1977.

———. *S.3197: Foreign Intelligence Surveillance Act of 1976*. Report No. 94-1035. 94th Cong., 2d sess., 1976.

Select Committee on Intelligence. *S.1566: Foreign Intelligence Surveillance Act of 1978*. Report No. 95-701. 95th Cong., 2d sess., 1978.

———. *S.3197: Foreign Intelligence Surveillance Act of 1976*. Report No. 94-1161. 94th Cong., 2d sess., 1976.

———. Subcommittee on Intelligence and the Rights of Americans. *Hearings: Electronic Surveillance within the United States for Foreign Intelligence Purposes*. 94th Cong., 2d sess., 1976.

Select Committee to Study Governmental Operations with respect to Intelligence Activities. *Hearings: Intelligence Activities*. Vols. 2-6. 94th Cong., 1st sess., 1975.

———. *Final Report*, Books 1-3. 94th Cong., 2d sess., 1976.

Government Publications

Commission on CIA Activities within the United States. *Report to the President*. Washington, D.C.: U.S. Government Printing Office, June 1975.

Comptroller General of the United States. *FBI Domestic Intelligence Operations—Their Purpose and Scope: Issues That Need To Be Resolved*. Report to the House of Representatives. Washington, D.C.: General Accounting Office, February 24, 1976.

———. *FBI Domestic Intelligence Operations: An Uncertain Future*. Washington, D.C.: General Accounting Office, November 9, 1977.

National Advisory Commission on Criminal Justice Standards and Goals. Task Force on Disorders and Terrorism. *Report: Disorders and Terrorism*. Washington, D.C.: Law Enforcement Assistance Administration, February 1977.

United States Central Intelligence Agency. *Research Study: International and Transnational Terrorism: Diagnosis and Prognosis*. Washington, D.C.: Library of Congress, April 1976.

United States Department of Justice. *Guidelines for Domestic Security Investigations*. Washington, D.C.: Department of Justice, 1976.

———. *1977 Annual Report of the Attorney General*. Washington, D.C.: Department of Justice, 1977.

———. *Report of the Department of Justice Task Force To Review the FBI Martin Luther King, Jr., Security and Assassination Investigations*. Washington, D.C.: Department of Justice, January 11, 1977.

———. *Report of the Department of Justice Concerning Its Investigation and Prosecutorial Decisions with Respect to Central Intelligence Agency Mail Opening Activities in the United States*. Washington, D.C.: Department of Justice, January 14, 1977.

Books

American Bar Association. Special Committee to Study Federal Law Enforcement Agencies. *Preventing Improper Influence on Federal Law Enforcement Agencies*. 1976.

Association of the Bar of the City of New York. *Report of the Special Committee on the Federal Loyalty-Security Program*. New York: Dodd, Mead, 1956.

Barron, John. *KGB: The Secret Work of Soviet Secret Agents*. New York: Readers Digest Press, 1974.

Bell, J. Bowyer. *Transnational Terror*. Washington, D.C.: American Enterprise Institute, 1975.

Berkinow, Louise. *Abel*. New York: Trident Press, 1970.

Berkley, George. *The Democratic Policeman*. Boston: Beacon Press, 1969.

Blackstock, Nelson. *COINTELPRO: The FBI's Secret War on Political Freedom*. New York: Vintage Books, 1976.

Blum, Richard H., ed. *Surveillance and Espionage in a Free Society*. New York: Praeger, 1972.

Bouza, Anthony V. *Police Intelligence: The Operations of an Investigative Unit*. New York: AMS Press, 1976.

Chafee, Zechariah. *Free Speech in the United States*. Cambridge, Mass.: Harvard University Press, 1941.

Cook, Fred J. *The FBI Nobody Knows*. New York: Macmillan and Company, 1964.

Copeland, Miles. *Without Cloak or Dagger: The Truth about the New Espionage*. New York: Simon and Schuster, 1974.

Crankshaw, Edward. *Gestapo*. New York: Pyramid Books, 1957.

Davis, Kenneth Culp. *Police Discretion*. St. Paul, Minn.: West Publishing Co., 1975.

Elliff, John T. *Crime, Dissent, and the Attorney General: The Justice Department in the 1960s*. Beverly Hills, Calif.: Sage Publications, 1971.

Emerson, Thomas I. *The System of Freedom of Expression*. New York: Random House, 1970.

Fund for the Republic. *Digest of the Public Record of Communism in the United States*. New York, 1955.

Gellhorn, Walter. *When Americans Complain: Governmental Grievance Procedures*. Cambridge, Mass.: Harvard University Press, 1966.

Goodell, Charles. *Political Prisoners in America*. New York: Random House, 1973.

Halperin, Morton H., *et al. The Lawless State: The Crimes of the U.S. Intelligence Agencies*. New York: Penguin Books, 1976.

Harvard University. Institute of Politics. *Report of the Study Group on Intelligence Activities*. February 1976.

Howe, Sir Ronald. *The Story of Scotland Yard*. New York: Horizon Press, 1966.

Kirchheimer, Otto. *Political Justice: The Use of Legal Procedure for Political Ends*. Princeton, N.J.: Princeton University Press, 1961.

Kirkpatrick, Lyman B. *The U.S. Intelligence Community: Foreign Policy and Domestic Activities*. New York: Hill and Wang, 1973.

Lowenthal, Max. *The Federal Bureau of Investigation*. New York: William Sloane Associates, 1950.

Mason, Alpheus T. *Harlan Fiske Stone: Pillar of the Law*. New York: Viking Press, 1956.

Mitford, Jessica. *The Trial of Dr. Spock*. New York: Vintage Books, 1970.

Morgan, Richard E. *Domestic Intelligence: Monitoring Dissent in America*. New York: Twentieth Century Fund, forthcoming.

Navasky, Victor. *Kennedy Justice*. New York: Atheneum, 1971.

Ransom, Harry Howe. *The Intelligence Establishment*. Cambridge, Mass.: Harvard University Press, 1970.

Reiss, Albert J. *The Police and the Public*. New Haven: Yale University Press, 1971.

Smith, Bruce. *Police Systems in the United States*. 2d rev. ed. New York: Harper and Row, 1960.

Smith, James Morton. *Freedom's Fetters: The Alien and Sedition Laws and American Civil Liberties*. Ithaca, N.Y.: Cornell University Press, 1956.

Thompson, Fred D. *At That Point in Time: The Inside Story of the Senate Watergate Committee*. New York: Quadrangle Books, 1975.

Ungar, Sanford J. *FBI: An Uncensored Look behind the Walls*. Boston: Atlantic-Little, Brown, 1976.

Watters, Pat, and Stephen Gillers, eds. *Investigating the FBI*. New York: Doubleday, 1973.

Whitehead, Don. *The FBI Story*. New York: Random House, 1956.

———. *Attack on Terror: the FBI Against the Ku Klux Klan in Mississippi*. New York: Funk and Wagnalls, 1970.

Wilensky, Harold L. *Organizational Intelligence: Knowledge and Policy in Government and Industry*. New York: Basic Books, 1967.

Wilson, James Q. *The Investigators: Managing FBI and Narcotics Agents*. New York: Basic Books, 1978.

Wise, David. *The American Police State: The Government against the People*. New York: Random House, 1967.

———, and Thomas B. Ross. *The Espionage Establishment*. New York: Random House, 1967.

Wright, Richard O., ed. *Whose FBI?* LaSalle, Ill.: Open Court, 1974.

Articles, Papers, Speeches

Amsterdam, Anthony. "Perspectives on the Fourth Amendment." 58 *Minn. L. Rev*. 349 (1974).

Association of the Bar of the City of New York. Committee on Federal Legislation. *Legislative Control of the FBI*. New York, 1977.

Committee for Public Justice, *et al.* "A Law to Control the FBI." New York, 1977.

Cotter, Richard D. "Notes toward a Definition of National Security." *The Washington Monthly* (December 1975), 4-16.

Cox, Archibald. "Reflections upon Watergate." The Louis D. Brandeis Memorial Lecture. Brandeis University, April 24, 1974.

Jackson, Robert H. "The Federal Prosecutor." *Journal of the American Judicature Society* (June 1940), 18.

Pyle, Christopher H. "Terrorism, Crime Control, and Civil Liberties." Paper presented before the Panel on Civil Liberties and Social Control of the American Political Science Association. Chicago, September 4, 1976.

Index of Names

General Index

Library of Congress Cataloging in Publication Data

Elliff, John T.
The reform of FBI intelligence operations.

Bibliography: p.
Includes index.
1. United States. Federal Bureau of Investigation. 2. Intelligence service—United States. 3. United States—National security. I. Police Foundation. II. Title.
HV8138.E57 353.007'4 78-70290
ISBN 0-691-07607-3